Moral
Phenomena

Library of Conservative Thought

Volume 1 of *Ethics*

with a new introduction by
Andreas A.M. Kinneging

Moral Phenomena

Nicolai Hartmann

Transaction Publishers
New Brunswick (U.S.A.) and London (U.K.)

Third printing 2007

New material this edition copyright © 2002 by Transaction Publishers, New Brunswick, New Jersey. Originally published in 1932 by The Macmillan Company.

This book is printed on acid-free paper that meets the American National Standard for Permanence of Paper for Printed Library Materials.

Library of Congress Catalog Number: 2001053504
ISBN: 978-0-7658-0909-4
Printed in the United States of America

Library of Congress Cataloging-in-Publication Data

Hartmann, Nicolai, 1882-1950.
  [Struktur des ethischen Phänomens. English]
  Moral phenomena : volume one of Ethics / Nicolai Hartmann ; with a new introduction by Andreas A. M. Kinneging.
    p. cm.—(Library of conservative thought)
  Originally published: Vol. 1 of Ethics. New York : Macmillian, 1932, in series: Library of philosophy. With new introd.
  Includes bibliographical references and index.
  ISBN 0-7658-0909-5 (pbk. : alk. paper)
  1. Ethics. I. Title. II. Series.

BJ1012 .H342 2002
170—dc21   2001053504

TRANSACTION INTRODUCTION[1]

DURING his lifetime, Nicolai Hartmann (1882-1950) was widely regarded as one of Germany's most distinguished philosophers. His works were widely discussed, and he figured prominently in various well-known general overviews of contemporary philosophy.[2] From 1931 until 1945 he held the most prestigious chair of philosophy in Germany. After his death in 1950, however, interest in his work rapidly declined. The number of publications devoted to his work in the past fifty years is limited, certainly when compared to what has been published on the work of his contemporary and rival Martin Heidegger.[3]

How to explain this decline in interest? After WW II, both in the English-speaking world and on the European continent, philosophical currents have come to the fore that are antithetical to Hartmann's philosophical position. Most of these fashionable currents are either strands of subjectivism and relativism in the broadest sense of the word, or strands of materialism and empiricism. Little of it is really new—most of it a reiteration—with marginal modifications of views originating in the nineteenth century.

The subjectivist and relativist currents are all heirs to a modern, post-Kantian idealism, subscribing to the idea that our knowledge of the world is mediated by 'categories' or 'language' posited by man, or alternatively, by the culture one belongs to. Knowledge of the world is always knowledge of what it is 'for us.' The world 'in itself' is unknowable or even non-existent.[4]

The various types of materialism and empiricism are successors to nineteenth-century positivism as developed by Comte, Mill, and Mach, and continued by the Vienna circle, or in a very different vein, successors to Marx and Freud. Notwithstanding the vast differences between the views grouped together here, they all reduce the world to that which is given by the senses: physical, material reality. All agree that spiritual and mental phenomena are nothing but manifestations—epiphenomena—of what are essentially physical, material things or events. And all agree that this world of physical, material things and events is governed by deterministic causal laws.

Hartmann's philosophy is developed in conscious and explicit opposition to both idealism and materialism and empiricism in their original nineteenth- and early twentieth-century shape. Since most of the fashionable currents in philosophy in the second half of the twentieth century are heir to these earlier ideas, it is no mystery why Hartmann has been relatively neglected in the past half century.

At the same time, however, this demonstrates Hartmann's importance to us. Here we have a philosopher who struggled with two views that, in different clothing but in essence unchanged, still dominate the philosophical landscape and are both unsatisfactory, one because of its subjectivism and relativism, and the other because of its reductionism and determinism. If these really are the only options we have of rationally making sense of the world, we are in the unenviable position of having to choose between the devil and Beelzebub. Hartmann's philosophy is an effort—one of the most impressive yet—to overcome this unpleasant dilemma.

I. LIFE, WORK, INFLUENCES[5]

Nicolai Hartmann was born in Riga, the capital of Latvia, which was at the time part of the Russian Empire, on the twentieth of February 1882. His parents belonged to the large German community that lived in the Baltic states at the time. He studied medicine in Dorpat (the present Tartu, Estonia) for a year, but then changed to St. Petersburg to study philosophy and classical philology. He stayed there from 1903 to 1905. Then he moved to Marburg, fleeing from the political upheavals in St. Petersburg. Hartmann remained in Marburg until 1925, interrupted only by four years of military service from 1914 until 1918. He studied with the neo-Kantians Hermann Cohen and Paul Natorp. In 1909 he became *Privatdozent*, in 1920 *Extraordinarius*, and in 1922 was appointed *Ordinarius* as successor to the chair of Natorp.

In 1923 Heidegger became Hartmann's colleague in Marburg, but a fruitful discussion between the two never ensued, if only because their daily schedule was incompatible. At five o'clock in the morning, when the lights in Heidegger's house were turned on, they were turned off at the Hartmann's, as a result of which one jokingly spoke of the actuality of the *philosophia perennis* in Marburg. When Heidegger's charisma drew more and more students away from Hartmann, and he was exposed to malicious attacks by the students of Heidegger, Hartmann gladly accepted a call to Cologne. Here he taught from 1925 until 1931, when he was appointed to the most prestigious chair in philosophy in Germany, at the University of Berlin.[6]

During the Nazi-period Hartmann was allowed to continue teaching. Like so many other Germans, he initially had some sympathy for the new regime, which seemed to solve the huge problem of mass unemployment. But on the whole, he kept silent and refused to express any political opinion. If his behavior was not heroic, he certainly was not involved in the Nazi-regime either.

In 1945, the uncertainty of the political situation, including the question of when and by whom the university would be reopened, induced Hartmann to accept an offer from Göttingen, where he taught and wrote until his death on the ninth of October 1950.

As a student Hartmann was very much under the influence of neo-Kantianism, but from about 1910 he gradually began to move away from idealism and turned towards a very different philosophy. His first important book, *Grundzüge einer Metaphysik der Erkenntnis*,[7] which appeared in 1921, constitutes a renouncement of idealism and a conversion to realism. With this work Hartmann meant to remove the epistemological impediments to a return to ontology: the science of reality qua reality.[8] Having done that, he spent the rest of his life developing and elaborating on his ontology.

His principal work, as he himself called it, is a general ontology in three volumes.[9] The first volume is entitled *Zur Grundlegung der Ontologie* (1935), the second *Möglichkeit und Wirklichkeit* (1938), and the third *Der Aufbau der Realen Welt* (1940).[10] Four other works, however, which might be called 'regional' ontologies, are equally important and a vital part of Hartmann's ontology: the *Ethik* (1926), *Das Problem des geistigen Seins* (1933), the *Philosophie der Natur* (1950), and the *Ästhetik*

(1953).[11] Moreover, Hartmann wrote a massive work entitled *Die Philosophie des Deutschen Idealismus* (1923/29),[12] several smaller books, and a substantial number of articles, the most important of which are collected in the *Kleinere Schriften* (1955/58).[13]

As even a superficial glance at these works makes clear, Hartmann's thought is decisively shaped by six writers: Plato, Aristotle, Kant, Hegel, Husserl, and Scheler. As this introduction is not meant to be an essay in the history of ideas, there is no need to go into these intellectual genealogies in depth. Moreover, from what follows below, Hartmann's debts will become sufficiently clear. However, a few words must be said here on these debts.

In a sense, Hartmann's work constitutes a return to a Platonic and Aristotelian ontology *cum* ethics, even though he differs with Plato and Aristotle in important respects. Many of these differences can be traced back to Kant, who always remained one of Hartmann's guiding-lights, even though he rejected Kant's transcendental idealism. Hegel was important to Hartmann both in his general ontology, influencing his views on the structure of the world, and also in his philosophy of the spirit. From Husserl, Hartmann mainly derived the phenomenological methodology of essence-perception (*Wesensschau*), which according to him was the basis and starting-point of good ontology. Finally, Max Scheler (1874-1928) needs to be mentioned, because he deeply influenced Hartmann's ethics. In fact, Hartmann conceived of his *Ethics* as a continuation and critical elaboration of Scheler's *Der Formalismus in der Ethik und die materiale Wertethik* (1913/1916).[14]

II. GNOSEOLOGY AND ONTOLOGY

In the first sentence of the introductory chapter of his *Grundzüge der Metaphysik der Erkenntnis*, Hartmann states that, phenomenologically, it is undeniable that 'cognition is not a creation, production, or bringing about of an object, as idealism [...] wants to teach us, but comprehending something, that is there, prior to all cognition and independent of it.'[15] Cognition is always cognition of a transcendent object 'in itself.' This phenomenological fact entails nothing conclusive as to the ultimate nature of cognition, but it does give realism a certain *prima facie* claim to truth. As a consequence, Hartmann argues, it is not for the realist to prove that cognition is cognition of reality, but for the idealist to prove the opposite.

In the *Metaphysik der Erkenntnis* Hartmann criticizes the idealist views of Berkeley, Kant, the neo-Kantians, and the later Husserl for not sufficiently grounding their departure from this phenomenological fact. In *Zur Grundlegung der Ontologie* he also provides positive arguments for realism. These are not to be found in the sphere of cognition, but in what Hartmann calls 'emotional-transcendent acts.'[16] In the sphere of cognition there will always be room for skepticism as to our ability to know reality as it is, because in a cognitive relation the subject remains relatively untouched and isolated from its object. In these circumstances, the question of how a subject, imprisoned in its own consciousness, can know a transcendent object is easily posed and hard to answer. In 'acts' such as suffering, on the other hand, the subject is 'overcome' by reality 'in itself.' In active involvement in the world the subject experiences the 'resistance' and 'opposition' of reality 'in itself.' Here, there is no room for doubt. '[T]he unfailing conviction of the being in itself of the world in which we live, does not so much rest on perception, as on the experienced resistance, that reality offers to the activity of the subject.'[17]

Hartmann's arguments are directed at a restoration of the dignity of the world 'in itself,' or 'being in itself' as he calls it, and a revocation of Kant's Copernican turn.[18] With this move, the epistemological—Hartmann uses the now archaic word 'gnoseological'—preoccupations of much of modern philosophy are put aside at one stroke, and ontology, the study of being qua being, is restored to its former status as *prima philosophia*.[19]

Here we are at the heart of Hartmann's concerns: the question what being 'in itself' is. As has been said above, his general ontology is set out in the *Grundlegung der Ontologie* and in two other works, *Möglichkeit und Wirklichkeit*, and *Der Aufbau der realen Welt*. We cannot go into the contents of these rich and profound works at length here. Two aspects of Hartmann's general ontology that are crucial in understanding the *Ethics* must be discussed here, however. First: his distinction between real being and ideal being. And second: his classification of real being in four strata, viz. inorganic being, organic being, mental being, i.e. being of the soul (*seelisches Sein*), and spiritual being (*geistiges Sein*). The first two strata constitute what the ontological tradition called 'nature,' the last two what it called 'spirit.'[20]

III. REAL BEING

Hartmann maintains that there are two different ways of being (*Seinsweisen*): real being (*reales Sein*) and ideal being (*ideales Sein*). Real being includes everything that is in or attached to the spatio-temporal world, including the incorporeal. The entities that partake of this kind come into existence and perish—they are impermanent, altering, and singular. Ideal being, on the other hand, is timeless and not spatial. We will go into Hartmann's analysis of real being first, and then return to the notion ideal being.

Real being consists of four different strata or layers (*Seinsschichten*), from the stratum of inorganic being at the bottom, through the strata of organic being and mental being, to spiritual being at the top.[21]

The categories of the inorganic and the organic are more or less self-evident, but what is the *raison d'être* of the distinction between mental and spiritual being? Mental being, writes Hartmann in *Das Problem des geistigen Seins*, encompasses everything that exists within the individual soul, consciously or unconsciously. Mental being everyone has for himself. It is an inner, esoteric being of the individual that is not transferable. Animals, at least the higher animals, also seem to have a mental life.

Spiritual being is built upon mental being, but it exceeds the mental. It is transferable, it is objective for every individual, and only man is a spiritual entity. 'Culture' is a term that renders the meaning of spiritual being quite accurately, if one defines it as including language, morality, law, politics, historical consciousness, ideology, the arts, religion, and philosophy.

Hartmann maintained that Hegel was the discoverer of this 'continent' of spiritual being, but Hegel wrongly metastasized spiritual being as something existing outside of the individual and with an inherent teleology. In reality, the individual is the exclusive 'carrier' of spiritual being, and if he neglects to carry it faithfully, spiritual being will deteriorate and disintegrate.

The lower a stratum, the stronger, the less fragile it is. The higher a stratum, the more vulnerable it is. Inorganic being is indestructible, spiritual being is the most perishable of all strata of being. This is an ontological law.

The lower strata are the ontologic base of higher strata. Higher strata are dependent on lower strata, in the sense that the lower strata are the matter out of which being at a higher stratum is formed. There is, however, according to Hartmann, no teleological relation between the lower and the higher strata. The lower strata are 'indifferent' towards the higher. That higher strata have developed is a cosmic coincidence.

The ontologic structure of the real world is described *in extenso* in *Aufbau der realen Welt*. Many characteristics or categories (*Kategorien*) of being of the lower strata return in the higher strata, but in each stratum some new categories are added, and others disappear. Hence, each stratum has its own nature and its own determinants.

Take, for instance, the three categories of temporality, spatiality, and causality. Temporality (*Zeitlichkeit*), i.e. being-in-time, is characteristic of all four strata of real being. The real world is a Heraclitean world, in which all things change and no one can cross the same river twice. Spatiality (*Räumlichkeit*), i.e. being-in-space, on the other hand, is a characteristic only of inorganic and organic being. Mental and spiritual being are not spatial, although both are attached to—carried by—spatial being.

The causal nexus is the principle of the motion characteristic of inorganic being, and it reappears in all the higher strata. But other, supra-causal (*überkausale*), determinants are added there. Already in the stratum of organic being, the vital sphere, a pre-existing form, a system of predispositions, somehow molds the

causal process. The organic process is in some way directed towards a goal (*Zweckmäßigkeit*). And it is in the stratum of spiritual
being that we encounter purposiveness, i.e. the finalistic nexus
(*Zwecktätigkeit*). At this point Hartmann clearly follows Kant in
his opposition of the traditional Aristotelian view that purposiveness is a characteristic of being as a whole.[22]

Hartmann's criticism of idealism and materialism follows
immediately from this conception of reality. Both idealism and
materialism neglect the ontologic stratification of the real world.
In doing so, the idealist reduces the lower to higher strata, and
the materialist reduces higher strata to lower. 'The former
keeps to Reason, Spirit, Ideas, God, the latter to Matter, Laws
of Nature, Causality. The former spiritualizes matter and nature, the latter disparages the spirit as an annex to matter.'[23]
Both flatten the world to square it with an erroneous, monistic
worldview.

Hartmann suggests that this is due, at least partially, to the old
prejudice that the best explanations are those on the basis of a
single principle. In other words, simplicity is the seal of truth. Put
differently, monism, whether of the idealist or of the materialist
stamp, is a consequence of an *esprit de système*—Hartmann speaks
of system-thinking (*Systemdenken*)—which violently compresses
all that is phenomenologically given into one preconceived
scheme of interpretation.

Only problem-oriented thinking (*Problemdenken*), departing
from the phenomenologically-given, ideally without any theoretical preconceptions, can do justice to the complexity of the
world. Problem-oriented thinking is not unsystematic. Indeed, it
usually strives to achieve systematic knowledge. But here the
wish to be systematic is not compulsive, and problem-oriented
thinkers are prepared to acknowledge problems that seem to un-
dermine their system.[24]

IV. IDEAL BEING

In addition to the sphere of real being, the world encompasses a
sphere of ideal being according to Hartmann. This sphere consists

of ideal entities, such as mathematical units and laws, the laws of logic, the essence (*Wesen*) of concrete, existing things, acts and occurrences. And it includes values. Since the notion of value is at the heart of Hartmann's ethics, it is necessary to go into the concept of ideal being at a somewhat greater length.

'In ancient times,' Hartmann sets out in *Ethics*, 'it was seen that there is another realm of being than that of existence, than that of "real" things and of consciousness which is not less "real." Plato named it the realm of the Idea, Aristotle that of the *eidos*, the scholastics called it the realm of *essentia*. After having been long misunderstood and deprived of its right in modern times through the prevailing subjectivism, this realm has again come into recognition with relative purity in that which phenomenology calls the realm of *Wesenheiten*. *Wesenheit* is a translation of *essentia*. It means the same thing, if we disregard the various metaphysical presuppositions which have attached themselves to the idea of essence. But on its part, *essentia* is a translation, although a very faded one, of the Aristotelian phrase *ti èn einai*, in which the past tense *èn*, understood as timeless,[25] points to the sum total of the structural elements that are presupposed—that is, of that which in the concrete thing, act or occurrence constitutes the objective *prius* and on that account is always contained in it.'[26]

What is this *prius*? 'For Aristotle, of course, this "essence" possessed a logical structure. It was thought of as the complete series of the determinant elements of a definition, or as a series of the *differentiae*, which, proceeding from the most general, embrace the ever narrower, down to the "last," to the *differentia specifica*. The *eidos*, which thus arises, is then accepted as the formal substance, the complete structure. This logicism was conditioned by the identification of "essence" with "concept," or, more correctly, by the lack of any discrimination between them. It was this that also obscured the doctrine of "essence" in the Middle Ages, and gave support to the audacious metaphysics of conceptual realism.'[27] That is to say, it gave rise to the idea that ideal beings (*universalia*) were part of, existed in the real world, and only there. They were thought to be merely *in rebus*.

Hartmann believes that this view is mistaken, because the specific nature of being of the *essentia* is lost.[28] 'From this [view] it has been necessary for the principle underlying Plato's fundamental vision to free itself again. In Hegel's doctrine of "essence" this deliverance has been accomplished.[...] [I]t signifies a harking back to the ancient notion of the "ground," which belonged to the meaning of "essence" in Plato's Idea.'[29] This is to say that '[t]he kind of being peculiar to the "idea" is that of an *ontós on*, the kind of being of that "through which" everything participating in it, is just as it is.'[30] Ideal being manifests itself in real being, but it is not absorbed in it. Ideal being is an independent sphere of being.[31]

Hartmann's indebtedness to Plato on this issue is obvious.[32] He disagrees with Plato on the status of the sphere of ideal being, however. In Plato's view, the sphere of Ideas is the sphere of true being, and real being is merely an imperfect reflection of it. Hartmann rejects this 'nimbus of loftiness' surrounding Platonic ideas.[33] Ideal being 'is a "thinner," floating, insubstantial being, half-being so to speak, which still lacks the full weight of being.'[34] This nimbus of loftiness 'is the expression of a false idealism, which will have to be paid for in life; because it results in a devaluation and disregard of the real.'[35] This is tragic, Hartmann believes, because the truly valuable things in life are to be found precisely there, in the transient world of real being.[36]

In the units and laws of mathematics man first discovered ideal being.[37] The Pythagoreans already spoke about the being of numbers, and Plato followed in their trail. Geometry, he wrote, is *epistèmè tou aei ontos*: knowledge of eternal being. Mathematical units and laws are *aei on*, their being is beyond time and space, beyond genesis and disintegration, which are typical of everything in the real world.

But although mathematical being differs fundamentally from real being, it pervades the latter. The Pythagoreans already saw that the principles of mathematics are the principles of reality.[38] Things, acts, and occurrences in the real world necessarily comply with the principles of mathematics. It is possible, by eliminating or adding one or more axioms, to develop a mathematics that has little to do with the real world, but it is not possible for the real world to escape from the grip of mathematical principles. The real contains and is molded by the ideal.

The real world is suffused with mathematical principles, but these principles cannot be observed empirically.[39] Moreover, the validity of mathematical principles is universal and stringent, whereas empirical observation can only render probable results. Therefore, knowledge of mathematical principles must be the product of a different kind of observation that is not empirical and can claim absolute validity. Plato called it an inner perception, a perception with the mind's eye, so to speak. Kant's synthetic judgment a priori also bears upon this kind of knowledge.[40] Following the latter, Hartmann speaks of a priori knowledge as 'an inner grasping of a state of affairs, that has immediate certainty, and can claim generality and necessity.'[41]

What goes for mathematics goes for all other types of ideal being as well, viz. for the laws of logic, for the essence of concrete, existing things, acts and occurrences, and for values. All of these cannot be observed empirically, but are perceived a priori. Our knowledge of these ideal entities is a priori knowledge.

This is the gist of Hartmann's general ontology and 'gnoseology,' i.e. epistemology. Doing justice to the richness and profoundness of his thought would require a much less condensed and cursory exposition. But as a preparation to what has to be said by way of introduction to Hartmann's ethical ideas as expounded in the *Ethics*, it suffices. So let us now turn to these ethical ideas.

V. VALUES

Philosophy, Kant famously said, is ultimately concerned with only three questions. What can we know? What should we do? And what may we hope for? The second of these is generally regarded as the fundamental question of ethics.[42]

This question is of more than theoretical, academic interest, writes Hartmann. 'It grows out of what is next to us, out of the current of everyday life no less than out of life's great decisive moments, with which the individual is occasionally confronted.[...]

Every moment we stand face to face with the question: what ought we to do? Every situation brings it up afresh. Step by step in life we must answer it anew, and no power can deliver us, or lift us above the necessity of answering it.'[43] No god or *causa efficiens* can release us from this awesome responsibility.[44]

'[E]very act has consequences, and the possibility is always present that they weigh heavily where we least suspect it. And what holds good on a small scale, concerning the conduct of the individual, is true on a larger scale of the conduct of a community, a generation, an age. On what we determine today, depends perhaps the future of generations.[...] Here the seriousness of the question "what ought we to do?" becomes self-evident.'[45]

Behind every 'ought to do' lies a conception of what was formerly called a 'good' (*kalon*, *agathon*, *bonum*), but to which modern philosophers, including Hartmann, usually refer as a value.[46]

Most values are valuable merely in a conditional sense. They are valuable because they are means to realize other, more ultimate values. But these too are in most cases only instrumental in realizing still more ultimate values. Yet, at the end of these chains stand one or several values, which are considered valuable in themselves and ultimately determine what we think we ought to do.

Nor do (ultimate) values pertain only to our doing—and refraining from doing—something. Values are pertinent not only with regard to how we act, but also with regard to 'the inner attitude of man, his ethos as deciding for or against, as acceptance or rejection, reverence or disdain, love or hate.'[47] There is no doing, no action here, but that does not mean that the inner attitude of man is ethically irrelevant, if only because our inner attitude determines what we eventually do.

Hence, the question of value is the question that ethics must deal with first and foremost, according to Hartmann. 'What is valuable in life and in the world generally?'[48] After all, 'I can gauge what I ought to do only when I "see" what in general is valuable in life.'[49] The question of what we ought to do is not, *pace* Kant, the fundamental moral question. It is a corollary of the more fundamental question of value. Values are the moral *principia*.

What kind of principles are values? In his theory of value, Hartmann follows the lead of Scheler's *Der Formalismus in de Ethik und die materiale Wertethik*—a work he describes as epoch-making[50]—although he is critical of many of Scheler's ideas and differs with him at many, sometimes crucial, points.[51]

The first question that usually arises with regard to values concerns their foundation. What is the nature of the authority of moral principles? Is it a genuine, absolute and objective authority, or is it subjective and relative to time and place? 'From the time of the sophists, who were the first to distinguish between what is *phusei* and what is *thèsei*, this question has never ceased to attract attention; and it rightly stands at the center of every conflict of opinions and theories.'[52]

Contrary to what is often presumed, Hartmann argues, the subjectivity of values cannot be proved by referring to the historical fact that values have differed at various times and places. If values are absolute, that historical fact would prove only that most men at most times are blind to at least part of 'the empire of values.'[53] Facts can teach us nothing here. Which of the two contradictory views is superior depends upon which is more tenable as a theory.

In the modern world, values are widely considered to be subjective. That is to say, they are regarded as the outcome of an act of valuation, and hence as something that is invented, made up, created. Hartmann's ethics are in essence an effort to do away with this view and vindicate the pre-modern conception that values cannot be invented but can merely be found, and are therefore objective and absolute.

Nevertheless, Hartmann admits that, in a specific sense, values are subjective. Values hold good only 'for' man. But they do so in the same way as geometrical laws hold good only 'for' spatial figures, mechanical laws only 'for' real bodies, and physiological laws only 'for' organisms. These laws are relative to certain kinds of being, but this does not mean that they can be created or abolished. They are laws to which the being for whom they hold good is unconditionally subjected. Values hold good for man as a spiritual being, and he is unconditionally subjected to them.

Neither are they subjective in the Kantian sense, according to Hartmann. Values are not transcendental categories of consciousness that structure our experience of the world. They are not posited by us, but subsist independently of our consciousness. Values have being in themselves (*Ansichsein*). They belong to that realm of being that Plato first discovered: the sphere of ideal being. Values are entities 'of an ethically ideal sphere, of a realm with its own structures, its own laws and order. This sphere is connected organically with the theoretical ideal sphere, the logical and the mathematical, as well as with that of pure essences in general.'[54]

VI. KNOWLEDGE OF VALUES

'Knowledge of values is genuine knowledge of being. In this respect it stands absolutely on a level with every kind of theoretical knowledge. Its object is for the subject just as independent a reality as spatial relations are for geometrical knowledge or things are for knowledge concerning things. The grasping of them [...] is just as much an act which goes out to something beyond itself as every other cognitive act [...]. In its "beholding" of them the subject is purely receptive; he surrenders himself to them. He sees himself determined by the object, the value as it is in itself; but he himself, on his side, determines nothing. The value abides as unaffected by his beholding as does any object of knowledge by the fact that it is known.'[55]

How do we perceive values, how do we come to know them?[56] It is impossible to observe values empirically. Only acts, things, and events are perceived empirically. To know the value of what is observed empirically is possible only if one has already comprehended the relevant value *in abstracto* of what is observed, and can use that knowledge as a standard to assess what has been realized. Knowledge of values is a priori knowledge, like knowledge of mathematical and logical being, and knowledge of the essence of real entities.

Epistemologically, values are not entirely on a par with the other classes of ideal being, however. The other classes have a categorical hold over the real world. Real being is wholly conditional on them. All real entities conform to them inexorably.

That is not the case with values. Real being can, but need not be in agreement with the values. It can be valuable or not. Regarding the class of values, the real is independent from the ideal. The real world does not necessarily conform to values in the way it conforms to the other classes of ideal being. Real being can be without value or even contrary to value (*Wertwidrig*). Hartmann maintains that '[t]his denial has nothing to do with theoretical negation. It does not at all question the being of the thing denied, it is more a refusal to recognize it despite its being, it is in tendency a nullification.'[57]

The independence of real being and values vis-à-vis each other deepens the epistemological problem. Due to the indissoluble bond between the real and the other classes of the ideal, it is possible in those cases to direct our thinking to the ideal through the real by bracketing the ephemeral.[58] In the case of values, this is impossible. So what does 'grasping' mean, when we speak of grasping a value?

Grasping a value is sensing it, or more precisely, being gripped by it (*Erfaßtsein von ihm*), writes Hartmann.[59] The specific 'organ' with which man perceives values is his sense of value (*Wertgefühl*). This sense of value is neither a cognitive nor a conative, but an affective, an emotional capacity.[60]

Not everyone has the same capacity to sense values, and not everyone's capacity is equally well developed, Hartmann argues. 'There are such things as education and lack of education of the sense of values, talent and lack of talent for the discernment of them.'[61] '[I]t is here just as it is with mathematical insight. Not everyone is capable of it; not everyone has the eye, the ethical maturity, the spiritual level, for seeing the situation as it is. Nevertheless, the universality, necessity and objectivity of the valuational judgment hold good *in abstracto*. For this universality does not at all mean that everyone is capable of the valuational insight in question. It only means that whoever is capable of it— that is, whoever spiritually gets hold of its meaning—must necessarily feel and judge thus and not otherwise.'[62]

Value blindness is quite a common phenomenon. In extreme cases it brings about a complete loss of meaning of life and the world. 'He who stolidly passes by men and their fates, he whom the staggering does not stagger nor the exalted exalt, for him life is in vain, he has no part of it. The world must be meaningless and life senseless to one who has no capacity to perceive the sense of life's relationships, the inexhaustible significance of persons and situations, or correlations and events. The outward emptiness and monotony of his life are the reflex of his inner emptiness and his moral blindness. The real world in which he exists, the stream of human life which bears him up and carries him along, is not without manifold wealth of content. His poverty amidst abundance is due to his own failure to appreciate life. Hence for the moral nature of man there is, besides the narrow actuality of action and ought-to-do, a second requirement: to participate in the fullness of life, to be receptive to the significant, to lie open to whatever has meaning and value.'[63]

The sense of values can be narrow and broad, not only in the individual, but also in collectivities. But even when it is broad, it seems to be a fact that we, individually and collectively, always appreciate only a limited section of the realm of values, while we remain blind to other sections.[64] One cannot be gripped by all values at the same time. On the contrary, each and every value tends to claim absolute allegiance. Such is the gripping power of values.

Hence, there is a real danger that one or a few values become tyrannically dominant in a man, driving out his sense of other values, and turning him into a one-sided fanatic. And the same can happen to a group of men or a whole society. The broadening of the sense of values, on the other hand, while ruling out fanaticism, can easily effect a decrease in intensity and immediateness and result in a degree of sloth.

The sense of values varies constantly. In Hartmann's view, this is the reason why values seem so alterable and relative, both historically and geographically. In truth, 'this shifting and variability do not constitute a "transvaluation of values," but a revaluation and reorientation of human life. Values do not change, but our insight into them changes.'[65] Actions, outlooks, and associations which yesterday passed as good, may today be held to be bad, due to the fact that some values have been unveiled and others have fallen into oblivion.

This process of transformation of the sense of value is not always calm and orderly, Hartmann thinks. 'In certain epochs it leads to sharp crises, breaks forth violently, seizes hold of the emotions like a whirlpool and sweeps them along into historic action. The valuational discovery which gave its penetrative power to primitive Christianity was such a crisis—the discovery of the peculiar moral significance of love of one's neighbor. One central value, or even a whole group of them, enters the ethical consciousness and radically transforms the view of the world and life.[...] In criticism of the old, in opposition to things consecrated, the new vision springs up, ripens and waxes strong. It must destroy so as to achieve; it must do this even where it takes up the existing order into itself and builds upon it. It is born under the sign of conflict; and the conflict lasts until it triumphs or succumbs.'[66]

'Here the great ethical leaders appear, the heroes of the spirit, prophets, founders of religions, the champions of ideas. From them the movement proceeds; they revolutionize the crowd. It is natural enough to think that such leaders are "inventors" of the new forms of value, that the birth of values themselves takes place in the thought of the champion of ideas.[...] [T]hat is a great mistake. The champion himself invents nothing; he only discovers. Indeed, even his discovery is conditional. He can only discover what already lives darkly in the valuational sentiment of the crowd, and presses forward to expression. It is he who, as it were, reads in human hearts the values newly felt; there he gleans them, draws them into the light of consciousness, lifts them on to his shield and invests them with speech.'[67]

This process of the transformation of values Hartmann calls the primary discernment of values (*primäre Wertschau*). There is also a secondary discernment of values: philosophical ethics. It is derivative and dependent on the primary discernment of values and can only follow in the footsteps of the latter, but it can nonetheless make a positive contribution to our moral knowledge. It can offer a synoptic view of the empire of values—at least of those parts of it which have been discovered until today—and clarify the connections, order, relations, and regularities which exist in the realm of values. This is the task Hartmann has set for himself in writing the *Ethics*.

VII. MORAL VALUES

What is the content of the empire of value? What types of value can be distinguished? How are they related to each other? Is there a hierarchical relation between them? Are there any or even many antinomies between them? It is in volume II of the *Ethics* and not in volume I that Hartmann discusses these and other questions *in extenso*. They will therefore be largely passed over here. However, in order to fully appreciate what is said on these matters in volume I, a few remarks have to be made at this point on the distinction between values in general and the special category of moral values (*sittliche Werte*).

In a sense, from a practical point of view, everything that exists somehow falls under the category of 'values.' Even the most remote and indifferent thing, act or event either has a positive or a negative worth. The world of things and their relations is at the same time and no less a world of goods and evils.

All of these goods are values, and all of these evils are 'disvalues' (*Unwerte*), but to Hartmann's mind it is impossible to call all the goods and evils *moral* values and *moral* disvalues. A piece of property, for instance, can be a good, can have a value, but as such it is not a moral value. A book, a vacation, peace of mind, anything may be a good, and anything may be an evil. But this does not make these things morally good or evil, moral values.

Moral values are necessarily affixed to man, more specifically to his acts and to his personality, which is shaped by and expressed in these acts. In the latter case, when values are inherent in a person, we speak of virtues. Man, and man only, is the carrier of moral values. Honesty would be an example of a moral value. Only an act or a person can be honest or dishonest, things or situations cannot.

Nevertheless, non-moral goods and evils are intimately related to moral values. Moral values presuppose other, non-moral goods. '[W]herein would an honest man be superior to a thief, if the things purloined were not somehow of value? What one man can steal, what another can treasure as a possession, is not merely a thing but a good. Honesty then, if it is a moral value, necessarily presupposes the positive worth of material (i.e. non-moral, AK) goods. It is inherently dependent upon the latter.'[68] And the same goes for all other moral values.

A moral value will often be a non-moral value at the same time. 'The fidelity of a person is a good thing for another towards whom it is practiced; trust is a good thing for him to whom it is shown; vigor and self-sacrifice for him to whom they are offered. To the beloved he who loves, to the friend a friend is a good.'[69] But the moral worth of a person who keeps faith, is trustworthy and vigorous, sacrifices himself, shows his love or friendship, et cetera, does not lie in the goods-value (*Güterwert*) he has for someone else. 'It inheres in himself, even when he brings no benefit to another, even when it is not a "good" "for" anyone.'[70]

Hartmann obviously follows Kant here. The moral value of an act depends on the intention of the actor, the virtue of a person on his disposition—not on the measure in which a good is achieved. All types of consequentialist ethics, ancient and modern, fail to take this fundamental phenomenon into account. 'Consequences do not depend upon the will alone, but it is the will alone which in an action can be (morally, A.K) good or bad. Upon it alone therefore depends the moral quality of the person.'[71]

VIII. THE REALIZATION OF VALUES

The world contains two essentially different kinds of being in itself: one real and one ideal. The former includes all things, acts, and events, everything that is 'actual,' whatever has existence. The latter consists of the configurations of pure mathematics and logic, and, over and above these, of the essences of every kind—including values—that persist throughout the changes of individual existence and permit of being discerned a priori. Between the two kinds of being subsists a fundamental relationship that is profoundly characteristic of the whole realm of being and of the knowledge of being: the design of ideal being in itself reappears in that of the real. As a consequence, the aprioristic knowledge of ideal being constitutes an inner foundation of all knowledge of the real, especially since this reappearance is categorical. There is not one real entity in which the corresponding ideal entity does not recur.

That is, except in the case of values. With values it is otherwise. They can of course be realized, but they can also be unrealized. It does not lie in their essence as principles that the real must correspond to them. Values are not inviolable determinants to which everything is subordinate. This leads to the question: what, if any, is the relation between values as ideal entities and the real world?

At this point Hartmann reintroduces the notion of the *ought*. Values and the ought are indissolubly bound together. The ought belongs to the essence of the values. It is not principally an ought-to-do, which refers to a volitional subject, but more generally an ought-to-be. Value and ought-to-be stand in strict correlation, in reciprocal conditionality. The ought-to-be is the mode of being of a value, its proper modality, and a value is the content of the ought.

Not every ought-to-be is attached to an ought-to-do. 'I ought to do what ought to be, in so far as it "is" not, and in so far as to make it real is in my power. This double "in so far as" separates these two kinds of ought.'[72]

The ought-to-be of the values refers to the real world. Sometimes the ought-to-be and the real are in harmony. But often they are not, and the ideal finds itself in opposition to the real; it is unrealized (*irreal*). Then the ought-to-be becomes actual.[73] The ideal 'calls out' to be realized.[74]

To be heard—and acted upon—Hartmann writes, there must be '[i]n the stream of real existence, i.e. in fluctuating reality itself, [...] a point of support, upon which the ought-to-be impinges. There must be something or other within the real course of the world, which is placed in the world as an element of it and is dependent upon its general conditions; it must come under the laws of the real world, share completely in the world's existential mode of coming into being and perishing, it must be a thing that passes away like the world's other entities. And yet it must at the same time be able to be a carrier of the imperishable, the ideal; it must in this one respect be more than the other entities, must be distinguished from all other reality by this essential feature, must stand in opposition to it.'[75]

There is one such point of support: man. He and only he is capable of sensing values, and at the same time capable of acting upon them. He and only he can convert the ought-to-be into reality. The rest of existence is dull and dead to the call of the ideal. Man is the administrator of the ought in the world of real being. In man only the ought-to-be is transformed into the ought-to-do, and in man only the ought-to-do is transformed into a moral act.

This transformation is anything but mechanical, Hartmann argues. The mediation between the ideal and the real presupposes that man considers the ought-to-be an end (*Zweck*), and that he subsequently takes action to realize it. Whether he really does consider it an end and takes action is up to him. There is no law of nature compelling him to mediate between the ideal and the real, at least not in the way a stone is 'compelled' to obey the law of gravitation. Indeed, man very often betrays his duties as administrator of the ought-to-be, because he does not comprehend the ought-to-do, or for some reason, such as weakness of will, he fails to act upon it.

Hence, the determining force of values is in one sense weak. Values do not rule unconditionally. Without 'outside' help by man they cannot be realized. And this 'outside' help is frequently absent.

At the same time, however, values have an unparalleled strength, according to Hartmann. Values 'can transform not-being into being. The *generatio ex nihilo*, which is otherwise an impossibility in all realms of being, here is possible.'[76] The laws of logic and all the other classes of ideal being rule within the real world. They do not add anything new to this world. Values, on the other hand, if they are realized, bring in a new, 'axiological' determination,[77] on top of the ontological determination that is always there.

Hence, if values are realized they literally change the world. And they depend on man to be realized. This demonstrates the uniqueness and greatness of man's position in the world as a practical, i.e. acting agent, and the awesome responsibility that is his. In his theoretical capacity, man merely mirrors the world, he is a mere consciousness of being (*Fürsichsein des Seins*), his thoughts only represent the world's structure. As a practical agent, on the other hand, he molds, transforms and builds up the world: he is a world-creator in little. Man as a practical agent is the restless point in the world, in which it loses its ontological equilibrium. He is the intersecting point between two heterogeneous determinations, the axiological and the ontological, the battlefield where these determinations clash.

A man who senses a value and acts upon it adds an axiological determination to the ontological determination of the real world. To comprehend what this means, we must take another look at the notion of value.

Values are ends. They do not impel from behind and push forward, but draw unto themselves. Hence, the determining power of values is teleological or finalistic. As has been remarked earlier, Hartmann, following Kant, recognizes that the traditional Aristotelian conception of the real world as *in toto* a finalistic nexus has been discredited. But he argues that it fits well with the stratum of spiritual being.

The finalistic nexus is introduced into the real world through man, on top of the causal nexus that pervades the real world. It is the reverse of the latter. The dynamic of a causal series is that of a blind forward push, indifferent to its results. The dynamic of a finalistic series, on the other hand, anticipates the final point and predetermines the whole series.

How can these two contradictory ways of determination coexist in one and the same world? This is one of the central problems of modern philosophy. Volume III of the *Ethics* is in its entirety devoted to it. But towards the end of volume I this discussion is introduced. Hartmann wants to avoid sacrificing one of the ways of determination to the other, but he is not content with a Kantian juxtaposition of an empire of nature (*Reich der Natur*) and an empire of values (*Reich der Sitten*) either. According to him, the finalistic determination inserts itself without conflict into the causal, because the course of its realization is itself causal. In the achievement of the end the actual process is a causal process, in which the means are real causes which, step by step, bring about the good aimed at. Hence, the lower, ontological form of determination is built into the higher and more complex axiological form as a constituent part of the latter. Axiological determination, though qualitatively superior, is dependent upon ontological determination.

This is not inconsistent. On the contrary, it is in line with the general ontological laws governing the relation between the various strata of being. 'In the graded realm of principles (of the strata of being, A.K.) it is precisely the dependent which is always and necessarily at the same time the superior: the higher principle is always the more complex, more conditioned and in this sense the weaker; the lower is always the more unconditioned and more general, more elemental, and in this sense the stronger, but at the same time the poorer. The higher cannot dispense with the lower nor break through it; it can construct nothing by violence against the lower determination, but upon the lower as a basis and upon its structures it may well form another and higher edifice. In this alone consists its superiority. This and no other superiority is possessed by values in their passage out of the ideal into the real world.'[78]

IX. PERSON AND PERSONALITY

Man is the intersecting point between two heterogeneous determinations, the battlefield where these determinations clash. Thus, man has a double nature. In Hartmann's terminology, he is both a 'subject' and a 'person.' As a subject he is a purely ontological being, as a person he is at the same time an axiological being. Man as a subject belongs to the stratum of mental being; man as a person is part of the stratum of spiritual being.

Subjectivity is the precondition of personality. 'Personality is the higher and therefore the more fully conditioned; the subject on the other hand is the lower, and therefore the conditioning form.[...] Personality exists only on the basis of subjectivity, just as subjectivity exists only on a basis of organic life, and life only on a basis of the whole structure of subordinate nature,' i.e. of inorganic matter.[79] The higher entity is autonomous vis-à-vis the lower, in the sense that it introduces new structures and laws, which are not in any way contained in the lower entity. They cannot exist without the lower entity, however. The freedom of the higher level can never displace or nullify its basis.

Only a person is a moral subject, on Hartmann's view. Personality involves the power or the freedom to take hold of a value or not, and to place one's acts in its service or not. For both the perception (or lack of it) and the action (or lack of it), the person is held responsible, precisely because of this power or freedom. Each is attributed to him and for each he is blamed in case of failure. If he does not sense values, or does sense them but fails to take steps to realize them, he bears the guilt. The moral value of his acts and his person depend upon this.

This conception of the person and personality, which is set out in the final chapters of volume I of the *Ethics*, is presented in explicit contradistinction to the conception of the person and personality put forward by Scheler in *Formalismus in der Ethik*. The differences between Hartmann and Scheler at this point are indeed considerable, but they rather concern the implications of the conception of the person and personality, than the conception itself of man as a person, i.e. as, in part, a spiritual being with moral responsibility. Nevertheless these differences exist, and they are of considerable interest.

Most importantly, Hartmann reproaches Scheler with a 'metaphysical personalism,' extending the concept of the person and personality beyond the boundaries of the phenomena the essential features of which it correctly depicts, to various kinds of other phenomena, even when they are completely different. Scheler thus makes a mistake typical of monist system-thinking.

'That the individual, isolated and for himself, is an abstraction, that he does not emerge except in larger contexts of persons and is conditioned not only in his existence but also in his ethos by this context, is an ancient insight,' writes Hartmann.[80] But Scheler mistakenly conceives of these contexts as persons of a higher order, as collective persons. According to him, family, tribe, nation, state, culture, and humanity also act, and they are also carriers of moral values. Indeed, Scheler seems to assume that these persons of a higher order are carriers of higher moral values than the individual. Moreover, Scheler's conception of a collective person culminates in an absolute and all-embracing person: a personal God.

The ascription of personality to social units is false in Hartmann's view. 'There are, of course, collective spiritual structures; there is an "objective spirit" [...] which never is absorbed in the individual consciousness, but in which all participate. Art, science, the morality of an age, the national, political, or religious life, is collective spirit in this sense. The way of being of such structures is a thoroughly real one, as they have their beginning and end, their history and laws of development.'[81] The individual is shaped by these structures to the extent that he finds scope for his individuality only within its bounds, or at the most, very little beyond them. But collective spiritual structures 'possess the character neither of a subject nor of a person.'[82]

These structures are not persons of a higher order: they are persons merely by analogy. Those who act, carry, or fail to carry values, and are responsible, are ultimately individuals. They can 'lend' their personality to a collective structure by acting in the name of the whole, but the fact that the community can set itself in opposition to such a representative individual proves that the collective structure is but a quasi-personal entity. By implication, Hartmann concludes, God—if there is one—is not the absolute and highest person, the carrier of the supreme values, but an absolutely impersonal being. Hence, 'neither God nor the state, nor anything else in the world is a moral being, but singly the primary carrier of moral values and disvalues: man.'[83]

A Note on the Translation

The style of German philosophers is justly notorious. The writings of Kant, Hegel, Marx, and Heidegger—to name only the most renowned—are, whatever one thinks of the merit of their ideas, hardly a pleasure to read. In view of this fact, one might be tempted to assume that Hartmann must be as hermetic a writer as are his countrymen. This would be unjustified, however, because he is the proverbial exception to the rule. His German is down-to-earth, his style transparent and often graceful.

This is not to say, of course, that Hartmann is effortlessly understandable. As a post-Kantian, post-Hegelian philosopher, Hartmann inevitably uses technical terms common in modern German philosophy, such as 'being in itself,' 'the transcendent' and 'the transcendental,' 'a priori' and 'a posteriori,' et cetera. Hence, notwithstanding Hartmann's stylistic virtues, reading his work—the *Ethics* not excepted—can be demanding.

If reading Hartmann is not easy, one can image what a feat it must be to translate him. The translation of the *Ethics* now being republished by Transaction was made by Stanton Coit in the years immediately after the appearance of the German original. As the translation of German philosophical texts in English is frequently rather poor, it is of some pertinence to say a few words about the quality of this particular translation.

A meticulous comparison of the German and the English text brings to light quite a number of mistakes, but most of these mistakes are of little weight. Page 184 of volume I may serve as an example. Coit, on that page, translates 'Inbegriff dessen was an Stukturelementen vorausgesetzt ist' as 'conception of that which in the structural elements is presupposed.' It should be 'the sum total of structural elements that are presupposed.' 'Auch' becomes 'even'; it should be 'also.' 'Gewagt' becomes 'attempted,' instead of 'audacious' or 'bold.' 'Die Tugend-Ideen' is rendered as 'the ideal virtue,' whereas it means 'the ideas of virtue.' Errors such as these one finds on every page. While they are not serious enough to obscure the meaning of Hartmann's words, it must be admitted that, on the whole, they tend to make the *Ethics* somewhat less transparent in translation than in the German original.

One more substantial error has crept into the translation. It concerns the technical terms 'being' (*Sein*) and 'existence' (*Existenz,*

Dasein). Coit frequently translates the German 'Sein' as 'existence.' Most conspicuously, the title of chapter sixteen, 'Das ideale Ansichsein der Werte' is rendered as 'The ideal self-existence of values.' This is erroneous, because 'being' is a broader concept than 'existence.' The first includes both the real world and the ideal world, the second refers only to the real world. The ideal world has no existence. The beings that belong to it have no spatio-temporal being. One cannot say of them that they are 'there' (*Dasein*). One can only say 'what' they are (*Sosein*). Ideal beings are the *essentia* of scholasticism and the *eidè* of Platonic and Aristotelian philosophy.

Notwithstanding these imperfections, however, Coit's translation of Hartmann's *Ethik* is of a good quality. The purist might take comfort in the well-known fact that, as the Italians say, 'traduttore traditore.' A translator is necessarily a traitor. Anyone who wants to study Hartmann pure and unadulterated should learn to read German.

ANDREAS A.M. KINNEGING
University of Leiden, Faculty of Law

NOTES

1. The *Ethics* consists of three volumes. Volume II and III will be published by Transaction in the following years and will be separately introduced by the present author. Aside from preparing the reader for volume I, the introduction at hand aims to give an idea of Hartmann's philosophy as a whole. A word of appreciation is due to miss Emma Cohen de Lara, M.A., and Mr. Michiel Visser, M.A., LL.M., for their help in preparing this introduction.

2. Cf. I.M. Bochenski, *Europäische Philosophie der Gegenwart*, Bern: Francke Verlag 1947, pp. 226-238, is positive; W. Stegmüller, *Hauptströmungen der Gegenwartsphilosophie*, Stuttgart: Kröner Verlag, 4th rev. ed. 1969, pp. 245-287, is disparaging.

3. H. Heimsoeth and R. Heib (eds.), *Nicolai Hartmann, der Denker und sein Werk*, Göttingen: Vandenhoeck & Ruprecht 1952 and A.J. Buch (ed.), *Nicolai Hartmann 1882-1982*, Bonn: Bouvier Verlag 2nd ed. 1987 (1982) contain bibliographies. H. Schnädelbach, *Philosopie in Deutschland*, Frankfurt a/M.: Suhrkamp 1999 (1983), p. 259, concludes 'that Hartmann has left a mark on his epoch, but has not—like Heidegger—been epoch-making.'

4.   Of course many strands of idealism, today and in earlier days, do not
        adopt Kant's notion of the transcendental subject.
5.   Cf. Martin Morgenstern, *Nicolai Hartmann, zur Einführung*, Ham-
        burg: Junius Verlag 1997, pp. 7-29. This small book is a good gen-
        eral introduction to Hartmann's philosophy.
6.   V. Farias, *Heidegger et le Nazisme*, Lagrasse: Verdier 1987, ch. 6
        gives an account of the vicissitudes surrounding the appointment to
        this chair, for which Heidegger and Ernst Cassirer, among others,
        were also candidates.
7.   In English: *Outlines of a Metaphysics of Knowledge*. With the ex-
        ception of the *Ethik* and a smaller work entitled *Neue Wege der
        Ontologie*, which was translated by R.C. Kuhn as *New Ways of
        Ontology*, Westport Ct.: Greenwood 1975 (1952), there are no trans-
        lations into English of Hartmann's works.
8.   Of course, Aristotles' classic definition of ontology or metaphysics,
        Metaphysics 1003a21, is 'the science which considers being qua
        being,' *epistèmè hè theórei to on hei on*. In paraphrasing Aristotle,
        'reality' is here taken as synonymous to 'being.' On Hartmann's use
        of the notions of reality and being, see *infra*.
9.   *Grundlegung de Ontologie*, Vorwort, cf. note 9.
10.   In English respectively *The Foundations of Ontology*, *Possibility
        and Actuality*, and *The Structure of the Real World*.
11.   In English: *Ethics, The Problem of Spiritual Being, Philosophy of
        Nature*, and *Aesthetics*.
12.   In English: *The Philosophy of German Idealism*. It originally ap-
        peared in two volumes. The first volume, published first in 1923, is
        on Fichte, Schelling, and the romantics, the second, published in
        1929, is on Hegel. In the second edition (1960) the two parts were
        published in one volume.
13.   Cf. the bibliography of Hartmann's major works at the end of this
        introduction. A complete bibliography can be found in Heimsoeth
        and Heiß, o.c., pp. 286-289
14.   M. Scheler, *Der Formalismus in der Ethik und die materiale
        Wertethik*, 6th ed., Bern & Munich: Francke Verlag 1980, translated
        in obscure English as, *Formalism in Ethics and Non-Formal Ethics
        of Values*, Evanston: Northwestern University Press 1973.
15.   *Metaphysik der Erkenntnis*, Einleitung.
16.   *Grundlegung der Ontologie*, ch. 27-32.
17.   *Ibid.*, ch.27a.
18.   *Metaphysik der Erkenntnis*, ch. 35d.
19.   However, Hartmann's ontology differs in two ways from what had
        passed as ontology from Aristotle to Wolff. First, it omits ultimate
        questions such as those dealing with the existence of God and the
        immortality of the soul. Second, it starts from below, with the facts
        of everyday life and of empirical science, and regressively deduces
        from these the fundamental categories of being, instead of starting

from above with a few a priori principles, as the old ontology did. Hence, for Hartmann ontology is *philosophia prima* in the order of being, but *philosophia ultima* in the order of knowing. Cf. *Grundlegung der Ontologie*, Einleitung.

20. *Aubau der realen Welt*, ch. 20a.
21. Cf. In 'Die Anfänge des Schichtungsgedankens in der alten Philosophie,' *Kleinere Schriften* vol. II, pp. 164-190, Hartmann traces this idea back to the ancients. Similar conceptions can be found in contemporary philosophers such as: M. Scheler, Die *Stellung der Menschen im Kosmos*, 14th ed. Bonn: Bouvier Verlag 1998 (1928); H. Plessner, Die *Stufen des Organischen und der Mensch*, 2nd ed. Berlin: Walter de Gruyter 1965 (1928); A. Gehlen, *Der Mensch, seine Natur und seine Stellung in der Welt*, 13th ed., Wiesbaden: AULA Verlag 1986 (1940).
22. Cf. Kant, *Kritik der Urteilskraft* (1790), 2nd part.
23. *Problem des geistigen Seins*, Geschichtsphilosophische Einleitung, § 6.
24. *Kleinere Schriften*, vol. I, 'Systematische Selbstdarstelling,' pp. 1-50. Hartmann names Plotinus, Proclus, Thomas Aquinas, Duns Scotus, Hobbes, Spinoza, Fichte, Schelling, Hegel, and Marx as instances of system-thinkers. He regards Plato, Aristotle, Descartes, Hume, Leibniz, and Kant, among others, as problem-oriented thinkers.
25. Cf. W.K.C. Guthrie, *A History of Greek Philosophy*, vol. VI, Cambridge etc.: Cambridge University Press 1981, p. 147n1.
26. *Ethics* I, pp. 183-184.
27. *Ethics* I, p. 184.
28. *Grundlegung der Ontologie*, ch. 43b.
29. *Ethics I*, p. 184.
30. *Ibid.*
31. *Grundlegung der Ontologie*, ch. 43b, ch. 44d, ch. 50b and passim.
32. *Ibid.*, ch. 38b Does this imply that Hartmann, like Plato, believes in a *chorismos* between the ideal and the real? He explicitly denies it in ch. 50b, but he also rejects Aristotelian 'immanentism.' The truth, according to Hartmann, ch.46b, lies in a synthesis between Plato and Aristotle. At ch. 50b he metaphorically describes the relation between the ideal and the real as the 'floating of the sphere of ideal being.' Cf. J. Notbüsch, 'Nicolai Hartmanns Lehre vom idealen Sein,' in: A.J. Buch (ed.), *o.c.*, pp. 238-251 for an excellent discussion. This author remarks, p. 245, that 'more or less all who have commented on Hartmann's theory of ideal being have concluded that at this point much in Hartmann's utterances remains unclear.'
33. *Ibid.*, ch. 50d.
34. *Ibid.*
35. *Ibid.*
36. *Ibid.*
37. *Ibid.*, ch. 38-45 on mathematics.

38.   Aristotle, *Metaphysics*, 985b25ff.
39.   *Metaphysik der Erkenntnis*, ch. 45.
40.   On Hartmann's view, Kant was mistaken in taking the a priori as transcendental, i.e. as a precondition of experience that lies within the subject, instead of as transcendent, i.e. pointing out a basic structure of the real world. Cf. *Ibid.*, ch. 46.
41.   *Ibid.*, ch. 45c.
42.   Actually Kant, *Logik*, Einleitung, iii, said that philosophy was concerned with four questions, the fourth being the question 'what is man?' 'The first question,' writes Kant, 'is answered by metaphysics, the second by morals, the third by religion, and the fourth by anthropology. Essentially, one could include all this in anthropology, as the first three questions involve the last.'
43.   *Ethics I*, pp. 27-28.
44.   The problem of the freedom of the will is the subject of volume III of the *Ethics*.
45.   *Ibid.*, p. 29.
46.   Cf. H. Reiner, *Die Grundlagen der Sittlichkeit*, Meisenheim am Glan: Anton Hain 1974. This is a much-expanded new edition of: *Pflicht und Neigung*, Meisenheim am Glan: Anton Hain 1951. § 21 contains an excellent historical overview. There is a good translation of the 1974 edition of this book: *Duty and Inclination, the Fundamentals of Morality Discussed and Redefined with Special Regard to Kant and Schiller*, The Hague etc: Martinus Nijhoff 1983. For some mysterious reason, however, chapter five of the German original has been left out of the translation, and some of essays put in at the end of both books differ as well.
47.   *Ethics I*, pp. 34-35.
48.   *Ibid.*, p. 37.
49.   *Ibid.*, p. 49.
50.   *Ibid.*, p. 15.
51.   Nor did Scheler see Hartmann as an acolyte. See *Formalismus in der Ethik*, Vorwort zur dritten Auflage (Preface to the third edition), pp. 19-23.
52.   *Ethics I.*, p. 51.
53.   This is the title of *Ethics II*; cf. *Ethics I*, pp. 55-56.
54.   *Ibid.*, p. 221.
55.   *Ibid.*, p. 219.
56.   *Grundlagen der Ontologie*, ch. 49k; *Ethics I*, ch. XVII.
57.   *Ethics I*, p. 233.
58.   *Grundlagen der Ontologie*, ch. 49b.
59.   *Ibid.*, ch. 49c.
60.   Hartmann's account of this important point is somewhat meager. Cf. *Ethics I*, ch. XIII, entitled 'Critique of intellectualism.' The German original is better: 'Schelers Kritik des Intellektualismus.' Hartmann largely follows Scheler here, who has much more to say about our

sensing of values, not only in *Formalismus in der Ethik*, but also in much of his other work. Cf. for instance the essays 'Ordo Amoris' and 'Liebe und Erkenntnis' (Love and Knowledge), in: M.Frings (ed.), *Von der Ganzheit des Menschen (On the Wholeness of Man)*, Bonn: Bouvier Verlag 1991. Cf. also the works of D. von Hildebrand, for instance, *Sittlichkeit und ethische Werterkenntnis (Morality and Knowledge of Ethical Values)*, 3rd ed., Vallendar-Schönstadt: Patris Verlag 1982 (1922).

61.   *Ethics I*, p. 228.
62.   *Ibid.*, pp. 225-226.
63.   *Ibid.*, p. 35.
64.   *Grundlagen der Ontologie*, ch.49d; *Ethics I*, pp. 228-229.
65.   *Ibid.*, p. 229.
66.   *Ibid.*, pp. 89-90.
67.   *Ibid.*, pp. 90-91.
68.   *Ethics II*, pp. 24-25.
69.   *Ethics I*, p. 211.
70.   *Ibid.*, p. 211.
71.   *Ibid.*, p. 142.
72.   *Ibid.*, p. 248.
73.   *Ibid.*, p. 249 Hartmann speaks of 'aktuales Seinsollen,' inaccurately translated by Coit as 'positive ought-to-be.'
74.   *Ibid.*, p. 257.
75.   *Ibid.*, p. 256.
76.   *Ibid.*, p. 238.
77.   From the Greek *axia*: value.
78.   *Ibid.*, p. 251.
79.   *Ibid.*, pp. 325-326.
80.   *Ibid.*, p. 334.
81.   *Ibid.*, p. 338.
82.   *Ibid.*, p. 339.
83.   *Ibid.*, p. 343.

HARTMANN'S MAJOR WORKS

1.   *Das Seinsproblem in der griechischen Philosophie vor Plato* (The Problem of Being in Greek Philosophy before Plato), dissertation, 1907.

2.   *Platos Logik des Seins* (Plato's Logic of Being), 1909, 2nd ed., Berlin: Walter de Gruyter 1965.

3.   *Des Proklus Diadochus philosophische Anfangsgründe der Mathematik* (Proclus Diadochus' Philosophical First Principles of Mathematics), habilitation, 1909

4.   *Die philosophischen Grundlagen der Biologie* (The Philosophical Foundations of Biology), 1912

5.   *Grundzüge einer Metaphysik der Erkenntnis* (Outlines of a Metaphysics of Knowledge), 1921, 5th ed., Berlin: Walter de Gruyter 1965

6. *Ethik* (Ethics), 1926, 4th ed., Berlin: Walter de Gruyter 1962
7. *Philosophie des deutschen Idealismus* (Philosophy of German Idealism), 1923/29, 3rd ed., Berlin: Walter de Gruyter 1974
8. *Das Problem des geistigen Seins* (The Problem of Spiritual Being), 1933, 3rd ed., Berlin: Walter de Gruyter 1962
9. *Zur Grundlegung der Ontologie* (The Foundations of Ontology), 1935
10. *Möglichkeit und Wirklichkeit* (Possibility and Actuality), 1938, 3rd ed., Berlin: Walter de Gruyter 1966
11. *Der Aufbau der realen Welt* (The Structure of the Real World), 1940, 3rd ed., Berlin: Walter de Gruyter 1964
12. *Neue Wege der Ontologie*, 1942, 3rd ed., Stuttgart: W. Kohlhammer 1949. Translated into English by R.C. Kuhn as *New Ways of Ontology*, Westport, Connecticut: Greenwood Press 1975
13. *Einführung in die Philosophie* (Introduction to Philosophy), 1949, 7th ed., Osnabrück: Hanckel 1960
14. *Philosophie der Natur* (Philosophy of Nature), 1950, 2nd ed., Berlin: Walter de Gruyter 1980
15. *Teleologisches Denken* (Teleological Thinking), 1951, 2nd ed., Berlin: Walter de Gruyter 1966
16. *Ästhetik* (Aesthetics), 1953, 2nd ed., Berlin: Walter de Gruyter 1966
17. *Kleinere Schriften* (Smaller Works), 3 vols., vol. I: *Abhandlungen zur systematischen Philosophie* (Essays on Systematic Philosophy), Berlin: Walter de Gruyter 1955; vol. II: *Abhandlungen zur Philosophie-Geschichte* (Essays on the History of Philosophy), Berlin: Walter de Gruyter 1957; vol. III: *Vom Neukantianismus zur Ontologie* (From Neo-Kantianism to Ontology), Berlin: Walter de Gruyter 1958

Moral
Phenomena

EDITOR'S INTRODUCTION

As Editor of the series in which the translation of Professor Hartmann's *Ethik* appears I have been asked by the translator to write a short Introduction to it. Leaving Dr. Stanton Coit himself, in the Preface which follows, to supply a more personal introduction of the author to his British and American readers and to explain his reasons for undertaking the work, I shall perhaps best do my part if I try as briefly as possible to indicate the relation in which Professor Hartmann's book seems to me to stand to the present state of Moral Philosophy as that is understood by English-speaking students. What follows may also serve for an apology, if such is needed, for the addition of so large a work (and that a foreign one) to the extensive literature of the subject that already exists in their own language. In the last century ethical thought in England and America, as elsewhere, has been more profoundly influenced by Kant than by any other philosophical writer. Starting from the idea of duty, or "the ought," as of the essence of moral consciousness, Kant found it impossible to explain the authority with which this speaks to us on the ground of feelings connected with the satisfaction of natural instincts, inclinations or desires. If this authority is to be justified we must seek for its source elsewhere. Kant, as is well known, sought for and found it in the a priori announcements of the reason, conceived of as emanating from a transcendental or supranatural ego. Rejecting this aprioristic view, as being founded on a mistaken idea alike of the objects of instinct and desire and of the relation of these to reason, Kant's followers yet sought to retain the doctrine of a supranatural ego or self as the source of ideals that go beyond the objects of natural desire, and at the same moment include that of its own moral perfection—the Kantian good will or will to good— as itself an unconditioned end. On the basis of this revised version of Kant's doctrine an ethical theory was developed in the latter part of last century which took as its watchword the idea of self-realization as the ultimate end of action and the standard of reference in moral judgment. In spite of the great names associated with this theory on both sides of the Atlantic, the last quarter of a century has witnessed a strong reaction against it. Besides the ambiguity of a phrase which carried with it an inexpugnable suggestion of egoism, there was on any interpretation of the "self" the difficulty of distinguishing between this theory and that which, after the manner of Utilitarianism, laid the main stress on the consequences of action in the furtherance of a well-being, defined, if not in hedonistic, at any rate in non-moral terms,—as the criterion of goodness in conduct. Whatever the value of the phrase in pointing to concrete good instead of to any formal consistency with "reason," as the aim of the actions we call good, an indispensable link seemed to be missing to justify the derivation from it of the idea of moral obligation. Unless itself carrying with it the implication of an "ought," unless implying something which there is an *obligation* to realize, even the perfection of the self as an end loses all authority, and we seem to be thrown back on the old alternatives (in however revised a form) of Utilitarianism and Intuitionalism—the one asserting the priority of good to right, after the manner of Bentham, the other that of right to good, after the manner of Kant.

It was in some such circumstances as these that the rise into prominence (owing to causes it would take too long here to attempt to recount) of the idea of Value and the Values inherent in objects and situations seemed to offer a point of view from which the whole subject might profitably be revised and fresh solutions reached. It was not of course a new idea. It had been anticipated, like so much else in modern philosophy, by Plato, who saw in the Idea of the Good, or the Purpose of things, a principle in the light of which not only the knowledge but the very being of the world might be explained. Unfortunately the Idea, as Plato meant it, had become infected with the subjectivism, which had, in so many fields, been a prominent note of modern philosophy ever since Descartes's announcement of the thinking of the self as the one ground of certainty. If our thinking is the source of certainty as to the existence of things, it seemed to follow that our feeling and desiring must be the source of their value. It was Kant's merit to see the fallacy of this whole contention, but he was unable to escape from the subjectivism of his age, and still sought for the determinant of value in a "reason" divorced from the world of common interests. What was wanted was a return to the Platonic idea of the world as a depository of values of different degrees, each with its claim to be its own "ought" as we might say, revealed directly to the eye that is trained to see it as it is in itself and in its relation to the whole of Good.

It is towards some such essentially objective conception of value that thought in England and America is now moving, and much has already been accomplished by the younger men in the direction of the reorientation of the study of Ethics to the new horizon—to which perhaps less than justice has been done by continental writers. Yet it remains true that it would be difficult to name any single British or American work devoted to an advanced and exhaustive treatment of moral values from the new point of view. The writers who have done most in this direction have tended to approach the subject with a certain anti-idealistic bias, while those who approach it from the side of idealism have tended to treat it too hastily as merely the starting-point for the vindication of higher religious values. A field thus seems to be open for a comprehensive treatment of the whole subject of moral values, as relatively independent and autonomous, from a point of view which unites the fundamental truths contained in the two great traditions which we may call respectively the Platonic and the Kantian.

It is this field that Dr. Hartmann's book aims at occupying. This is not the place to attempt a review of its scope, which is sufficiently indicated in the Table of Contents that follows.

But there are one or two points to which attention may perhaps usefully be drawn.

1. There are sections of it which call for exceptional effort even on the part of advanced students of the subject—particularly the section (Part II, §2) where under the guidance of the Kantian list of categories the author deals with what he calls the Antinomic of Values—the modal, relational and the qualitative and quantitative polar opposites that are traceable in what he happily calls "valuational space." Yet it is just in this section that the originality of Dr. Hartmann's treatment is most likely to strike the attentive reader, and, should he allow himself, as he legitimately may in a first perusal, to pass rapidly over it, he will find it will amply repay him to return to it for more careful study.

2. A further difficulty in the same part may be caused by the author's references to German writers (e.g. Max Scheler and W. v. Hildebrand) who are perhaps too unfamiliar to English readers. But ample compensation for unfamiliar allusions will, it is hoped, be found in the central place in the exposition of the "Special Moral Values" assigned to the treatment of these by Plato and Aristotle which is the common property of Western students. In his brilliant interpretation of the Platonic ἔρως in Part II, § 8, and elsewhere, and of the Aristotelian doctrine of the μεσότης, Dr. Hartmann seems to the present writer to have placed the readers of the *Dialogues* and the *Ethics* under a particular obligation.

3. There is one quite fundamental point on which students who have followed the recent development in England and America of a theistic philosophy, founded on the interdependence and inseparability of moral and religious values, may find a difficulty, perhaps a ground of disagreement with the author. His whole scheme is built upon the view that while the higher values depend upon the lower and more basal, the latter are independent of the higher and autonomous in their own field. Applied to the relation of the ethical to the religious, this seems to veto any attempt to found theistic conclusions

on any alleged presuppositions or postulates of the moral consciousness. I believe that on a closer study of Dr. Hartmann's meaning there will be found to be less incompatibility than appears between what he calls the autonomy of ethics and what is historically known as the Moral Argument for the Being of God. What he has in view is the falsification of moral values that must inevitably result from any suggestion that the love of man owes the chief part, or indeed any part, of its value to its being regarded in the light merely of a step to the love of God as a transcendent Being, *a fortiori* that loving actions are a way of laying up treasure in heaven. On the other hand, so far from denying, he insists on the presence in the higher moral values of an element of Faith, essentially religious, in the potentialities of human nature, and of Hope that these will find their fulfilment. In this faith and hope, as he himself says, in Chapter XXX, "man sees himself caught up into a larger Providence, which looks beyond him and yet is his own." Whatever ambiguity remains we may hope will be dispelled by the author in some future work, devoted, in the same spirit and with the same admirable thoroughness as the present one, to the subject of Religious Values.

In conclusion I may perhaps be allowed to express my sense of obligation to Dr. Stanton Coit for the infectious enthusiasm with which he has thrown himself as a pure labour of love into his long and arduous task of translation and to congratulate him on his success in carrying it to completion. As it leaves his hands the book seems to me not only an entirely accurate but (what is saying a good deal more) an entirely English rendering of the text.

J. H. MUIRHEAD

TRANSLATOR'S PREFACE

THE German original of Dr. Hartmann's *Ethics* is published in one volume of 746 closely printed pages. But as English readers of philosophy, unlike German students, would be repelled rather than attracted by so formidable a tome, the Editor and Publishers of this version have deemed a one-volume edition inadvisable. The book might have appeared, however, in two volumes of some five hundred pages each. But as the work consists of three nearly equal parts, each of which within itself constitutes an organic body of thought, it would have been necessary to separate the first from the second half of Part II, whereas a three-volume edition envisages the threefold structure of the work.

There was also a practical reason for the adoption of the present form. As Dr. Hartmann is as yet unknown to that portion of the English public who do not read German, the price of the whole work might have delayed by some years their acquaintance with him, whereas now many may venture to purchase the first volume by itself for less than a third of the entire price; and those who find it to their taste will probably buy the second without hesitation and then the third.

Dr. Hartmann's critical acumen and close reasoning, his ripe scholarship and power of systematic arrangement, his moral insight, his transparent love of spiritual values and his profound belief in man's responsibility and creative capacity may awaken in many readers—as they have awakened in me— a sense of indebtedness to the author and a not unworthy curiosity to know something more of his personality and of the influences which have stimulated and directed his investigations. To such it will be gratifying to learn that Dr. Hartmann is still in the full vigour of middle life. Only last spring he was called to the Chair of Philosophy in the University of Berlin, which was occupied a century ago by Schleiermacher and recently by Professor Ernst Troeltsch. Prior to that he had held (since 1925) the Chair of Philosophy in the recently refounded University of Cologne, having been invited thither from Marburg, where he had become *Privatdocent* in 1909 and professor in 1920.

Dr. Hartmann was born of Protestant German ancestry on February 20, 1882, in Riga, Latvia, then a province of Russia. His later school years were spent at St. Petersburg, where he responded to the many formative influences which at that time streamed into the Russian capital from the leading countries of Europe. From the age of twenty to twenty-seven he studied, first, medicine at Dorpat, then philology at St. Petersburg, and finally philosophy in Marburg, where he took his degree in 1907.

The great thinkers of the past who have most influenced him have been, in the order of his approach to them, Plato and then Kant; later Leibniz and Hegel, and finally Aristotle. At the same time he was making an intimate study of the metaphysics of Hermann Cohen, the author of *The Logic of Pure Knowledge*, the methodology of Edmund Husserl and Max Scheler's phenomenological investigations in the domain of concrete ethics.

In 1921 he published his first great work under the title, *Outlines of a Metaphysic of Knowledge*. In that work (the second edition of which appeared in 1925) he broke altogether with Neo-Kantianism and Idealism, and took up a new line of ontological Realism. Since then he has published nothing in the same direction, but has prepared much new material which has not as yet received its final shaping.

The present work was begun during the Great War. The laceration of the peoples of Europe—children of one civilization and of one moral heritage—the senselessness of the universal misery and the yearning for peace caused Dr. Hartmann to concentrate his attention upon the nature of the human ethos. It was during the winter of 1916–17, while he was a soldier in the trenches on the Eastern Front, under the incessant firing of the Russian guns, that he made his first analyses of "moral values." At that time the only books to which he had access were Aristotle's *Nicomachean Ethics* and one volume of Nietzsche. From these beginnings arose the masterly chapters embodied in Volume II of this work, although the author's investigations in concrete ethics were not completed until ten years later.

Before the War he had already been making systematic research into the metaphysical implications of morality. These are set forth in Volume III. Volume I contains the fruits of later reflection and was written last. It is devoted, as a sub-title in the German original indicates, to the phenomenological structure of values.[1] The whole of this massive body of thought was not co-ordinated until the years 1923-24, after its author had repeatedly examined and discussed it in seminar with his students at the University of Marburg.

I owe my first acquaintance with Dr. Hartmann's *Ethics* to an adverse criticism of its philosophical basis, which appeared in the *International Journal of Ethics* for January 1930.[2] Although representative of an antagonistic school of thought, the reviewer conceded that, as regards analysis of the actual ideals for and by which men live, "Hartmann has had only one great predecessor—Aristotle," that by virtue of its detailed contributions to specifically ethical problems his book is the most important treatise on the subject in the present century, and that it is the most impressive statement of intuitive ethical realism in print. These judgments, substantiated by the reviewer's quotations from Dr. Hartmann and by summaries of Dr. Hartmann's position, induced me to purchase the book. The reviewer likewise called attention to the fact that it is the most comprehensive treatise on ethics which has ever been published. But even this information did not repel me. For I have often wondered why so vast, urgent and complex a

[1] It is with the author's sanction that I have given to the volumes of this version the sub-titles: "Moral Phenomena," "Moral Values" and "Moral Freedom."
[2] *A Critique of Ethical Realism*, by Sidney Hook (of New York University).

subject should be presented in the condensed and fragmentary fashion characteristic of nearly every writer on ethics—except Plato. Have they perhaps feared lest it might divert their genius from more important questions? But what questions can these be?

After my first reading of the German text, I secured from the author the privilege of translating it. And it has been my good fortune that Messrs. Allen & Unwin were willing to risk publishing the English version and the Editor to include it in the "Library of Philosophy." I am also much indebted to Miss Virginia Coit, who translated six of the chapters in Volume II, to Dr. Muirhead, Dr. J. E. Turner (of Liverpool University) and Mr. A. F. Dawn (B.A. of London), who checked my version with the German text, and to Miss H. M. Aird (M.A. of Edinburgh), who prepared the manuscript for the printer.

To all these I am most grateful. They have made it possible for me to render what I believe will be a lasting service to the English-speaking public—to bring to leaders of Church and State, in finance and industry, in education, domestic relationships and personal life, the fundamental principles of ethics in a form detached—without injury—from dead tradition, and protected—with untold gain—against the newfangled novelties of mechanical behaviourism, of impulsivism, subjectivism and ethical relativism.

The old foundation of the established moral order—Authority—has been blown to atoms. And that is well. But it is not well that many popular leaders are to-day busy devising and advocating ingenious superstructures, which have no foundation at all, save shifting sands. Happily, it is at this juncture that ethical realism has entered upon the scene, constructive, absolutistic, idealistic, and yet undogmatic, schooled in critical philosophy, drilled in scientific method, statesmanlike in purpose and humane in motive.

In his Introduction, Dr. Muirhead intimates that he sees in Professor Hartmann's system no occasion for a sharp division between moral and religious values and certainly no antagonism. Now the author's own sense of a clash here is, I think, due to his identification of religion with what he calls metaphysical personalism. Many, however, who have been recently making investigations in the phenomenology of religion are tending to detach religious, just as Dr. Hartmann detaches ethical, values from a personalistic interpretation of the cosmic background. They are identifying Deity—the objective factor in religion—with "Whatever-is-Holy" and Piety—its subjective side—with the "Sensing-of-Holiness."

This sensing of holiness is, they say, the rudiment of worship. They are also perfectly clear as to what they mean by holiness: "Those objects are holy which on account of their inherent worth must be loved to the uttermost but never touched, feared absolutely but never hated." These religious realists are likewise inclining to the belief that the supreme, self-existent, ideal values, which the human spirit discerns, constitute "The Holy," independently of any question as to a Reality beyond.

I would, moreover, point out that Dr. Hartmann's *Ethics* embraces not simply moral, but all values, that these from the lowest to the highest are presented by him as forming a hierarchy and that, although he does not use religious terms, he nevertheless betrays throughout an attitude of worship; and the object worshipped is the Ideal, Self-existent Realm of Values as a Creative Power impinging upon the world of the senses and of human society and calling for man's co-operation. Is not this the interpretation of the meaning of life, which the lacerated nations need and towards which they have always been blindly groping their way?

STANTON COIT

THE ETHICAL CHURCH
   LONDON, W. 2

October 1931

FOREWORD

TRUE to the modern interest in everything subjective, the ethical philosophy of the nineteenth century spent itself in an analysis of the moral consciousness and its acts. It was far from troubling itself about the objective contents of moral claims, commandments and values. There stood Nietzsche, a solitary figure, warning us with his startling assertion that we have never yet known what good and evil are. Scarcely listened to, misinterpreted by over-hasty disciples as well as by over-hasty critics, his momentous call for a new inspection of values died away. It has taken decades for the capacity to develop within us, whereby, from out the distance which has already become historic, we could understand his call. And only in our day, slowly and against great odds, the consciousness of a new phase in the ethical problem manifests itself, the supreme concern of which is once more the contents, the substance, of ethical Being and Not-Being.

In the following investigation I have undertaken to go counter to the long-settled tradition and to take account of the new order of things, in that I have chosen as my central task an analysis of the contents of values. I have done so in the belief that only in this way will it be possible in the future to grapple afresh with the problems of conduct. For, while these certainly are not to be neglected, they may very well for a time be left in the background, in order that other problems may be brought forward, which have been ignored and yet for the moment are most urgent.

So at least I understand the present situation. Nor am I alone in this. Max Scheler has rendered us the service of making it obvious to us. The idea of a concrete ethics of values is far from being submerged in his criticism of Kant's formalism. It is indeed the fulfilment of that ethical apriorism which even in Kant formed the essence of the subject. Epoch-making judgments are recognized by their power to fuse organically apparently heterogeneous and conflicting factors. Concrete ethics, by showing us the gates to the kingdom of values, achieves the synthesis of two fundamental concepts which had historically grown up in very different fields, and in sharp contrast to each other. One was the Kantian apriority of the moral law and the other the manifoldness of values which Nietzsche—though only from a distance—had discerned. Nietzsche was the first to see the rich plenitude of the ethical cosmos, but with him it melted away in historical relativism. On the other hand, Kant had, in the apriority of the moral law, a well-considered and unified knowledge of the absoluteness of genuine ethical standards; he lacked only the concrete perception and the breadth of sympathy which would have given this knowledge full recognition. The concrete ethics of value is the historical reunion of factors which have really been intimately associated from the beginning. Indeed it is, above all, the rediscovery of their inherent connection. It gives back to ethical apriorism its original richness of content, while to the consciousness of value it gives the certainty of a firm foothold in the midst of the relativity of human valuations.

Herewith our path is indicated. It is, however, one thing to point it out, and another to follow it. Neither Scheler nor anyone else has trodden it, at least not in ethics proper, and this is surely no mere chance. It simply shows that in the realm of values we are only novices, and that with this fresh insight, which at first looked like finality, we stand again at the very beginning of a work the greatness of which is difficult to measure.

This situation is deeply significant for the new orientation of the problem. It is the more serious because it is in this untrodden realm that we deal with decisive discoveries, concerning, for instance, the meaning and contents of moral goodness itself. In retrospect over long years of labour it now seems to me doubtful whether a step forward could have been taken, if help from an unexpected quarter had not been forthcoming: namely from Aristotle, the ancient master of ethical research. Among all the new views which the present stage of the problem has yielded to me, scarcely one has astonished and at the same time convinced me more than this, that the ethics of the ancients was a highly developed concrete ethics of values, not in concept or conscious intention, but certainly in fact and in actual procedure. For it does not depend on whether correct terminology is used but whether, and how, goods and virtues in their manifold gradations have been grasped and characterized. Upon closer inspection the Nichomachean Ethics is discovered to be a rich mine of suggestion. It shows a mastery in the description of values which is evidently the result and the culmination of a whole development of careful method.

That a new systematic examination entails a new understanding of an historical treasure is a well-known fact. That Scheler's idea could, without in the least aiming at it, throw new light upon Aristotle is a surprising test of the concrete ethics of values. But that the naïvely developed point of view should win for us indications and perspectives from the seemingly exhausted work of Aristotle by enabling us to understand and appreciate it better than before proves most clearly that we are here dealing with an unexpectedly profound interpenetration of old and new achievements, and that at the turning-point in ethics at which we now stand we are experiencing an historical synthesis of greater range than that of Kant and Nietzsche: a synthesis of ancient and modern ethics.

As yet, however, this exists only in idea. To carry it out is the task of our age. Whoever grasps the idea is called to the task. But the work of one individual can be only a beginning.

NICOLAI HARTMANN

MARBURG
September 1925

CONTENTS

PART I

THE STRUCTURE OF THE ETHICAL PHENOMENON

(PHENOMENOLOGY OF MORALS)

SECTION I

CONTEMPLATIVE AND NORMATIVE ETHICS

SECTION VI

THE ESSENCE OF THE OUGHT

SECTION VII

METAPHYSICAL PERSPECTIVES

INTRODUCTION

1. THE FIRST FUNDAMENTAL QUESTION

THE tradition of modern thought presents philosophy as asking at the outset of its task three vital questions: What can we know? What ought we to do? What may we hope? The second of these is recognized as the fundamental problem of ethics. It is that aspect of the human problem in its entirety which gives to ethics the character of practical philosophy. It is the kind of question which aims at more than the merely intellectual grasp of reality and yet at less than what hope yearns for. Independent of any guarantee of attainment, independent equally of knowledge of the conditioned and accessible and of belief in the absolute, it stands midway between the hard realities of life and the hovering ideals of the visionary. It does not even turn its face towards anything real as such; and yet standing very near reality—indeed nearer than any theory or aspiration—it plants itself in the real, and sets before its eyes the reality of that which is unreal in the existing conditions.

It grows out of what is next to us, out of the current of everyday life not less than out of life's great decisive moments, with which the individual is occasionally confronted. Such moments are those which through the weight of reasons for and against, presented once but never again, lift the individual above half-conscious drifting into a fresh decision in his life, into a perspective of unavoidable and unforeseeable responsibility. But the same is in fact true also of the little things in experience. The situation before which we are placed shows the same aspect in petty details as in affairs of great moment. It forces us to a decision and to an act, and it gives us no dispensation from the necessity of deciding; yet it does not tell us how we ought to decide, what we ought to do or what consequences we ought to accept and to prefer.

Every moment we stand face to face with the question: What ought we to do? Every new situation brings it up afresh. Step by step in life we must answer it anew, and no power can deliver us, or lift us above the necessity of answering it. To the ever-new question our action, our actual conduct, is the ever-new reply. For our action already contains the decision. And even where we were not conscious of it, we can afterwards recognize it in our act, and perhaps repent of it. Whether in every choice we decide aright does not enter into the problem, nor into the situation. For that, there is no guarantee; and the hand of another does not guide us. Here everyone is thrown back upon himself, and makes the decision alone, and from himself. Afterwards, if he has erred, he alone bears the responsibility of the guilt.

Who foresees the sweep of his action? Who knows the chain of its consequences, or measures the greatness of his responsibility?

A deed, once done, belongs to reality and can never be undone. What was defective in it is in the strictest sense irreparable. The situation arises once for all, never returns, and, like everything real, is individual. But it is also there irrevocably, woven into the web of the cosmic process as a part of it. The same things hold good of an act, when it has occurred. Its effects extend to ever-wider circles, it propagates itself after its own kind. When it is once woven into existence, it lives on, it never dies out—even if the beat of the waves which proceeds from it grows weaker and is cancelled in the greater stream of the world's course—it is immortal as all reality is.

However unreal and unmotived its origin may be, when once it is incorporated into existence it follows another law, the law of reality and of efficacious activity. This law gives to it a life of its own, a power to build up and destroy life and being, in the presence of which repentance and despair are powerless. A deed passes beyond the doer, sets its mark upon him and judges him without mercy.

Not of every act do we see the chain of consequences. But every act has consequences, and the possibility is always present that they weigh heavily where we least suspect it. And what holds good on a small scale concerning the conduct of the individual is true, on a large scale, of the conduct of a community, a generation, an age. On what we determine to-day depends perhaps the future of generations. The coming time always reaps what the present sows, as the present has reaped the harvest of the past. In a pre-eminent sense this holds good where the old has outlived itself and the new, the untried, seeks to establish itself, when fresh energies burst forth and dark unknown powers begin to stir. It is here that under the weight of an unforeseen responsibility the modest participation of the individual in the initiative of the whole can last for centuries.

Here the seriousness of the question "What ought we to do?" becomes self-evident. One forgets the real significance of this fundamental question only too easily amid the clamouring problems of the day—as if it were not exactly these latter which have their root in the former and by it alone can be solved. Not, indeed, that philosophic ethics should always speak out directly. Its task is not the positive programme, not the bias of partisanship. The reverse is true: a holding aloof, on principle, from the given, the present, the disputed, makes ethics free and renders it competent to teach.

2. The Creative Power in Man

Ethics does not teach directly what ought here and now to happen in any given case, but in general how that is constituted which ought to happen universally. This may vary and may be manifold. But not all that ought to take place can occur in every situation. The passing moment, with its claims, here has scope within that which ethical reflection requires. Ethics furnishes the bird's-eye view from which the actual can be seen objectively. From it the tasks of individuals and the tasks of ages appear equally specific. It keeps the same distance from both; for both it means an elevation above the special case, escape from extraneous influences, from suggestion, falsification, fanaticism. Herein ethics proceeds not otherwise than does philosophy; it does not teach finished judgments, but how to judge.

In this sense it takes the question: "What ought we to do?" It does not determine, describe or define the proper "What" of the Ought; but it gives rather the criteria, by which the What is to be recognized. That is the inner reason why it stands high above all the strife of particular tendencies, interests and parties. Its perspectives stand to those of private and public everyday life as those of astronomy to acquaintance with terrestrial things. Nevertheless the points of view even of these particular tendencies have their justification in it alone. The distance is not a separation, not a losing hold of the particular case, but only a perspective, a conspectus, a comprehensive vision and—in idea—a tendency towards unity, totality, completeness.

Here the character of practical philosophy loses all its aggressiveness. It does not mix itself up with the conflicts of life, gives no precepts coined *ad hoc*; it is no code, as law is, of commandments and prohibitions. It turns its attention directly to the creative in man, challenges it afresh in every new case to observe, to divine, as it were, what ought here and now to happen. Philosophical ethics is not casuistry and never should be: it would thereby kill in man the very thing which it ought to waken and educate—man's creative, spontaneous, living, inner sense of what ought to be, of what in itself is valuable. This is not a renunciation of the high task of being "practical." Only in this way can it be practical: by drawing forth, lifting up and maturing the practical in man— that is, the active in him, the spiritual ability to generate. Its aim is not man's disfranchisement and imprisonment within a formula, but his advance towards full self-direction and responsibility. The freeing of man from tutelage is the true making of man. But only ethical reflection can set him free.

In this sense ethics is practical philosophy. It is not a shaping of human life regardless of man's intelligence, but is precisely his own advance towards his own free fashioning of life. It is his knowledge of good and evil which puts him on a level with divinity; it is his ability and authority to help in determining the course of events, to co-operate in the workshop of reality. It is his training in his world-vocation, the demand upon him to be a colleague of the demiurge in the creation of the world.

For the creation of the world is not completed so long as he has not fulfilled his creative function in it. But he procrastinates. For he is not ready, he is not standing on the summit of his humanity. Humanity must first be fulfilled in him. The creative work which is incumbent upon him in the world terminates in his self-creation, in the fulfilment of his ethos.

The ethos of man includes both the chaotic and the creative. In the former lie his possibilities but also his danger; in the latter he finds his vocation. To fulfil it is to be human.

Ethics applies itself to the creative power in man. Here human intelligence is seeking and finding the pathway to the meaning of life. But in this it is practical. Man thus moulds life. Ethics is not primal and foundation-laying philosophy; its knowledge is neither the first nor the most certain knowledge. But in another sense it is the primal concern of philosophy: its original and innermost obligation, its most responsible task, its μέγιστον μάθημα. Its limitation is something not willed, something conditioned from within. Its domain is a natural sanctuary of wisdom, for ever esoteric—if judged by the rules of the understanding and its fixed concepts—a sanctuary, in which even the wisest treads with reverence and awe. It is, nevertheless, that which is nearest and most comprehensible; it is given to all and is common to all. It is the first and most positive philosophical interest of man; historically it is this interest which first divided philosophy from mythology. It is the source and innermost motive of philosophical thinking, perhaps indeed of human intelligence in general. It is, furthermore, the final goal and the widest outlook of this very thinking. And the reason why it is preoccupied with the future and always directs its gaze upon the remote and the unactualized and that it sees even the present under the guise of futurity, is because it is itself super-temporal.

3. THE MEANING OF "PRACTICAL" IN PHILOSOPHY

What ought we to do? is harder to answer than: What can we know? As for knowledge, its object confronts it, is fixed, immovable, existent in itself. Thought can fall back upon experience. What does not tally with the data of experience is false. But what we ought to do is not yet done, is unreal, without previous existence in itself. It can first attain existence through the doing. Yet the inquiry is concerning the "what" of this doing, in order thereby to direct the doing.

Here the fixed object, the immediate presence, is lacking. Thought must anticipate it. Thought here lacks the corrective of experience. It rests on itself alone. Whatever can here be perceived must necessarily be discerned a priori. The autonomy of this apriorism may indeed be an object of pride for the moral consciousness; but in it lies the difficulty of the problem. What credibility has ethical perception, if it lacks every criterion? Is the nobility of the human ethos so sure a testimony that it cannot even be disputed when it says dictatorially "You ought"? Is it not condemned to remain floating for ever in the hypothetical? Indeed, does not multiplicity rule here, relativity, subjectivity, variation from case to case? What I ought to do to-day under determined circumstances ought I not perhaps to leave undone to-morrow under different circumstances, and perhaps never do again in my life?

Now it is clear that at this point the false perspective of casuistry has again been introduced—a partisan approach to the particular and the given. Nevertheless, the problem is not to be settled by aloofness from the actual. Who would wish to say where the boundary is of the legitimate question as to the "What" of the Ought? Practical interest always attaches precisely to the actual and this always threatens to foreshorten the wider perspectives. Thus it comes about that, in spite of its acknowledged universality and dignity, the subject-matter of ethics is nevertheless exposed at the same time to the most serious doubt.

In this sense ethics is once more the most disputed department of philosophy. Is there a unity in morals? Does not the ethos itself vary from people to people and from age to age? And ought one then to believe that the nature of the good itself changes according to the actuality of the moment? Would not that again mean a denial of the autonomy of the ethos, a casting of suspicion upon the essential meaning of the Ought and the good?

Thus at the first step ethics brings us face to face with its insurmountable difficulty: how are ethical principles to be arrived at and how can one be certain of them? No experience can teach them; in contrast to that which can be experienced they must be intuitively discerned. But where, in contrast to the actual, we find them intuitively discerned and set up as claims, there we also find them variable, displaceable, exchangeable, transformed, dislocated. To what then can ethics as a science cling?

To this question the peculiar meaning of the "practical" in ethics corresponds. Other domains of practical knowledge are always aware through other sources what in the last resort the goal is. In all technique, hygiene, jurisprudence, pedagogy, the ends are fixed, are presupposed; there is only a question as to the ways and means. Ethics is practical in a different sense, one might almost say in the reverse sense. It ought to point out the ends themselves for the sake of which all means are there, the highest, the absolute ends, which cannot be regarded as in turn means to anything else. Although within

certain bounds an ethics of means can be legitimately maintained, the emphasis is still upon the ends.

The meaning of the practical is therefore in fact the reverse
of what it is in other fields. How are pure, absolute, irreducible
ends discovered? As they can be found in nothing real or are
verifiable only afterwards, what cognitive pathway leads to
them? That is the insurmountable difficulty with the question:
"What ought we to do?" It is a unique kind of difficulty, it
is peculiar to ethics and constitutes a part of its nature. And
yet it allows of no disavowal, it is propounded irremissibly
to man. Each person must somehow solve it for himself, in
action if not in thought. He cannot take a step in life without
actually settling it in one way or another. It is the highest
claim which confronts him. Its import is the necessary correlate
of that dignity of autonomy, of that highest privilege, which
distinguishes the ethos of man. Man carries it with him as
long as he breathes.

Not for idle play is this superb capacity given to him.
What is at stake is always himself—including his high power.
For even this he can lose through folly, can gamble away.

4. The Valuational Wealth of the Real and Participation Therein

All this, however, is only one half of the fundamental problem
of ethics. The other half is less positive, less obtrusive and
exacting, but correspondingly more general, concerned more
with the whole of man and of human life. The first question,
as regards himself, referred only to man's action and, as
regards the world, only to that part of it where the power
of his action can make itself felt. Notwithstanding the urgency
of its hold upon him, this portion of existence which makes
a claim upon him and, loading him with responsibility, depends
upon his decisions, resolutions and will is an imperceptibly
small part of the world.

But the inner attitude of man, his ethos as deciding for or

against, as acceptance or rejection, reverence or disdain, love or hate, covers an incomparably wider area. This deciding-for-or-against manifests its highest intensity, no doubt, only concerning things near to oneself; as the radius increases, it grows pale: at a certain distance it bears the character only of an accompanying emotional tone that for the most part remains unnoticed. But this tension nowhere entirely disappears. It accompanies the accepting consciousness, it transports it to the limits of the powers of comprehension, in the form of admiration, interest and finally of theoretical alertness of the will to understand. A purely theoretical consciousness of objects is a mere abstraction. Actually, the practical interest is always there, like an undercurrent, and occasionally it breaks powerfully through and disturbs the serenity of contemplation.

Here there is no question of outward efficiency, of decisions weighty with consequence. There is here no Ought. Yet in the mere inward attitude taken there is something highly positive and involving great responsibility. For the nature of man himself is not indifferent to the range of his interest and its strength. His nature widens and grows proportionately, or again shrivels.

He who stolidly passes by men and their fates, he whom the staggering does not stagger nor the inspiring inspire, for him life is in vain, he has no part in it. The world must be meaningless and life senseless to one who has no capacity to perceive life's relationships, the inexhaustible significance of persons and situations, of correlations and events. The outward emptiness and monotony of his life are the reflex of his inner emptiness and his moral blindness. The real world in which he exists, the stream of human life which bears him up and carries him along, is not without manifold wealth of content. His poverty amidst abundance is due to his own failure to appreciate life. Hence for the moral nature of man there is, besides the narrow actuality of action, a second requirement: to participate in the fulness of life, to be receptive of the significant, to lie open to whatever has meaning and value.

This claim upon him is more inward and calm and keeps its secret better than the claim of the Ought-to-Do and of the will. And yet to this it is fundamentally related, it is the same ever-new and living need of an inner decision for or against. It demands the same taking up of a moral attitude on the basis of the same inward autonomy, of the same ethical principles.

Philosophical ethics has misinterpreted this often enough, has allowed itself to be deluded by the more positive and elemental pressure of the other claim, and through this bias has reacted perniciously upon the development of the human ethos. Every ethics of duty and of the Ought alone, all purely imperative morals, commits this blunder—the blunder of overlooking the fulness of life. Whoever has fallen under the spell of such a rigorism may at this stage foolishly ask: Is not that which is valuable always given up first of all? Is not moral value always in its very essence an eternal Not-Being, an Ought-to-Be? Are there, then, actualized values in the world? Whoever asks this question has not noticed what a failure to appreciate life, what a thanklessness and arrogance hold him in their grip. As though the actual must necessarily be bad and of poor quality! As though human life were in itself a senseless game, the world a vale of tears, and as though all existence had only waited for him in order to attain through his will and his action light, meaning and value!

An ethics exclusively of the Ought is a moral delusion, is a blindness to the value of the actual. No wonder that, historically, pessimism follows in its track. In a world stripped of values and profaned, no one could tolerate life.

5. THE SECOND FUNDAMENTAL QUESTION

When once we have grasped the fact that the very same values which alone can guide our purpose and action are a thousand-fold realized in life by persons and situations, that they confront us in relations and events, surround us all the time, carry us forward and fill our existence with light and splendour—far

beyond our limited power of comprehension—we stand face
to face with the second ethical question: What are we to
keep our eyes open for, so as to participate in the world's
values? What is valuable in life and in the world generally?
What are we to make our own, to understand, to appreciate,
so as to be man in the full meaning of the word? What is it
for which we still lack the sense, the organ, so that we must
first form our capacity, sharpen and educate it?

This question is not less important and serious than the
one concerning what ought to be done. In fact, it is infinitely
broader in content, richer, more comprehensive. In a certain
sense it includes the other question. For how shall I recognize
what I have to do, so long as I do not know about the values
and disvalues within situations, the approach to which alone
requires me to decide, will and act! Shall I not fumble about
in the dark, be exposed to every kind of error, shall I not
necessarily with clumsy hand ruin the valuable thing which,
possibly, like all else that is real, cannot be replaced?

Thus the second question surpasses the first in importance.
It proves to be definitely precedent, conditioning the other.

And it is superior, as well in its wider metaphysical significance as in its practical positive bearings. For the meaning
of human existence is not exhausted in man's proud vocation
as a builder and fashioner of the world. What is the good of
working, if it dies with the work? Wherein is the meaning of
creation itself, if the thing made does not contain the meaning,
if it is not significant to someone capable of judging? Is it
not man's metaphysical meaning in the very same world in
which he also works and fashions, that the world may have
meaning for him? In him alone the world has its consciousness,
its existence for itself. What he is to the world, no other of its
creatures can be to it. His cosmic littleness, transitoriness
and helplessness do not impair his metaphysical greatness and
his superiority to the lower forms of being.

He is the subject among objects, the recognizer, the knower,
the experiencer, the participator: he is the mirror of Being

and of the world, and, understood in this way, he is the world's meaning. This view is not an arbitrary or speculative fancy, it is a straightforward expression of a phenomenon which can be explained but not explained away: the phenomenon of man's cosmic status. We do not know whether there is another mirror of the world than that which consists of our human consciousness. In this matter free play may be permitted to fancy; but that changes nothing as to man's place in the world. This place is for us certain, about this we know; and this is enough, in order to recognize in it the metaphysical meaning of human existence. Although man may be a dim mirror of the real, nevertheless he is still a mirror and in him Being is reflected. For him Being has a meaning. Whether it would have without him, or whether without consciousness the world would be meaningless, eludes our judgment.

This meaning of human existence is not exhausted in the mere taking up of the idea. Acceptance without interest, the purely theoretical enlistment of consciousness, is, as was said, an abstraction. Man is primarily practical, only derivatively is he theoretical. His apprehension is from the first a preferring of one thing to another. His portion in the coming and going of events is participation with feeling, interest, the sense of valuing. Impartial calmness of thought is a later distillation. And here everything depends upon the energy, reach and right orientation of the evaluating sense. The common phenomenon is the narrowness of the sense of value, petty-mindedness, a lack of appreciation of the comprehensible extent of the real. For most persons the limit of life's narrowest interests, of the most positive egoistic relations, dictated by the stress of the moment, is at the same time the limit of their moral universe. Their life is a cramped, diminished life, a shrivelled, distorted caricature of humanity.

One does not need the great metaphysical perspectives in order to gauge the low moral level of such narrow-mindedness. The apathy of feeling for values bears on its brow the stamp of inner misery. It avenges itself immediately on man. To it correspond his moral poverty and the emptiness of his life. The stress of existence becomes a burden, for which life does not compensate him. Not from its excessive fulness but from its impoverishment comes satiety.

And in what harsh contradiction does such impoverishment stand to the riches of real life, to life which is always at hand and surrounds us with its munificence. The tragedy of man is that of one who, sitting at a well-laden table, is hungry but who will not reach out his hand, because he does not see what is before him. For the real world is inexhaustible in abundance, actual life is saturated and overflows with values, and when we lay hold of it we find it replete with wonder and grandeur.

These statements of course do not admit of "proof," just as we can prove to no one that a thing is there which he is not in a position to see. And whether one can operate upon another for moral cataract—whether ethics as a science can— that must certainly remain doubtful. In general, however, it is possible to teach another to see, to wake up his emotional activity, to educate and train the capacity to discriminate values. There is such a thing as moral guidance, a leading into the abundant riches of life, an opening of eyes by means of one's own vision, an admitting to participation through one's own participation. There is a training of others in humanity as well as a training of oneself therein.

6. THE VALUATIONAL CONSTITUENTS OF PERSONS AND SITUATIONS

The claim which we are considering must begin with the simple question: What, then, is it that we fail to heed in life? What is it that escapes us?

Here in fact lies the whole difficulty. It is not to be solved simply by pointing it out. For every constituent value a corresponding sense must be awakened. The constituent parts of value are everywhere. We see them close before us at all times and yet again we do not see them. Every person, every human peculiarity is filled with them, is significant and unique down to the most impalpable shades of colouring. Each is a world in miniature, and not only as a specific structural entity but also as a specific structural value. Not less so is every actual juxtaposition of persons, every situation when some wider or narrower connection in life calls it forth: it may be a complex of interacting obligations, tensions and relaxations, a dove-tailing into one another of purposes, passions, quiet emotional dispositions, or even noisy, rough acts of partisanship—every-thing bound variously to every other and reciprocally con-ditioned, intensified and complicated by their very reactions, over-woven with released sympathies and antipathies and carried to a higher plane of the ethos; finally, in a brighter or darker consciousness of the situation, lived through again as a whole by the participants, and presented as a total impression subjectively distorted in the imaginative concept of the persons themselves. The moral situation is never wholly merged in persons, it is always something else lying above and beyond them, even if not something existing independently of them. It is, besides, a cosmos in itself with its own manner of Being and its own legitimacy, not less a determinant factor for the person than the person is for it. And the unique value corre-sponds to the unique entity. Situations are something individual, only existing once and not returning. Whoever has stood in a situation and not comprehended it, for him it is lost, is wasted and has irrevocably passed away.

Our human life, seen at close range, consists of nothing else than a running chain of coming and going situations—from the most fluid, most accidental, relations of the moment to the most inward and weighty and enduring fetters which link man to man. Communal as well as individual life is rooted in them and wears itself out in them. They are the ground upon which conflicts grow and press on to settlement. They are the contents of hope and disappointment, joy and suffering, of valiant strength and of weakness.

When a poet moulds a human situation and sets it before

our eyes, we easily see its constituent parts in their ethical fulness; we somehow suddenly feel their values throughout, although obscurely and with no consciousness of the special complexity of their valuational structure. Thus we feel the great as great and the sublime as sublime.

In actual life only one thing is different from what it is in dramatic art. There is lacking the guiding hand of a master, who unobtrusively brings the significant into the foreground, so that it also becomes evident to the eye of the common man. But life throughout is a drama. And if we could only see plastically the situation in which we are placed, as the poet sees it, it would appear to us just as rich and as filled with values as in his creation. The proof of this is the fact that in looking back upon our past life the highest points of value are for us those moments which hover before us in entire concreteness and fulness of detail—independently of whether at the time our sense of value realized the ethical content or not—yes, often in contrast to our former crude perception, and with perhaps a secret pain at the thought that it has for ever vanished, that it was ours and yet not ours.

7. Passing By on the Other Side

Failure to appreciate is a special chapter in the life of man. If we were to leave out all that we pass by without noticing, without looking, not to mention without appreciating, there would remain in the end little of the substance of life which really was ours spiritually.

The paths of life cross one another at many points. One meets innumerable beings. But there are few whom one "sees" in the ethical sense, few to whom one gives the sympathetic glance—one might almost say the loving glance, for the glance that appreciates value is loving. And, conversely, how few are they by whom one in turn is "seen"! Worlds meet, surface lightly grazes surface, in their depth they remain untouched and solitary; and they part again. Or for a lifetime or more they run parallel, externally united, perhaps chained to one another, and yet each one remains locked out from the other. Certainly no man can or ought to sink and lose himself in everyone he takes a fancy to. Deeper participation remains individual and exclusive. But is it not true that, in this general passing-by, everyone at the same time wanders about with a silent yearning in his heart, a yearning to be "seen" by someone, to be sympathetically understood, responded to, to be trusted beforehand? And does not everyone find himself a hundred times misunderstood, neglected or overlooked? Is not the great and common disappointment of all in life just this: to go empty away, unseen, unsensed, to be dismissed unvalued?

This is human fate. But is it not the acme of unreasonableness, when we consider that each one deep down is aware of the yearning of others for a recognizing glance, and, notwithstanding, passes by without having looked—each one alone in the secret suffering of his solitude?

Is it merely haste and discontent with one's own life which inhibits each, or is it not perhaps the narrowness of one's own perception of values, the fetter of the isolation of each, the inability to extend one's hand to another?

There is no doubt that, together with natural egoism, fear of others and false pride, there exists above all an incapacity to "see" morally. We do not know what riches we daily overlook; we do not dream how much we lose, what escapes us; hence we go by unheeding. Hence the abundance of life's highest values is wasted on us. What we are longing for is there in unnumbered hearts. But we let it perish and we go away empty. Superabundant as the human ethos is, it sickens and dies, because of the poverty and crudity of our ethical perception, the perception of just the same men for the same human ethos.

And in great affairs does not the same picture appear, magnified and coarsened? Is there not a moral participation and understanding also on a large scale, and an ignoring of great issues? Is not party prejudice the same thing in the life of the State; is not chauvinism the same thing in the history of the world? One people is struck with blindness as regards the distinctive character and world-mission of another. But the party spirit is blind to the just claim and political value of the opposite party. Each is acquainted only with its own aims, lives only for them, harnesses to them the life of the whole as well as of the single individual. So the individual is oblivious of the true life of the whole which is not sacred to him; he lives only for the life of his own group, just as he finds it, forced into the narrow formulas of his time and of his understanding. No one has penetration into the great correlations which constitute the peculiar life of the whole; no one traces sensitively the pulse-beat of history. Nevertheless everyone is in the midst of history, has a hand in the game and is called upon to be a seer and fashioner of the whole. He lives without regard to his era, its values and tasks, its distinctive life which is revealed only to him, its contemporary. Is it any wonder that an age which has an excess of partisans and party leaders suffers from a critical dearth of loyal citizens and statesmen?

Certainly there is, besides, an historical consciousness, even an historical science, which re-establishes the whole. But this consciousness does not keep pace with the historical life. Science much later reconstructs from traces of a vanished life, and shows, as posterity sees it, a faint general picture of what was, but is no longer, our life. It comes too late. It cannot take the place of the participating sense of values which the contemporary had. It lacks the immediateness of actual experience and the intense feeling of participation. The interest of the descendant is not the correlate, equal in rank, of historical life. His love does not come to the rescue of the past, and the past no longer loves him.

The moral world in little and the moral world on the grand scale resemble each other startlingly. They reflect each other more closely than an unsophisticated man might believe.

He who, as a single individual, does not look lovingly about him will also, as a citizen of the State, misunderstand and hate and, as a citizen of the world, will sow slander and discord. To pass a human being by unnoticed, to pass a community by, to brush past an historical crisis of the world—in all this appears the same aspect of the same ethos, the same going empty away, the same self-condemnation and self-annihilation. It is the same blindness to values and the same squandering of them. Only once is given to a generation what returns neither to it nor to any other; as only once to an individual is given the one-time fulness of the moment. And it is the same sin against the meaning of life, against the metaphysical significance of human existence—the same absurdity.

8. The Modern Man

If there is such a thing as an awakening of the consciousness of value, it is our time that has need of it. How far it is possible, no one can estimate. It can hardly emanate from philosophy. For all that, however, this is a field for philosophy to explore. There are prejudices which only it can uproot. And there are emotional obstacles which reflection and the turning of the eye of the soul inward can meet.

The life of man to-day is not favourable to depth of insight. The quiet and contemplation are lacking, life is restless and hurried; there is competition, aimless and without reflection. Whoever stands still for a moment is overtaken by the next. And as the claims of the outer life chase one another, so likewise do the impressions, experiences and sensations. We are always looking out for what is newest, the last thing continually governs us and the thing before the last is forgotten ere it has been fairly seen, much less comprehended. We live from sensation to sensation. And our penetration becomes shallow, our sense of value is blunted, by snatching at the sensational.

Not only is modern man restless and precipitate, dulled and blasé, but nothing inspires, touches, lays hold on his innermost being. Finally he has only an ironical and weary smile for everything. Yes, in the end he makes a virtue of his moral degradation. He elevates the *nil admirari*, his incapacity to feel wonder, amazement, enthusiasm and reverence, into a planned habit of life. Callously passing lightly over everything is a comfortable *modus vivendi*. And thus he is pleased with himself in a pose of superiority which hides his inner vacuity.

This morbid condition is typical. It does not appear to-day for the first time in history. But wherever it has made its appearance, it has been a symptom of weakness and decadence, of inward failure and general pessimism.

What is bent on being destroyed one should allow to go to ruin. Yet from every downfall young healthy life shoots forth. Even in our time this is so. Whether the rising generation, with its still somewhat planless attempts, will open up the way, whether it is reserved only for future generations to press powerfully forward to a new ethos, who to-day would dare to foretell? But the seed is there. It never was dead. It is incumbent upon us to be the awakener out of spiritual misery, to have before our eyes the idea, in our hearts the faith.

Ethical man is in everything the opposite of the precipitate and apathetic man. He is the seer of values, he is *sapiens* in the original sense of the word: the "taster." He it is who has a faculty for the fulness of life's values, that "moral faculty," of which Franz Hemsterhuis prophesied: to it gleaming riches open.

The philosophical ethics of to-day stands under the banner of this task. It stands at the parting of the ways between the old and the new kind of philosophizing. It is taking the first steps in the conscious investigation of values. How far it will lead us, we men of to-day cannot know. But its goal lies clear before our eyes: to bring man into the conscious possession of his "moral faculty," to open to him again the world which he has closed against himself.

After what has been said there can be no mistake as to what the new ethics will and must be. Whether it is such and can be so at all, the future will show. But in its whole attitude it is undoubtedly one thing: it is in itself a new ethos. It signifies a new kind of love for the task in hand, a new devotion, a new reverence for what is great. For to it the world which it will open is once more great, as a whole and in its smallest part, and is filled with treasure, unexhausted and inexhaustible.

The new ethics also has once more the courage to face the whole metaphysical difficulty of the problems which arise out of the consciousness of the eternally marvellous and unmastered. Once again the primal passion of philosophy has become its attitude—the Socratic pathos of wonder.

PART I

THE STRUCTURE OF THE ETHICAL PHENOMENON
(PHENOMENOLOGY OF MORALS)

SECTION I

CONTEMPLATIVE AND NORMATIVE ETHICS

CHAPTER I

THE COMPETENCY OF PRACTICAL PHILOSOPHY

(a) MORAL COMMANDMENTS, THE GENERAL TYPE, THEIR CLAIM TO ACCEPTATION

THE two questions which have been raised in the Introduction contain together the whole programme of ethics. They do not, however, divide it into two independent parts. Their connection is too inward, too organic for that. They cannot be separated, they are the two sides of one fundamental problem. I can gauge what I ought to do only when I "see" what in general is valuable in life. And I "see" what is valuable only when I experience this "seeing" itself as a valuable attitude, as a task, an inner activity demanding expression.

This interpenetration of the two questions is no merely indifferent matter as regards our method of investigation. The extended front of the problem disperses the energy of our forward thrust. Dividing it, we must take up one special problem at a time, and from what is then acquired recover a comprehensive survey. But the success of this method is assured only where, from the start, the interpenetration of the problems guarantees such a recovery. It is a favourable feature of ethical research that this condition applies to the cleavage of the fundamental question. We may quietly pursue by itself the narrower and clearer problem of what ought to be done, without thereby incurring the danger of ignoring the other and wider problem concerning the valuable in general. Both questions concern the same ethical principles, the same values. Only their respective domains are markedly different in extent. To obtain our first points of contact we must start with the narrower one; and for a while we may follow the traditional methods of ethics, which deal almost exclusively with what ought to be done. To bear in mind the partial character of the question will serve as an adequate corrective.

When we are seeking for principles, we must first of all ask: What kind of principles?

It is not enough to answer concisely: Values. What values are is precisely the question. And this question is more difficult than might be supposed. If we commence with the narrowest interpretation of ethical principles, as being the principles of what ought to be done, they unmistakably bear the character of commandments, of imperatives. They set up demands, constitute a sort of tribunal, and before this tribunal human conduct—either as a doing or as a mere willing—is to vindicate itself. But they themselves offer no account of their own right, they recognize no court superior to themselves which could legalize their demands as just claims or could unmask them as a usurpation. They come forward as an absolute, autonomous, final court. Thereby, however, they themselves conjure up the question of legitimacy.

What is the nature of the authority of moral principles? Is it a genuine, really absolute authority? Or is it relative to times and interpretations? Are ethical laws absolute? Or do they come into existence, and can they sink back into Non-Being and into oblivion? For example, is the commandment "Love thy neighbour" super-temporal and eternal? Is its validity independent of whether or not men revere it and aspire to fulfil it?

Evidently the question is not to be solved by referring it to the historical fact that there have been times when man did not know this law. If it is absolute, that fact was only a fact of ignorance or of the moral immaturity of mankind, but not a refutation of the law. If, however, it be not absolute, the historical moment of its first appearance is the moment of the birth of an ethical principle.

Facts, therefore, can here teach us nothing; just as, in general, facts never can decide a question of right.

These two contradictory interpretations confront each

other: the one absolutistic, aprioristic; the other relativistic, historically genetic.

Which of the two is right depends upon which, in its consequences, is tenable as a theory. If moral commandments are absolute, it is necessary to prove the absolute in them to be an autonomous, undeniably certain principle. But, contrariwise, if they have come into being, it is necessary to show how their genesis is to be understood and how with it the positive right to acceptation and the appearance of absoluteness arise. From the time of the Sophists, who were the first to distinguish between what is φύσει and what is θέσει, this question has never ceased to attract attention; and it rightly stands at the centre of every conflict of opinions and theories.

(b) Ethical Relativism

This question is definitive as to the essential nature of philosophical ethics. If moral commandments have come into being, they are the work of man; human thought has the power to raise up and overthrow them. In that case, philosophical thought also has the power to issue commandments, just as political thought has the power to issue laws; consequently, positive law and positive morality stand on the same level. Ethics then is "practical philosophy" in the normative sense, and the claim to declare what ought to happen is no empty presumption. For the principles of the Ought must be invented, devised. Their place of origin is the laboratory of ethical thought.

Even if it is a fact that norms commonly arise and acquire acceptation, but do so apart from philosophical reflection and prior to it in time, their entire vindication would still devolve upon philosophical ethics. For to it as intellectual referee would belong the task of reviewing the norms, of weighing them in the scales, of acknowledging or discarding them. Ethical thought would be the appointed law-giver of human life, would have the power and the duty of declaring the truth to man.

That philosophical ethics does not actually assume this enormous responsibility can easily be apprehended in a vague way; but it needs a more rigid proof from the structure of ethical phenomena. This will of itself be forthcoming with increasing certainty in the course of further investigation.

But what is clear immediately and without proof is that no philosophical ethics, even if such a vindication really devolved upon it, could sustain it. For human thought is exactly as relative as the norms, the relativity of which it should overcome. Ethical theories diverge from one another to exactly the same degree as the varying norms of positive morality. If ethics wished to take up this impossible task in earnest, it must needs become guilty of the same arrogance which it would have to unmask in those norms which have sprung up.

Rather it must itself avoid the pretention of absoluteness, which it attacks in them. On this point there can be no serious doubt.

(c) ETHICAL ABSOLUTISM

It is otherwise, if moral commandments are absolute. There is then nothing for philosophy to do but to establish and present them clearly, to seek the inner grounds for their absoluteness and to bring these into the light. For here thought is only a reproduction of that which is pre-figured, and ethics is contemplative, not normative; it is pure theory of the practical, not itself "practical philosophy." It stands apart from life, has no influence, cannot teach what we ought to do; it cannot revise, form or re-form, and it assumes no responsibility. It has no actuality, but follows real life only at a serene distance. Its value exists only for itself, for the thought-structure as such, not for life.

But this again cannot be the true situation. It is true that philosophy does not in general guide actual life. But if therein lay the limit to significant philosophical enterprise, why does not the very simple knowledge of the limit check the enterprise once for all? Why does not the long series of philosophers break off, who from ethical reflection and insight expect directive illumination? Is this an ominous aberration, a shadow of that arrogance of the legislator's self-glorification? Or, indeed, is there here a hidden reason which ever anew deludes the earnest seeker with the autonomy which he does not possess?

Is not the reverse in reality true? Is not this deeper insight nevertheless somehow a guide and builder of life for those who take up seriously the problem of moral commandments? And are not teaching and learning here exactly that which this guidance and edification introduce into the life of others? If one looks to the philosophical science of the ancients, one cannot doubt that this phenomenon is a fact, and that in many ages it has had no narrow scope among the educated. The belief then will not die out, that instruction and salvation must come from the depths of philosophical insight.

And must one not say: even if that phenomenon should be questionable and this belief vain, still we must, in spite thereof, categorically demand instruction and normative guidance from philosophy? Is not exactly this its meaning and its Ought? It is an undeniable fact that of ethical commandments there are many, differing according to time and people, and all presenting themselves as of equal authority, whereby their claims to absoluteness are contradicted. Since, therefore, there are as many historical errors as there are positive laws, a categorical demand must be made for a court of appeal which separates, sifts, restrains arrogance—even if it cannot itself produce anything better.

Philosophy can be the only court. Every other would once more be a presumptuous authority. By its very nature philosophy is the court which judges with understanding and according to principles. And even if it should not be so as yet, it is its essential nature to be so. Therefore it must become so. It is the appointed court of appeal.

CHAPTER II

CAN VIRTUE BE TAUGHT?

(a) THE PROPOSITION OF SOCRATES

BUT how then is the practical and normative character of ethics to be understood? And how is it to be defined? Ethics cannot assume the defence of commandments. It cannot be positive legislation. What competence has it then of a practical kind?

The same problem was involved in the initial question of ancient ethics: Can virtue be taught? The ancients decided it almost without exception in the affirmative. Their fundamental thought was intellectualistic. It is best known in its Socratic form. No one does evil for evil's sake; a good which he is striving for always hovers before him. He can be mistaken only in what he holds to be good. It all depends on whether he knows what is good. If that is known to him, he cannot will the bad; thereby he would contradict himself. Hence the two fundamental propositions which rule the whole later ethics of antiquity are: Virtue is knowledge; and therefore, Virtue can be taught.

Even the Stoic doctrine of the emotions did not contradict this teaching. It is indeed the feelings which prevent the will from willing the good; they must on that account be destroyed. But feelings themselves are regarded from the intellectualist point of view—that is, as inadequate knowledge (ἄλογος ὁρμῆ). The overcoming of them is none other than a knowing, the dominance of the logos.

Herein lies the extreme normative conception of ethics; not only is ethics competent to teach what ought to happen, but it also has the ability to determine volition and action. The morally bad man is the ignorant man, the good man is he that is wise. The ideal of the wise man dominates ethics.

(b) THE CHRISTIAN CONCEPTION OF "SIN"

Christian ethics subverts this doctrine by its concept of human weakness and the power of evil.

Man knows the commandment of God, but he nevertheless transgresses it. He has not the power to fulfil it, his knowledge is impotent, he "sins." One may describe the concept of sin as the specially revolutionizing factor in Christian ethics. Sin is neither a mere mistake nor simply guilt. It is a determining, seductive power in life. Certainly upon man falls the consequence—the wages of sin—but he is not its master. He must give way to it. The ancient Greek is indeed also aware of being overcome; but he is overcome by feeling, and the feeling is his ignorance. But the Christian is convinced from the first that it does not rest with him. For it is not a question of knowledge. It is a question as to the ability or inability to follow the better knowledge. For man does not necessarily follow it. Much more, once he knows the law, he still has to decide for or against it. There is a dark irrational power which takes part in this decision. It is the stronger power. Man has not the strength to wrench himself free from it. The flesh is weak. God alone can help and can deliver from the evil power.

It is a matter of indifference how one metaphysically interprets the power of evil, whether as devil or as matter, as an anti-moral impulse or as radical evil. The fact is always the same; and it contains, just as does the proposition of Socrates, a fragment of truth which is not to be lost. It is the antithesis of the doctrine of Socrates. Translated into the language of the ancients it reads: Virtue cannot be taught; for only knowledge can indeed be taught, but knowledge does not avail. In the language of our present-day concepts it is: Ethics can indeed teach us what we ought to do, but the teaching is powerless, man cannot follow it. Ethics is certainly normative in idea, but not in reality. It does not determine and guide man in life, it is not practical. There is no practical philosophy. Religion alone is practical.

The latter statements express a view which, once more, shoots far beyond the mark. Although the overcoming of human weakness and of the power of evil may be a question by itself, which is outside the question whether virtue can be taught, we nevertheless must know the moral commandments beforehand; we must in some form know what is good, and what is evil, in order to be confronted by a decision. Although virtue "is" not knowledge, a knowing must belong to it. And in so far as man does not possess this knowledge, the task of ethics is to give it to him. It must confront him with the decision for or against what is presented. It would have to point out the moral commandments to him.

This presentation of the problem is not changed when we interpret it in the conceptual language of religion. Here the law given of God plays the rôle of the norms. The law abides, even in the work of redemption: "I am not come to destroy, but to fulfil." As the first condition, man must be confronted with the law. His failure is failure before it. But the representation of God, as law-giver, is not a disavowal of ethics as man's recognition of the norm, but is the strongest acknowledgment of the absoluteness of its content. The authority of the law-giver is the form of this absoluteness. Here the autonomy of the moral consciousness is transferred to God. Whether this transference corresponds to the phenomenon, whether man does not thereby deprive himself of his birthright, is not the question here. It belongs indeed in its essence to the concept of sin. Sin is not guilt before men or before one's own conscience, but guilt before God. In this sense sin is no longer an ethical concept and has no connection with the question before us.

(c) Schopenhauer's Purely Theoretical Ethics

With both these conceptions, the ancient and the Christian, we can link up a longer series of further gradations of the normative. But for our problem only the extreme case is of importance—the complete disappearance of the normative. Schopenhauer was the best representative of an ethics of this kind.

According to his view, ethics as a philosophical discipline is entirely unpractical to exactly the same extent as are logic and metaphysics. Not only can it prescribe nothing, it cannot even treat of precepts. There is no power, whether in man or outside of him, which could hold up an Ought against him. Truly, there is a principle of moral conduct which is deeply anchored in the metaphysical nature of man. But ethics can only lay it bare, draw it into the light of consciousness, so far as it is already active in him. It cannot incite the principle to activity where it slumbers buried and choked with earth. Ethics is not an energizing factor in real life, it can only behold, analyse, comprehend in a contemplative way, like all philosophy. It is pure theory.

The life of man goes on its way untroubled about it. How man determines his course depends upon his "intelligible character"; his character is the moral decision. But it never enters into the world of appearance, not even in ethical theory. Ethics accordingly not only cannot invent what ought to be but cannot even discover and teach it. What ought to happen is always there; indeed, the decision for or against is already made. The primal deed of choice does not lie in consciousness at all, but precedes it.

If one compares this interpretation of ethics with the two views stated above, one may discriminate a threefold gradation.

(1) The ancient view: Ethics is normative; it teaches what ought to happen, and indeed successfully. It has influence upon life, its teaching sustains man's responsibility.

(2) The Christian view: Ethics is indeed normative in the sense of a doctrine, but not in the sense of efficacy or of influence. Doctrine alone is without effect. Strength and help must come from another quarter.

(3) Schopenhauer's view: Ethics is not at all normative;

it can neither determine life nor throw any light on how it should be determined. It is without influence for good or evil.

It is easy to perceive that the two extreme theories are furthest removed from the ethical phenomenon. In the ancient conception we have seen the source of the error. In the Christian, the error is removed. Schopenhauer's view suffers from the opposite embarrassment: How could the consciousness of the principle be a matter of complete indifference for the attitude towards life, since all consciousness has practically an emotional undertone, and since pure theory exists only in abstraction? And how can ethics as a doctrine be wholly unpractical, since it is a knowledge of the principle, and this knowledge is the presupposition of volitional decision? For, although moral conduct "is" indeed not knowledge, it presupposes knowledge.

The intermediate view comes closest to the phenomenon of the moral life. It limits the normative in ethics without discarding it on principle. That it in fact limits it too much is matter for further investigation.

(d) PLATO'S "MENO" AND THE SOLUTION OF THE DIFFICULTY

But we have not yet closed the controversial question of the ancients concerning the possibility of teaching virtue. The erroneous presupposition in it was that knowledge, as such, guarantees right conduct. If we set this aside, if we correct it, knowledge still retains the basic significance of a prior condition. But if we fall back upon this more modest proposition, the old question returns with clearer outlines.

It now exclusively concerns this knowledge which first brings man face to face with decision, and in this sense is the condition of right conduct. If we for a time disregard the further question whether and how far man is free to apply such knowledge, the problem still remains: What sort of knowledge is this? Is it, as such, capable of being taught or not? Can ethics communicate its contents—the moral commandments? Or is it powerless here also? Is it condemned merely to confirm afterwards and to analyse what the living moral consciousness already possesses?

It is in fact this problem which Plato takes up and treats in the *Meno*. Herein he has opened up the way for philosophical ethics.

The perplexity arises from the alternative: Virtue is either something that can be taught (διδακτόν), something that by practice can be acquired (ἀσκητόν), or it is something that is inborn in man by nature (φύσει παραγενόμενον). This either-or is to be understood as a strict disjunction. If virtue can be taught, its contents cannot be an original possession of the moral consciousness (the soul). They must be received from without, and be capable of being acquired by study. But then it is an affair of legislation (θέσει), a thing humanly devised, and has no absoluteness, no universal obligatoriness. The sophistical relativity of knowledge holds then for moral perception also. And the dependence of right conduct upon knowledge signifies the abandonment of the fixed invariable standard of good and evil.

And conversely: If virtue is inborn by nature, it is indeed an invariable standard of value, a possession raised above all affirmation and all arbitrariness of thought, a possession originating in the soul, the basis of moral perception; but it cannot be taught. No one can communicate it to the soul: the soul can only create it out of itself. But for ethics that means banishment into theory, into the unpractical, the contemplative.

Here we have in a nutshell the fundamental predicament of the normative. Both sides of the alternative are equally unacceptable, both are in conflict with the situation found in ethical phenomena. And now begins the famous dialectical investigation which proves the alternative itself to be false.

If in ethical "knowledge" the διδακτόν and the φύσει παραγενόμενον exclude each other, they must exclude each other also in every other kind of knowledge. Is this the case? Mathematics is accounted a subject-matter for teaching; one ought therefore to conclude that mathematical propositions are not objects of innate knowledge. One must examine the phenomenon of teaching and learning. Plato elaborates this phenomenon fully in the cross-examination of the slave.[1] The slave is placed before the figure of a square and is questioned concerning the side of a square double the size. It is shown that at first he gives false answers, but that then he sees his error from the nature of the thing itself (the geometrical figure). Finally from the same nature of the thing he perceives in the diagonal of the given square the side of the one which is sought. He knows it suddenly, without its having been told him. The cross-examination had only directed his attention to it. Evidently, therefore, he had the knowledge in himself as an original possession. His "learning" is only a becoming conscious of the factual contents in him. The "teaching" by the one who knows is only the directing of attention to the matter in hand. The pupil must see it himself, he must be convinced by it himself, otherwise there is no real insight. "Teaching" is merely the midwifery of cognition.

Herewith the situation is fundamentally reversed. In geometry at least the διδακτόν and the φύσει παραγενόμενον do not exclude each other. Here the alternative itself is false. Conversely: Only what is already present in the soul as innate knowledge can be learned. "Learning" is the apprehension of inborn knowledge, the "anamnesis." The epistemological significance of anamnesis has no connection with the mythopsychological notion of "recollection"; it is determined by its definition: "To recover of oneself knowledge from within oneself."[2] This "recovery" points to the depth of the soul into which he must reach, who, already knowing, wishes to assure himself of the truth. In Plato the expression appears to have a certain fixity of meaning, as a parallel passage in

---

[1] *Meno*, 82b–86e.
[2] Ibid., 85d: ἀναλαμβάνειν αὐτὸν ἐν αὑτῷ ἐπιστήμην.

the *Phædo* shows, where the nature of learning is defined as a "recovery of inborn knowledge."[1]

"Anamnesis" is the Platonic concept of the aprioristic in knowledge. Geometrical knowledge is aprioristic. That does not prevent its being "teachable." Teaching is the leading of another to make his own descent into the depth. Might it not be the same with ethical knowledge?

Manifestly the morally good man knows in some form or other what the good is. From what source can he know it? He cannot fall back upon any authority, he cannot swear by the word of any master; just as little has he from birth a clear consciousness of the good. It is otherwise if he carries the knowledge of the good hidden in himself, in the depth of the soul, as inborn knowledge and can draw it up into the light of consciousness through his own reflection and penetration, and on occasion through the midwifery of one who knows, who teaches, in that he incites to reflection. In this sense then virtue can be taught, just as geometry can. Its teachability does not contradict its inner origin, the φύσει παραγενόμενον. This is only a vague expression for the apriority of moral knowledge contained in the essential nature of virtue. It can be taught only because and in so far as it is an aprioristic insight.

[1] *Phædo*, 75e: ἆρ οὐχ ὃ καλοῦμεν μανθάνειν δικείαν ἐπιστήμην ἀναλαμβάνειν ἂν εἴη.

CHAPTER III

THE RIGHT MEANING OF THE NORMATIVE

(a) The Indirectly Normative

ETHICAL perception is perception of norms, commandments, values. All knowledge of norms is necessarily aprioristic. The Platonic philosophy is the historical discovery of the aprioristic element in the whole realm of human knowledge. It is in a pre-eminent sense a justification of all normative perception, including that of the normative character of ethics itself.

Ethics can in fact teach us what is morally good, as geometry can teach what is geometrically true. But it can force nothing upon the moral consciousness, it can only direct attention to its own contents and principles. It can only bring out of consciousness what is contained in it. In this also it resembles pure mathematics. The difference is only that the principles and contents which it brings into consciousness are commandments, norms, values. It therefore is normative according to its contents, but not according to its method or its kind of teaching. For the apriority of insight and the art of leading another to it are the same here as there. Philosophical ethics is the midwifery of the moral consciousness.

It can accordingly set up and teach principles of which without it no consciousness could perhaps be aware. But these it cannot evolve out of itself nor invent; it can only bring to consciousness what as a principle is a faculty in the human soul, or more correctly—since the very concept of a faculty is ambiguous—what is in itself an ethical principle. Ethical principles must have such an existence—whether these be commandments, norms, or simply values.

What such a Being of the principles in itself signifies, what sphere of existence they belong to, and what modality they have, is a further question which involves a peculiar series of inherent difficulties. In their own place it will be necessary to investigate them. For the moment the Platonic parallel of ethics with mathematics must instruct us up to this point, teaching us that there are undoubtedly spheres of Being of this order in general—which are neither real nor merely subjective—and that we, in daring to cope with this question, do not assume more than what the theory of knowledge in other departments recognizes without hesitation.

The character of the normative in ethics as a philosophical discipline is therefore justified; but, in contrast to all the exaggerated representations of its power to mould life, it suffers a considerable limitation. That is to say, ethics in itself is not at all normative, but only its subject-matter, the principle, or rather the realm of principles, which it is to uncover. This normative character of the principles is transferred indirectly to ethics itself. Hence in it the normative character is paler, is weakened, and is by no means necessary. Ethics is normative only in so far as it brings to consciousness principles, the influence of which upon human determination, disposition and valuation of the real is first mediated through elevating them into rational consciousness. Only within these boundaries is its art of midwifery a condition of such influence, and only in these boundaries does it really assist moral principles to be efficient in real life.

But that is by no means always the case; perhaps it is only so as a rare exception. Ordinarily commandments, norms, valuational views are actively at work in life before they have been raised by subsequent ethical reflection into the full light of consciousness. Rather does philosophical ethics usually discover them first through having hit upon their embodiments in life, and having its attention turned by means of these to the presence of the principle—not as if the knowledge of principles becomes in this way aposterioristic. The principle as such can only be discovered a priori, that is, as something independent, primal, immediately evident, which exists behind those embodiments—and under embodiments must be understood those very facts, the valuations, dispositions, resolutions of the moral life. This aprioristic insight, nevertheless, is occasioned through the a posteriori.

(b) The Visible Field and the Idea of Ethics

It is accordingly important to make clear that all those exaggerated expectations with which the inexperienced man is accustomed to enter upon the task of ethical research, all the high-flying dreams of world-improvement and of the rapid reorientation of life, must be dropped at the very threshold of real ethical work. Philosophical investigation is a modest absorption in the ethical phenomenon, not an eager hunt for actualities and sensations.

On the other hand, one must not fail to appreciate the fact that the scope of the indirectly normative in ethics is very considerable. The possibility is always at hand that it may with its methods discover values which are lacking in moral life, or have ceased to be recognized; and in view of the great significance of the task this possibility alone is sufficient to lead the ethicist to unresting search, notwithstanding the danger of gaining only meagre results. Who, however, would to-day presume to form a rigid judgment as to the prospects of such a search! In the realm of values we are at the very beginning of deliberate investigation. No one can know whither it will lead. And as for the history of ethics itself, it seems to us old and worthy of respect, as though fixed on its rails; but what is the short span of the known history of the mind compared with what we do not know and with what is to come! Ethics by its very nature looks towards the future. From the same point of view, it must regard itself and its peculiar, arduous work; and here it has no occasion for sceptical resignation. However modestly it keeps itself close to the phenomena and eschews presumptuous ideals, its essence and its principle still remain this: To be a transforming power in life. And while it can be this only in so far as it turns its attention towards values which are in real life lacking, its principle is to open the eyes, and to present to life what it teaches the eyes to see.

In principle, it is certainly practical philosophy—however much or however little it may ever discover or indirectly transform. But in its essential purpose the only question concerns its fundamental attitude and has nothing to do with actual achievements upon which it could perhaps already look back. It is normative not with regard to results, not according to experience, but in regard to the task which falls to it in human life and which, as such, is intuitive in a priori fashion.

(c) ETHICS AND PEDAGOGY

One must not forget, moreover, that in all educational activity there is a narrow but perfectly definite practical field for ethical research, whether this activity consist of instruction by a professional teacher, or of that inevitable influence and stimulation which issue forth in all the intercourse of the morally mature.

The more of the realm of values which the one who influences embraces in his view, so much the more of course he necessarily opens the vision, understanding and perspective for life of the person he guides. Imperceptibly valuational problems arise in connection with subjects of study and questions of life; and involuntarily everyone who reproves, advises, calls attention to or speaks about literary matters, directs the uneducated person's sense of value to its permanent object, ethical values. The younger and the more unripe the learner is, so much the more responsible and weighted with consequences is the teacher's influence. A too narrow valuational perception on the part of the teacher is always a serious danger for the youth entrusted to him. The consequence is a premature forcing into a one-sided, limited or even biased interpretation of life—a moral distortion, a systematization, a reducing of all youth to one pattern. These are mistakes from which educational institutions seriously suffer. But the cause of the evil is the educator's lack of ethical culture.

In this field philosophical ethics has a highly positive task. It must educate the educator, as he must educate youth. Thus indirectly ethics is that which haunted the vision of Plato: it is the educator of humanity in general.

Stated universally: If the consciousness of moral principles were to remain indifferent to their application in life, the "practical" significance of ethics would be limited to the rare achievements of original discovery in values. But such is not the case. Developed, matured, schooled consciousness of value is far superior practically to unawakened, obscure, unclear, perception—least, perhaps, in regard to resolution and action, but surely as concerns the purely inward attitude, the emotional response to persons and situations, participation in the valuational fulness of life, and man's inward moral growth.

Here, in the narrowest confines of everyday life, far from the great perspectives of mankind's development, ethics finds a wide practical field. It co-operates in the awakening of the sense of value. The fact that this work is carried on only through the mediation of a single person or of a few makes no difference. Born educators will always be few, but they are the salt of the earth.

(d) THEORETICAL AND ETHICAL APRIORISM

If now one asks: Which was right, antiquity or Schopenhauer? Can the good be taught, or is ethics purely contemplative? the answer must be: Both are right and both are wrong. The Platonic raising of the disjunction between "teachable and inborn" into a conjunction gives the synthesis of the two views by removing their exaggerations. Ethics indeed does not of itself dictate anything. But nevertheless it teaches what is good, in so far as our knowledge concerning goodness is never completed. It teaches only what it finds before it, what it beholds; and its teaching is nothing else than allowing another to behold.

But in so far as the thing beheld contains a demand, a commandment, ethics is at the same time the consciousness of the command, and thereby a consciousness that is itself commanding.

This state of things has a far wider range than the mere presentation of the normative would lead one to suppose. It touches the innermost kernel of the ethical phenomenon: the relations of principles, i.e. values, to consciousness. If this relation were one of knowledge merely, the fundamental problem involved in it would be already solved by the key of Platonic apriorism in the doctrine of anamnesis; but, besides that, it is also a relation of willing. It contains the question: How do valuational principles acquire efficacy and the power to mould the real?

It is easy to see that consciousness herein plays an integrating rôle, that values operate otherwise than categories of existence —not directly, but, if at all, through the mediation of the consciousness of value. But in this way ethical apriorism itself also acquires a significance totally different from the purely theoretical. It has a different and an incomparably greater metaphysical import; and here is the limit of the Platonic analogy between geometry and ethics.

Geometry as pure knowledge does not need to carry over into reality the laws which it discerns a priori. The real is already geometrical so far as it can be geometrical at all. But what ethics discerns a priori (the values) is not contained wholly in the actual; indeed reality is in great mass saturated with value, but it lacks distinct valuational form so far as it is capable of being formed. There are un-actualized masses of value; and there is a real which is contrary to value. Along with the good there exists the morally bad.

Here the problems divide. The boundary is between the merely cognitive a priori and the demanding, commanding, a priori. Here is at the same time the frontier beyond which even the problem of ethical "knowledge" is no longer a merely cognitive problem. Here begins the jurisdiction of life's actuality and of the Ought-to-Do, since every value once conceived has a tendency to realize itself, however unreal it may be. Valuational discernment and valuational effectiveness upon the real conduct and life of man are separated from each other only through freedom of choice.

The whole burden of the responsibility falls upon a priori discernment. Even if it does not, as such, command what ought to happen, the contents which it discerns nevertheless command. And thus it itself incorporates the weight of the commandment.

Can it bear the burden of such a weight? Is it so certain, so absolute, so incapable of deception? Or is there still some criterion for it, an opposing court of appeal wherein it might find a corrective? Theoretical apriorism possesses such a criterion in experience, which rests upon the testimony of the senses. Ethical apriorism has no such thing, for reality which can be experienced does not at all need to contain the values discerned; and the values are condensed into commandments exactly there where reality—that is, the actual conduct of man —does not correspond to them.

In ethics apriorism rests wholly upon itself. It is altogether autonomous; and that is exactly the questionable element in it. At this point the insurmountable difficulty of the normative in ethics comes up again in another sense—as it were upon another plane. Suppose this autonomous apriorism did not rest on a firm footing, suppose there were a concealed arbitrariness in it, a veritable invention, a fictitious element, a wanton play of phantasy under the guise of a higher authority! Would not that be a trick played upon human life itself? Is it not seductively easy to invent commandments—either from private self-interest or under pressure of life—to attribute to them the authority of the absolute, and then, later, even to believe in them?

Here it is not enough to confine the act of commanding to an extreme minimum. Certainly ethics does not pretend to settle once for all what in any given case is commanded. Just as the theory of knowledge does not say what is true in this or that problem of existence, but only what truth is in general, whereby it can be known, what its criterion is, so also is it with ethics. It does not say what is good here and now; to decide that it would need to have insight into the single instance down to its most imponderable elements and to view it comprehensively; it would need also to trace out the consequences, to have a knowledge of the present and of the future. No human knowledge can lay claim to that. Ethics is not casuistry—not only in so far as it may not forestall the free creative resolution beforehand, but also in so far as it has not the capacity for so doing. But this changes nothing at all in the fundamental problem. For what the good in general is, what is commanded in general, that it declares and must declare. The criterion of good and evil in general is the minimum which we may expect from it. But the question is: Is ethics competent to furnish the criterion?

It is this question which has not been decided in the previous examination of the normative consciousness. Nor can it be decided by the merely a priori apprehension of value. Rather must the very question as to valuational apriorism at this point be opened out anew and more fully.

SECTION II

THE PLURALITY OF MORALS AND UNITY OF ETHICS

CHAPTER IV

MULTIPLICITY AND UNITY IN MORAL CONSCIOUSNESS

(a) THE HISTORICAL MULTIPLICITY OF MORAL COMMANDMENTS

WHEN once the general task of ethics is established, the more special question arises: Of what kind of morality ought it to treat? Is there then a unitary morality? Should we make that of our own time and country our point of departure? Or are we to go farther back and grasp the morality of Christendom which binds us to other peoples and ages? If one accedes to such an extension of the basis of orientation, one cannot stop short at any historically empirical boundary. Beyond the morality of "Love thy neighbour" one must survey the morality of "an eye for an eye." But then the field of the phenomena will become boundless. The ethics of Spinoza, Kant and Nietzsche, the classical ethics of the Greeks, the Stoic and Epicurean ideal of the wise man, the transcendant morality of Plotinus and the Church Fathers, yes, the moralities of the Hindus and Chinese—it makes no difference whether near to us or remote, whether living or dead in the life of our time— each one claims to be the genuine ethical good of humanity, to become the subject-matter of analysis.

In the interest of objectivity the wide extent of this problem is justified and may not be arbitrarily narrowed, out of respect for one's own condition or limitation. The task of philosophical ethics cannot consist of a more or less opportunistic selection from its multiplicity. But also it cannot waste itself in a mere juxtaposition of the details of the manifold. Yet the contradictions of these "moralities" forbid a simple comprehensive survey. Ethics must then be unitary in itself—it must be so in a sense more cogent than are other philosophical disciplines.

In pure theory cleavages are due only to a lack of vision and comprehension; but in claims and commandments they constitute an inner conflict among themselves, involving their reciprocal nullification.

The unity of ethics is the fundamental demand which raises its voice categorically above the plurality of morals, a demand which stands above all strife of opinions, which is evident a priori and unconditionally, and is intolerant of any doubt. Its absolute singleness appears at the very threshold of the investigation, in conscious contrast to the plurality presented in the phenomena themselves. Therefore the problem is: How can philosophical ethics overcome the cleavages and the contradiction? How can it achieve a synthesis of that which in itself is antithetical? How is unity in ethics possible?

(b) CURRENT MORALITY AND PURE ETHICS

To look for the unity in direct opposition to the multiplicity would be in this case far too simplified a procedure. The latter must not be set up outside of, but taken up into, or have predominant scope within, the unity.

Within certain limits the analogy to the unity of truth may yield us support. Every age has its "current truths." The physics of Aristotle was accepted, and that of Galileo "passed as truth." But all those current truths must be distinguished from "the truth" as such, from the ideal requirement which every science of a given time itself sets up—a requirement which it only imperfectly fulfils, but for which philosophy seeks the criterion. In the same manner every age and every people has its "current morality"—by analogy with "positive science" one may well say its "positive morality." It is always a system of accepted precepts, to which man subjects himself and which he recognizes as absolute.

Historically there is a morality of bravery, a morality of obedience, a morality of pride; likewise of humility, of power, of beauty, of strength of will, of manly loyalty, of compassion.

But from every positive morality, ethics, as such, is to be distinguished by its universal ideal challenge of the good, as it is implied and is presupposed in every special morality. Its affair is to show what in general is good. Ethics seeks for the criterion of the good, which is lacking in the positive moralities.

What herein becomes immediately evident is the fact that the relation between current morality and ethics, in spite of all divergences, is from the very beginning an inner connection, a relation of subjection, indeed of ideal dependence. There is no current morality which would not have the tendency to be absolute morality. Indeed, a current morality in general has acceptance only so long as there is a living belief in its absoluteness.

Herein it does not differ from all the other departments of thought. All positive knowledge has the tendency to be absolute knowledge; every positive law the tendency to be "righteous" (ideal) law. Everywhere in the realm of the positive is already immanent a reference to the Idea. It is the inner condition of acceptance itself, i.e. of positiveness. But as the Idea of morality in general is nothing else than the concrete essence of ethics, one may say that every current morality has the tendency to be pure ethics; indeed, it believes itself to be pure ethics. And only so long as it so believes does it prevail.

But if the Idea of pure ethics is contained in every morality, one would think that within this there would be somehow contained the sought-for unity of ethics. But then the unity would have to be found in current morality itself—not outside of it and not in opposition to it. Not of course as though a constituent part was to be found in other constituent parts; for it is not a conscious ferment in the varying moral commandments. It is rather perhaps as if conditions, primary presuppositions, may be demonstrated, in so far as the subject-matter rests upon them in the order of fact (but not in the order of consciousness).

Then, too, there would be the possibility, by mere reflection upon the likenesses in all moral commandments, which are current or have once been current, to penetrate through to the unity of ethics.

The success of such a method would be certain if we might assume that the sought-for unity is something in itself simple, as it were, a point, and besides is still capable of being understood in its unity, or at least as a thing which can be exhausted in some few characteristics. But this is highly questionable. Certainly a very widespread prejudice prevails to the effect that the essence of the good is simple, is plainly comprehensible, easily understood, altogether rational. But the very fact of the multiplicity and contrariety of moral commandments ought to have raised doubts on this point. If one goes deeply into the investigation of the realm of values, the assumption becomes more and more doubtful with every step. Not as though one must here give up the search for unity of some kind or other; but unity can also be comprehensive, indeed it can in itself be relational, in many ways articulated. But where it is a matter of grasping such unities, there it is indeed a question whether one can grasp them directly as such—that is, as unities; and consequently, even when one grasps them in their contents, whether one can also perceive the distinctive quality of their unity.

The ordinary fate of such a procedure, which starts with multiplicity, is the reverse: one succeeds only in grasping ever again the manifold; and one sees oneself obliged finally to seek the unity elsewhere. But if one grasps it from another quarter, then indeed the diversity permits of being comprehended under it. This is the old Platonic wisdom: Unity must be seen in advance, seen a priori. But then immediately arises the danger of finding the a priori perception in concrete opposition to the given multiplicity.

The question may accordingly be summed up as follows: Is there an a priori perception of what constitutes the unity of pure ethics in the multiplicity of the current moralities themselves?

(c) FURTHER DIMENSIONS OF THE MANIFOLD

But the question is still wider. The manifold of the moral consciousness is not exhausted in that of positive morality. The latter constitutes here, as it were, only one dimension of the organization, and indeed of an organization taken over empirically and only presented outwardly. In reality, then, not only do the views of different times and peoples diverge (not to mention those of the single philosophical systems rooted in them), but also, within these systems and moralities, clearly distinguishable ethical tendencies can be marked off from one another, tendencies which partly reappear in the various systems, partly are characteristic of particular views only, but which always somehow spring up interwoven with one another. Their classification, which one can reproduce only by hints in vague concepts, cuts across the other division; it stands, as it were, vertically upon it.

Thus there is a difference of principle between the morality of the community (the State) and of the individual; likewise between the morality of the man and the woman, and the child (ancient morality, for example, was almost exclusively that of the man); or between the morality of power, of justice and of love. Again, in another dimension lie such contrasts as the following:

(1) The morality of labour, of production—and that of moderation and contentedness with little;

(2) The morality of struggle, of competition, of expression of energy—and the morality of peace, of compromise, of charitableness;

(3) The morality of the highest or most secret desires—and that of the customary severe claims upon one, against which the inclinations and desires of our own nature revolt;

(4) The morality of authority, of subjection to recognized and accepted norms—and the responsibility of seeking, of watching for new norms, and of fighting for them (here, going-in-quest, understanding, and revolutionizing, are felt to

be duties, and one assumes responsibility for what has been discovered and for the ideal one represents in one's life);

(5) The morality of the present or of one's own immediate environment—and the morality of the future, of the distant, of the ideal (to which the present and actual persons and relations are subordinated, indeed sacrificed);

(6) The morality of action in general, of the active life— and the morality of appraising values and enjoying them.

To these pairs of opposites might easily be added a long series of others. Within each one of them both tendencies are justifiable; both grow out of the fulness of circumstances themselves. They are all different but unavoidable directions in which the general tasks of life move, directions which show the autonomous points of view or ends of individual philosophies and which as such cannot at will be manœuvred, interchanged or brought down to a dead level.

(d) The Unity Sought For and the Investigation of Values

It is clear that ethics must not assume an attitude of exclusiveness or indifference towards any one of these directions. Every exclusiveness would make it particularistic and biased, it would set itself up, not above the current types of morality, but alongside of them. Yet it is inherent in the Idea of ethics to stand above them, to be their unity.

But how do heterogeneous claims permit of being unified? Here one can no longer appeal to the fact that the multiplicity is something merely empirical, therefore "accidental." It proves also to be untrue that the deficiency is merely in the reflection upon unity, in the consciousness of it, while the unity itself inheres implicitly in reality. This point is no longer the question, because the specific types are by no means empirically apprehended; from the essence of the matter it is clear that every type as such, with its peculiar kind of claim, is entirely a priori. The unity therefore can only be a synthetical unity existing above the specific claims. Every one of these directions in morality implies a highest end of life of its own; but every one of these ends lays claim to a superior rank. It ignores the like claims of the rest which in themselves are equally justified, it denies its own co-ordination with them. It comes forward in exclusiveness as a tyrant, it has an evident tendency to overthrow the others, even sometimes to annihilate them. How then could the unitary, universal end be imposed upon the manifold?

And yet this very kind of assertion on the part of individual ends is a proof of the necessity of a unity of ends in general. To be a unity is of the very essence of striving. But ends are points of guidance in striving. As in space a human being cannot go two ways at once, but is compelled to choose one, so on the spiritual and moral plane he cannot strive in two directions at once, let alone in more than two. One he must choose. Plurality of supreme ends tears him to pieces, causes him to lose his unity, to be split up, to be inconsequent and to falter. It paralyses his energy and with it the striving itself. Unity of purpose is a fundamental requirement of the moral life. Therefore all ends which are capable of being pursued, all positive norms, commandments and types of morality, are necessarily exclusive and tyrannical. They must be so because otherwise they would defeat themselves. Their presumption may well be a limitation, but it is not arbitrariness, it is rather an unavoidable consequence.

And for the same reason, on the elevated plane of the ethical problem also, the dominating unity of the ends is an unavoidable consequence. It is a far more categorical demand than the unity of principles in the domain of theory. This latter unity is merely a supreme postulate of reason, of comprehension. But unity of end is a postulate of life and of conduct. Without it no step in life could be taken with conviction.

Actually therefore we do not possess a unity of ends. It is unknown. If one accordingly takes up in earnest the demand for unity, one must be clear on this point, that here the supreme insight is itself still lacking. And since we confront multiplicity as an objective phenomenon, the only possible way of solving the problem is to make this phenomenon our point of departure. It must therefore be asked: Do connections, references, binding relations exist among values and norms? Are moral commandments really disparate? Or can links, attachments, conditions and dependencies be pointed out among them? Even if there be no claim to unity, does there exist at least a gradation of moral claims among them, and a principle of gradation? But this question when applied to the unity of ends is equivalent to asking: Is there a system of ends? And inasmuch as values stand behind all ends—for only what appears to a man as valuable can he convert into an end—the question is transformed into one which is more general, more objective and much wider in outlook: Is there a system of values?

This question fixes the limit of the problem which we have before us. The order, or its principles, the system, would be the unity sought for. A unity can be only the unity of a system, for it must not exclude anything. It must be single without being tyrannical. The question is a typical one as to system.

Thus the investigation of values, even before it begins, is burdened with the most difficult task imaginable.

CHAPTER V

THE KNOWLEDGE OF GOOD AND EVIL

(a) COMMANDMENTS, ENDS AND VALUES

IT is at this stage that ethics takes up its real task—the doctrine of value (axiology), which, as regards content, constitutes its foundation. Not only the end of striving and of doing, but also the moral claim and its character of Ought, the commandment, the norm—all these have their basis in value—a structure peculiar in kind and in mode of existence. It is evident that one not only can never will nor take up as an end anything which one does not regard as "valuable," but also can never accept it either as a command or demand, as a commandment, as something that ought to be. One must somehow have conceived that a thing has value; only then and only thereby does it become a determining power in the moral life.

At first only a new name is hereby given to what we were seeking, and the actual advantage over other names cannot at once be discerned. The general nature of a value is indeed just as unitary as is that of an end or of a commandment. But here we are not inquiring concerning such a unity of nature, but are seeking for a unity of content. From the point of view of content, however, the realm of values manifests exactly the same bewildering multiplicity as the realm of commandments, or ends; indeed, a still greater multiplicity, for obviously there can be values which never appear as commands for the will or as ends of striving—whether it be because they are already actualized, or because according to their contents they never come into consideration as objects of effort. In the realm of value, therefore, we are confronted everywhere with the same problem: the order, the system, the unity is yet to be discovered.

But, precisely for the question of unity, the fact that the

sphere of concrete multiplicity is thus widened is of importance. If one is acquainted only with single, scattered members of a multiplicity, such as an inadequate point of view reveals, the prospect of finding their inner co-ordination is slight. The higher the point of view and the wider the circle of the elements perceived, so much the greater is the probability of a total view of the contents. It is thus in all fields of research. It cannot be otherwise in the domain of values. A value, indeed, always and necessarily corresponds to any commandment or end; but an end or commandment does not correspond to every value. Here, along with the question: What ought we to do? the other fundamental question[1] arises: What is valuable in life? What is it with which we are to come into contact? This question is the richer of the two in content. With it the outlook upon the realm of values is widened.

Under this fundamental question are co-ordinated, side by side, questions varying greatly among themselves: What is good and evil, what is virtue, what are "the virtues," what is happiness, what are the goods of life, of mind, of human society? In this expanded multiplicity we are to see the order, the principle; but the condition for this is the orientation in the multiplicity itself. Before making an investigation and closer definition of the single perceived values, every hankering after unity is premature. To secure the separate contents, to render them clearly comprehensible, is the immediate problem before us. Ethics must occupy itself with this, before and independently of any consideration of the required unity. To the latter, Part II of our investigation will be devoted.

(b) THE MYTH OF THE TREE OF KNOWLEDGE

We are still very uncertain about this problem. It is true that, up to the present, philosophical ethics has almost without exception held the opposite opinion. It has believed that it had solved not only this but also the problem of unity, or rather

[1] Cf. Introduction.

that it had found it already solved. The most contradictory tendencies of thought have at all times had this in common, that they professed to know already what good and evil are. The "good" has stood for the absolute unity of the morally valuable in general—an interpretation which one could the more readily accept since one had the name for the unity and did not observe the manifoldness of values. Neither did one see that all these tendencies of thought meant, in fact, fundamentally different things by the "good," and each denied the truth of the other.

That this belief was futile is one of the most recent discoveries; we have to thank Nietzsche for the first clear statement of it. In it two things forced their way to consciousness: (1) Values are many, their realm is a manifoldness; and (2) we know neither the entire manifoldness nor its unity. Each is still to be discovered, and is a task of ethics. This, however, if expressed in traditional concepts, means that we do not yet know what good and evil are.

It is not easy to take in at a glance the perspective which opens up to ethics at this turning-point. We cling too closely in thought and sentiment to the traditional. The myth of the tree of knowledge is the point around which centres the traditional ethics of Western Christianity. "In the day ye eat thereof, then your eyes shall be opened, and ye shall be as gods, knowing good and evil." This the serpent prophesies in Paradise. And man, albeit cheated out of innocence and happiness, believes. To this day he thinks that he knows what good and evil are. He believes this so firmly that even the most critical thought has fallen a victim to the great deception. All the profundity of thinkers is directed towards finding grounds for the nature of the good, which they think they understand. For this purpose they, one and all, build up a metaphysics of the moral consciousness. But they take no trouble to know good itself. It never occurs to them that they could fail in this. For they think they know what is good.

The prophecy of the serpent is the great deception. Sin has

not opened man's eyes, he has not become as God; to this day he does not yet know what good and evil are. More accurately, he knows only little about them—only fragments. And all the profound explanations have been futile, premature; they have been wasted on a supposedly sure possession of moral knowledge. The metaphysic of morals has lacked the foundation, which is the phenomenology of values, or, as we might call it, the axiology of morals. This is the first and chief concern of ethics. It lies, in fact, between us and every metaphysical theory. The realm of values contains the secret of "good and evil." Not until we know it as a whole can we know its parts. Not until we know its manifoldness and fulness can we taste of the real fruit of the tree of knowledge.

(c) NIETZSCHE'S DISCOVERY AND THE DISCOVERER'S ERROR

The knowledge of one's ignorance is always the beginning of knowledge. Even the knowledge of good and evil can take no other route than over this threshold of all knowledge alike.

To it Nietzsche's work brought us. Here for the first time, with full consciousness, "beyond" and independently of everything which in the course of the ages had been accepted as such, the question was raised concerning the content of good and evil.

This question is a hazardous undertaking, for it touches that which has been consecrated. And the hazardous undertaking avenged itself upon the daring doer. It dragged him beyond its true aim into destructive criticism, even into a premature laying hold of the new, the unknown, which was opened out before his gaze. His vision, only just freed, fell upon the realm of values, and in the first delirium of victory he thought he comprehended the whole. The discoverer, indeed, could not dream that what had opened itself before him was a field for intellectual work of a new kind, which could not as yet be completely surveyed.

But his mistakes were quite natural ones. His so-called

immoralism, his dream of the super-man, his morality of power with its craving for beauty—which unfortunately became only too quickly a fashionable philosophy and obscured the significance of his epoch-making discovery—all this should no longer mislead the serious student. Perhaps no one is ever wholly without blame for the misfortune of being misunderstood; but when the fault has been atoned for by the ill fate of being misunderstood and has become an historical fact, it falls back upon the one who misinterprets it. To extract the values from a thought is more than to criticize its defects. The time is ripe for this task. We must take possession of the now opened realm of values.

Seldom does a discoverer know fully what he has discovered. Nietzsche knew it as little as did Columbus. The successors inherit the field; to them falls the task of acquiring what they have inherited, in order to possess it.

It is in place here to say, although it cannot be confirmed until later, that the most fatal error on Nietzsche's part is to be traced precisely to that one of his doctrines which in his time won the greatest attention—to his doctrine of the "revaluation of all values." In that lay hidden the idea of valuational relativism. If values permit of being revalued, they also are capable of being devalued, they permit of being manufactured and of being destroyed. They are the work of man, they are arbitrary, like thought and phantasies. If this be so, the meaning of the great discovery is again immediately annihilated at the first step; for then the path over the threshold does not lead into a new and unknown realm which is still to be opened; there is nothing further to discover and to find; the bolt which had restrained is merely pushed back to admit free devising and inventing. But if that was the meaning of the liberation, one cannot understand why the long-checked source of invention does not now spring up and burst forth—or can it be that man is lacking in the spirit of invention?

In truth, the opposite has been proved. There has been no lack of fabrication, but what has been invented has had no power over man; it did not possess the force to convince his sentiment, to determine his real discriminating consciousness of value, to give a new orientation to his innermost being. For valuational consciousness, whatever else it may be, is in the first instance a sense of value, a primal, immediate capacity to appreciate the valuable. It has been proved that the sensing of value does not impotently allow itself to be transformed by a thing fabricated, that it is in itself something unaccommodating, incapable of being disconcerted, a unique entity, a law unto itself, a distinctive orientation of values.

What this unique entity is constitutes the very question. That it in some way or other exists in the closest connection with the essence of values themselves permits of being easily demonstrated from the fact of its power of resistance. But apart from that this phenomenon shows the idea of revaluation and of valuational relativism to be wrong. The phenomenon is different from what was imagined by the over-hasty sensation-mongers. Here, indeed, an unlimited field opens for fabrication and invention; but in this field the real moral values are not to be found—the values which convince the discriminating sense and stimulate life. These are of a different origin.

What origin may well be an enigma. But one thing is not to be overlooked: here exists a field different from that of things fabricated—the field of distinctive values. And this it is our task to discover.

CHAPTER VI

THE PATHWAY TO THE DISCOVERY OF VALUES

(a) REVOLUTION OF THE ETHOS AND THE NARROWNESS OF THE SENSE OF VALUE

THE further question arises: How are moral values discovered? The inquiry nearly coincides with that concerning the historical appearance and disappearance of commandments and norms—the contents of morality. Its range is simply extended farther. In it, moreover, one must not see a mere question of method. It is not concerned with the kind of knowledge, but with the realm of phenomena in which the values are to be met. Least of all, therefore, is a reference to the apriorism of valuational perception to be brought in. For the exact point of the question is: How does this apriorism enter into the world of appearances, and how does it prove its own truth in life?

In any case one may in a certain sense say that philosophical ethics discovers values. But very seldom is it a really original discovery. Generally it is a later appropriation of that which beforehand existed in the moral consciousness, and which was active there, whether as an accepted commandment of current morality or as an unconscious point of view in the sensing of values within their real setting. Numerous values are thus alive in human hearts, without being grasped by consciously seeking for them or without their structure being clearly discerned. But such a comprehension and such a discernment are possible; only philosophy, however, can achieve them. Yet precisely on this account they are a discovery at second hand.

But then, if one asks how the primary discovery takes place, one must reach down much deeper into the moral life. Throughout, in this discovery, the moral consciousness is at work in all its manifestations. Every new conflict in life sets a new problem before man, and can lead him to an apprehension of new values. The primary consciousness of value grows with the enhancement of the moral life, with its increasing complexity and intensification, with the multiplicity and the positive valuational height of its contents. But then it follows that the whole of mankind constantly is at work on the primary discovery of values, and indeed without pursuing this work as an end: every community, every age, every race does its part, within the limits of its own historical existence; and just so, on a small scale, every individual for himself, within the limits of his own circle of moral vision.

The consequence is: there is in general no absolute halt of the valuational consciousness. Here, also, as everywhere in the world, everything is in flux. Under the apparently still surface a steady revolution of the ethos is at work. In regard to this the accepted concepts may very well deceive one: they last longer than the actual boundaries of the momentary vision of values. They are made of another material; they are not the valuational sense itself; they appertain to the surface. If an age has impressed a name upon a perceived value, it is the very next generation which is certain not to give any longer the same meaning to the name. Words are sluggish, concepts are coarse and come hobbling after, but insight into values is inconceivably alert and highly differentiated; thought cannot tell what it will do next. Thought, indeed, follows the imperceptible shiftings of the circle of light upon the ideal plane of the values manifold—but always slowly, from afar, and often discontinuously, by jerks, with leaps over the more finely differentiated factors. Thus it comes about that in all ages the really discriminating minds hit upon nameless masses of value—"anonymous virtues" Aristotle called them.

There is accordingly a persistent elaboration of new ethical masses of value. This is no revaluation of values, but a revaluation of life. In the revolution of the ethos, the values themselves do not shift. Their nature is super-temporal, super-historical. But the consciousness of them shifts. From the whole realm it cuts out, for the time being, a little circle of something seen. And this little circle "wanders about" on the ideal plane of values. Every valuational structure which enters the section of the seen and vanishes from it means for the evaluating consciousness a revaluation of life. For, to the evaluating consciousness, the real is always ranged only among the values perceived during a given epoch.

In this way it happens that actions, dispositions, relationships, which yesterday passed as good, can to-day appear bad. Neither the real nor the values have changed; the only change has been in the assortment of the values which are accepted as the standard of the real.

The process of ethical revolution is a genuine process of discovery, a genuine unveiling, a disclosing of values; indeed, on the other side there is always at the same time a loss of values, a forgetting of them, a vanishing. This whole phenomenon of transformation shows a kind of "narrowness" of the valuational consciousness. There is abundant proof that this narrowness is not rigidly outlined, that consciousness can grow and diminish also in valuational content. But this, too, has its drawbacks. For with expanding volume the intensity and the immediateness of the sense of value decrease. On the other hand, it is the onesidedness of the ethos which gives to it its characteristic acuteness, its passion of devotion, its creative energy.

(b) THE CHAMPION OF IDEAS AND THE CROWD

The inmost kernel of the moral life, the self-development of the ethos, is identical with the primary discovery of values.

Hidden beneath the surface the perpetual process of revolution, however, is always far removed from being uniform. In certain epochs it leads to sharp crises, breaks forth violently, seizes hold of the emotions like a whirlpool and sweeps them along into action. The valuational discovery which gave its penetrative power to primitive Christianity was such a crisis—

the discovery of the peculiar moral significance of neighbour-love.

One central value, or even a whole group of them, enters the ethical consciousness and radically transforms the view of the world and of life. The antithesis to the old traditional valuations inflames to contest, and not only to intellectual contest. The passion of the newly awakened ethos challenges the passion of the old; but this defends itself against destruction. The inertia of things long sanctioned is an obstacle which grows with the momentum of the onslaught. The reason is that in the old ethos genuine discerned values are alive. Martyrdom is the perpetual accompaniment of crises. The course of ethical revolution has something essentially antithetical in it. In criticism of the old, in opposition to things consecrated, the new thought springs up, ripens and waxes strong. It must destroy so as to achieve; it must do this even where it takes up the existing order into itself and builds upon it. It is born under the sign of conflict; and the conflict lasts until it triumphs or succumbs.

On the other hand, the part which the individual actually plays in the ethical revolution is very different. The average man is a vanishing factor in the total process. But the totalities of the valuational consciousness solidify anew in the ethos of individual men, and in them first find form and expression. And from them they react upon wider circles. This phenomenon is most clearly discernible at historical points of upheaval in the process.

Here the great ethical leaders come into evidence: the spiritual heroes, prophets, founders of religions—the champions of ideas. From them the movement proceeds; they revolutionize the crowd. It is natural enough to think that such leaders are "inventors" of the new forms of value, that the birth of values themselves takes place in the thought of the champion of ideas. Even that is a great mistake. The champion himself invents nothing; he only discovers. Indeed, even his discovery is conditioned. He can only discover what already lives darkly in the valuational sentiment of the crowd, and presses forward to expression. He it is who, as it were, reads in human hearts the values newly felt; there he gleans them, draws them into the light of consciousness, lifts them on to his shield and invests them with speech.

Only that for which the times are ripe, only that which has matured in the living ethos of man, only that which through moral necessity and yearning has become ripe for utterance, has effective strength. The champion of ideas is himself only at second hand a discoverer. Before him the living sense of values, obscure and half conscious, eternally seeking and groping, was moving forward; and what the champion finds had life and energy always here in the depths.

This is the secret of the response he meets with in the crowd; this is what constitutes the strength of the Idea—a strength not like that of waves which grow weaker as they advance, but like that of wildfire which, kindled from a spark, reaches impetuously about and grows stronger as it advances. The strength does not lie in the spark alone, but in the tinder lying everywhere around. The idea already lives before it is discovered by self-conscious thought. Its life is only waiting for thought to give it form, like a crystal in solution. Here also perception comes limping after. Nevertheless, it arouses the hidden life of the Idea and causes it to assume visible structure.

But even that hidden life is neither entirely unconscious nor wholly conscious. When it is lifted into the light by the voice of the champion of ideas, not only is its content suddenly there, like a ripe fruit, but everyone already knows it, recognizes it, and believes his innermost being to be expressed therein. It is the genuine Platonic anamnesis on a grand scale. But the champion of ideas is the midwife of the crowd, and compels it at the fateful hour of its ethos to bring forth that which is most alive in it.

Every age carries in itself dark seeds of ideas. A new consciousness of values is always ripening. But the ground is not always ready for the champion of ideas. And where the ground is ready for an idea, the champion is not always at hand. Perhaps we stand to-day under the banner of dimly discerned values, which are entirely different from those now accepted and taught among us. Morally no age entirely comprehends itself. The real ethical life is a life deeper than consciousness.

There is also, of course, the reverse phenomenon: the champion of ideas who is not understood, who comes at an unfavourable time, and who dies in solitude with his truth. He does not disprove, he confirms what we have been saying; he is the exception which proves the rule. His idea lacks neither life nor force. But it has both only in him, not in the crowd. There is no echo from the human heart because the idea has not arisen from it. Its time may come, but its revealer will not see it. Who lives before his time is dead in his time.

Nothing is more instructive concerning the nature of values than the relation between the crowd and the champion of ideas. When the prophet stands alone, without response, we are perhaps justified in asking: Is not that which he promulgates a mere thought, a solitary dream? But this question cannot be raised when the spark takes fire, when the idea returns in unnumbered persons in whom it is awakened, when the idea is liberated through the word of the prophet. Then the opposite question must be put: Why do all those, who from the same need cherish the same yearning in their hearts, seize secretly and half-consciously upon the same idea, so that this is pre-figured, as it were, in them, and only waits for release? Why does not the ethos of the crowd split up into as many ideas as there are heads? It is not enough to answer that the social form of the times, the struggles, the ethical situations, are the same for all. Why, then, does not each one go a different way? Why does not each seek a different solution of the same problem of conscience? What constrains all to go on their quest and turn towards the same value?

There is only one answer. At the point to which all, because of the same need and yearning, must direct their gaze there lies only one value; as they contemplate the given situation they are not free to imagine at will different norms of good and evil. There exists only the one norm which corresponds to the question that confronts them; there is only one which gives an answer capable of being comprehended. This is the sought-for court of decision. No other can take its place.

But this means that values have actually an existence in themselves, independent of all imagination and longing. It means that the consciousness of them does not determine values, but that values determine the consciousness of them.

(c) BACKWARD-LOOKING AND FORWARD-LOOKING ETHICS

The philosophical outlook upon values is subordinate to the living well-spring of the valuational consciousness. It is even more subordinate than the outlook of the champion of ideas. For he is seldom a philosopher. In Socrates, Fichte, Nietzsche, we have perhaps examples of such a combination; but they are not examples on a grand scale. Possibly the reformers of the Middle Ages and of modern times are better illustrations; possibly also the legendary Pythagoras or Empedocles; but in their consciousness of values the philosophical element is not the pre-eminent factor. Plato, with his whole soul, believed in the world-calling of the philosopher as the ethical leader; but apart from his own historical influence, only the Utopias of solitary thinkers have conceded his point.

In fact almost without exception philosophical ethics takes another route. It occupies itself with values which others have discovered and strives to present them clearly, to force them into consciousness and to establish them. The principle is adopted: "One knows it already." The adoption of the principle and the work of establishing values are certainly not to be despised, particularly where the acceptance is extended to the whole mass of discovered values and where no narrow arbitrary selection is made. For the establishing of values a more circuitous route is needed; recourse to metaphysics is required, the practical view of the world is welded with the theoretical. By deliberation, what was obscure and a mere affair of feeling is raised to the plane of science. Thus ethics naturally presses on towards theory and a system of values.

But when once this latter is recognized as a task, the other tendency must necessarily set in. To the ethics of explanation must be added that of inquiry, of observation, of investigation of values. This must not be held back by the slight prospect of success—a discouragement borrowed entirely from a philosophical experience which has scarcely ever pursued such investigation in earnest. If only it is realized that not all values are known, or, what is the same thing, that we do not yet know what good and evil are, it becomes impossible for ethics to be satisfied with the retrospect upon what has long been known. From the new task ethics cannot escape; it cannot resist the pressure that is upon it, to investigate more values, for the understanding of which man is perhaps already ripe. Inevitably the forward-looking, constructive, inquiring and measuring tendency confronts the backward-looking and merely speculative tendency.

Only in the former, which has long enough been waited for, does ethics become really normative—in the sole sense in which it can be so. In it alone does ethics return to its own principle and become the leader of man. In it the Platonic ideal is not dead, the ideal of ruling and moulding mankind spiritually through the power of philosophical perception, through the vision of Ideas. In principle also it is not so utopian as are the only too well-known and premature attempts to actualize the vision. For the problem with which it deals is not one for an individual mind to solve; that would be presumption—it was the mistake of the Utopians; it is a matter for common investigation, a concern not of our time alone but of a wide, slowly advancing, scientific continuity. The individual investigator by his work can contribute only an inappreciable element.

But the turning-point has been passed. A beginning has been made.

(d) THEORETICAL AND ETHICAL INVESTIGATION OF PRINCIPLES

The question: How can values be discovered? arises *de novo* and in another sense. It is concerned with secondary and reflective discovery. How can the obscurely discerned treasures, which always and everywhere are maturing, be dug out? How can thought take cognizance of them, master them, in order to draw them into the light?

Scientific comprehension is more than emotional contact. Granted, then, that in the sentiment of our time a series of values has unconsciously become accessible, how are they to be transformed into a scientific possession? Where is a more exact presentation of them, a closer description and delimitation, a rational determination and logical construction, to be attained?

An investigation of values is an investigation of principles. So it must partake of the character of an investigation of principles. Principles are entities which are dependent only upon themselves, but which other things depend upon. It is perfectly clear how deductions can be drawn from principles, once they are given. But how it is possible to arrive at principles themselves when they are not given is not clear. There is nothing above them; and under them is only what is derived from them. But granted that this relation of dependence is a settled fact, a principle can be discerned, as a presupposition, in the structure of the thing dependent upon it.

In this way actual laws are discerned in the concrete events of nature; likewise categories of existence, so far as they are discernible at all; not otherwise also the categories of knowledge, and with the same limitation. The laws are always there beforehand; they are at work in the concrete fact which depends upon them. And never until afterwards are they known. Knowledge of laws and knowledge of categories do not precede. Insight into that which is first is never the first insight. It was a fundamental error to want to make the theory of knowledge an exception to this rule; there is no "pure methodological thinking" before experience—that is, before the concrete knowledge which is not attained directly but only by the circuitous route of the *posterius*.[1]

The condition for such a procedure is a basis of fact, a section of given and analysable phenomena, a factum. Theoretical philosophy is not embarrassed for lack of a fact. It possesses it in the sphere of Being, among the things that can be experienced, in the phenomenon of experience itself— whether this be naïve or scientific. Here analysis may begin; from it material, constitutional laws may be drawn out and lifted up or, if one prefers so to express it, inferred backwards. In this connection inference is nothing else than a making known of the unknown correlate on the basis of the fact that stands in fixed relation to it. The relation, of course, must itself be somehow perceived. But what name is given to such perception makes no difference.

Now ethics is in the same situation as regards the circumstance that principles are not given. It also must first disclose them or, having turned away from the concrete phenomenon, it must behold them. In willing, resolving and acting, in disposition, in one's attitude towards life or in quiet participation, the principles are contained in rich abundance as the regulative factor. Accordingly, it must be possible to discern them there. But with the presentation of these phenomena they cannot yet be seen; they are just as little known in themselves as are principles of knowledge. Here what is known is always only the instance, the situation, the special end of striving. When a man shrinks from taking unfair advantage of a competitor in the stern struggle for existence, when instead he springs forward to help him, shares with him his own acquired advantage, he by no means need know whether he does this out of a sense of justice or from love of his neighbour or from personal sympathy. He merely has the sure feeling that he is doing "good." The obscure sense of value does not discriminate the principle. It only qualifies in a general way the concrete case of conduct. In the knowledge that this action is "good"

[1] Cf. *Metaphysik der Erkenntnis*, 1925, pp. 251–253.

is contained no knowledge as to wherein this goodness consists; likewise no knowledge as to why it is good. The principle is present in the doer and it determines him; but he has no knowledge of it.

One might accordingly believe that procedure in the discovery of ethical principles is strictly analogous to that in the discovery of theoretical principles. There is ethical as well as theoretical experience. Indeed, it is still nearer to life, still less liable to be mistaken than are the phenomena. But just here the difficulty begins. For the principles themselves are of a different nature. Values are not laws of existence; they have no binding necessity over the actual. One can never know whether in the given conduct of a man they are actualized or not. At least from experience itself one cannot know this. Rather must one bring the knowledge of good and evil with one as the measure of experience in general, in order to be able to know whether the special case is of positive or negative value. In the instance cited above, this knowledge is already presupposed; it does not arise from the action; but in the doer it precedes the doing; and, just so, it also precedes in the moral evaluation, in the approbation which others render to it as due—however hidden in the moral consciousness the root of such knowledge may be. It is a purely a priori knowledge. On the basis of this knowledge alone can I choose an instance which I experience, as one in which the moral principle is determinant. Conversely, I cannot from experience of individual cases discover the principle. The experience, in which I should be able to find my bearings, from which I ought to be capable by analysis of discovering the principle, already presupposes therefore precisely the knowledge of the principle itself. For the experience must have been selected by the principle.

This, of course, turns the situation upside down. Here is an insurmountable difficulty, which does not confront the investigation of theoretic principles. It looks like a vicious circle that is inevitable.

(e) CATEGORIES AND VALUES, LAWS AND COMMANDMENTS

Expressed in general terms, ethical principles are not categories. Categories are uniformities which exercise unconditional compulsion, forms under which everything within their sphere irresistibly falls. They are, universally, what natural laws are for the special forms typified in certain strata of the actual. To them there are no exceptions; moreover, a single exception would prove that no law exists. Their kind of validity is impregnable. There is never a discrepancy between genuine laws of existence and concrete being. Cases rest entirely upon the laws. They "follow" the law in blind subjection. The laws are fulfilled in every "case." That is the reason why every "case" reveals the law to the investigator unmistakably, if, skilful in experiment, he knows how to isolate it. Every case, so far as it is at all open to observation, is representative of all. It is the representative of the categories under which it falls.

With values it is otherwise. They can, of course, be actualized and perhaps to a wide extent are so. But they can also be unactualized. It does not lie in their essence as principles that the actual should correspond to them. Here great deviations, indeed extreme contradictions, may prevail. That does not detract from value as a principle. For its nature is not the same as that of an existential law. It does not coerce, it does not dominate existence. Values exist independently of the degree of their fulfilment in reality. Over against the real they signify only a claim, an Ought-to-Be, no inevitable necessity, no real compulsion. What they are in Idea subsists in its own right beyond real Being and Not-Being. The claim holds good, even where it is not, indeed even where it cannot be, carried out. The exception, the deviation, the rebellious element in the existent, do not abrogate it.

Values are not to be recognized by the fact that they are, or are not, contained in the real. They subsist even where the given case, indeed where all actual cases, contradict them. The case does not reveal the value. For so long as one does not already know the value from some other source, it always remains questionable whether the case agrees with it or not.

If we limit the question to the still narrower and ethically more positive problem of the Ought-to-Do, the difference becomes still more striking. Moral principles in this sense are exclusively values not realized, or not yet fully realized. They represent commandments, express always a Non-Being, and precisely on that account a positive Ought-to-Be. In life the morally good is never simply real, a man is never simply as he ought to be. How could that which is commanded, as such, become evident from his real actions, resolutions and dispositions, as these can be experienced by us? Between the commandment and the actual conduct of a man stands his free decision, the open For and Against. And precisely where he acts against it, the commandment rises up in opposition to him, threatening and accusing. The unfulfilled value is not a natural coercion, but a requirement and a claim upon him, as the commandment expresses it. Nor does that mean for him a depressing burden; on the contrary, it transforms him into a moral entity. If the commandment were for him a law of nature, he would necessarily follow it blindly, as a stone follows the law of gravitation; then he would be purely a natural entity, and would be, in constitution, like a stone. The difference between commandment and law—the fact that along with all the uniformities of nature to which he is inevitably subjected there exist commandments which he can transgress— is a prerequisite of his humanity.

(f) Ethical Actuality and the Fact of the Primary Consciousness of Value

Ethical values are not to be discovered in the conduct of man. On the contrary, one must already have knowledge of them in order to distinguish whether his conduct accords with them or violates them. On this point ethical research cannot reckon upon any datum by the mere analysis of which moral principles can be made manifest. This is the basis of the fundamental difficulty in ethics. The discovery of values must take another route. The mere actuality of instances cannot be our guide.

If herewith the situation were exhaustively characterized, the pathway to the investigation of ethical principles would be altogether cut off. Before any further reflection, however, one feels that one cannot acquiesce. Even if the facts of human conduct cannot reveal the principle, it is not these facts alone which are here at hand. Rather is there also, accompanying them, an evaluating consciousness of the fact. This is not a consciousness of principles, not a pure beholding of values, but a sense of value, a clearer or obscurer acquaintance with the worth or worthlessness of the actual conduct.

That this cognisance is presupposed in the appraisement of facts does not indicate a vicious circle. For what is sought is the valuational structure in its ideal individuality, but only on the presupposition of an undifferentiated and often hazy consciousness of it, a consciousness that in general the instance contains something of value. This attendant, obscure consciousness, which must inevitably guide even the philosophical investigator, thus belongs equally to the realm of fact. By its presence ethical differs from ontological reality. Both are equally real, but the latter contains one further essential element. And on this the question turns. Both types of the real have in common the fundamental ontological structure of reality. Actions and dispositions are real in real persons, just as qualities and motions are in real things. But beyond this there is something else real in persons, which is not constructed out of laws of existence; namely, the accompanying feeling of value, which rejects and accepts, condemns and justifies.

Ethical is richer than theoretical reality. For it includes the reality of the moral consciousness. It is this latter alone upon the possibility of experiencing which the question turns. The moral consciousness consists not of resolutions and dispositions (these can just as well be bad as good—that is, can go directly contrary to the moral consciousness), but of the distinctive sensing of values, which separates the good from the bad in them and constitutes their ethical standard.

Moral consciousness in this sense is indeed never complete, and is perhaps never free from error in its application, that is to say, in the actual valuation which it confers upon actions and dispositions. But it is nevertheless always a genuine consciousness of values. And that is sufficient for the analysis of the phenomenon, in order to discover its valuational structure and to determine it conceptually.

Accordingly, if we relate the moral consciousness in this sense—which is an unquestionable fact in human life—to the objectively real, we can no longer allow that there is no datum upon which the search for ethical principles can be based. On the contrary, there is such a fact—only we must not seek for it upon a false plane of the real. It is never to be found in the actual conduct of man, nor in the actual adjustments and historical phenomena of human society, but simply and alone in the primary consciousness of good and evil itself—in so far as such a thing is ever in evidence. This is the primary ethical phenomenon, the "factum" of ethics.

Of course it is an altogether different sort of fact from the theoretical datum. It is real, is capable of being experienced, and yet in its essence not empirical. For even the primary consciousness of value is an aprioristic consciousness. We may, therefore, with a certain right speak here of an "aprioristic factum." The paradox is merely apparent. All a priori insight is actually in this sense to be called a factum. Even in the theoretical domain the theory of aprioristic knowledge plants itself upon its actuality. And if this latter did not exist there would be no problem of aprioristic knowledge. In the field of ethics this circumstance was long ago established and formulated by Kant; he it was who described the "moral law" as a "fact of Reason." This Kantian fact of reason is in reality exactly what we have named the fact of the primary consciousness of value

—that is, the sensing of values. In this respect ethical reality is richer than that which is understood as mere existence.

Neither is this fact affected by the difficulty, set forth above, as to deviation from valuational principle. The primary emotional consciousness of value, where it exists at all and in so far as it is present, cannot, to one's liking, agree or not agree with the principle, as is the case with disposition and action. It is necessarily in harmony with ethical principle, being nothing but its expression in consciousness; it is the way in which principle modifies consciousness and, in modifying it, is present.

Not everyone is conscious of every moral value, just as not everyone has insight into every mathematical proposition. But where anyone does have a real valuational consciousness, this is in him a direct witness to the value itself. The value itself therefore can be discerned by its presence in consciousness. This reality does not need to be further sought for. It reveals the principle immediately.

(g) The Possibility of Illusion and of a Spurious Moral Consciousness

One might possibly be in doubt as to what confidence could be put in judgments which are drawn from such a fact. The fact is not at all strictly universal, since men vary in their sense of value. And, moreover, should we not need for the fact of our valuational sense itself still another criterion, in order to distinguish it from other similar but not intelligible facts?

These misgivings betray a certain insecurity of knowledge in the presence of the phenomenon of the moral consciousness. It must be conceded that within certain limits the insecurity is indeed justifiable. But here the question is not as to whether the insecurity is generally justifiable, but as to whether it is fundamental and unavoidable. Only if it is absolutely unavoidable, only if human judgment is entirely helpless in its presence, does the situation become serious. But if acuteness of perception is lacking only in the case of mediocre persons, if only the morally inexperienced and the narrow-minded, or indeed merely the philosophically undisciplined, fail in this matter, then the insecurity has little significance. In other departments, especially in those in which purely a priori judgments are accepted, precisely the same insecurity occurs. But it is always in itself possible to train the perception of a phenomenon. And this kind of training is exactly the task of the ethicist. In this respect the situation is by no means more unfavourable in the realm of ethics than in other spheres of discipline. The group of phenomena, of which the primary consciousness of value is the witness, is unmistakable—if once its significance has been grasped. It embraces such manifestations as moral approval and disapproval, accusation, self-blame, conscience, the sense of responsibility, the consciousness of guilt and remorse. There can of course be a falsification of these phenomena. But ordinarily they are genuine, and are based upon a genuine sense of values. And even in the case of falsification is hidden a kernel of the genuine thing. Finally, moreover, it is the business of the ethicist to scent out falsification. Even in this, one's penetration permits of being sharpened, not otherwise than in the case of false judgments in art and of affectations on the part of the æsthetically perverted.

The criterion of the genuine and spurious is nothing else than the primary consciousness of value itself. Even the philosopher in his investigations brings such a thing with him. It is contained in his research work, just as it is in the phenomena of the moral consciousness in which he finds his bearings. The possibility of misleading others is accordingly not so great as at first glance it appears to be. In judging of the whole procedure, one should never forget that the knowledge of values—even secondary, philosophical knowledge—is never derived from the facts alone, is never knowledge a posteriori. Insight into values is and remains aprioristic insight, whether it have the primary form of the sensing of them or the derived form of reflective discrimination.

The roundabout way through the facts of the moral consciousness only means a leading, a guiding of one's own perception of value towards that which would not otherwise fall within range of one's vision. Objects presented, occasions and motives of discovery, are not discovery itself, any more than they are its subject-matter. Even if insight is led by way of the phenomena of the moral consciousness up to the structure-values, it must none the less behold these themselves directly, face to face. Valuational insight does not take on trust or by faith what the analysis of the "factum" furnishes; the analysis leads it only to the other, the deeper, phenomenon, which is in itself independent and is independently discerned: the intrinsic phenomenon of value, which is no longer a phenomenon of the actual, no longer banished into some realm of ethical existence. And this new, differently constituted and ideal phenomenon can only be perceived purely for itself and purely as an ideal phenomenon.

Here enters a knowledge *sui generis*, with its own laws and its immediacy, an aprioristic intuition, which is independent of the *posterius* of actual phenomena and of the part they play as guides. Even here the *posterius*—just as with the knowledge of theoretical principles—is only a roundabout way to autonomous aprioristic insight.

CHAPTER VII

THE VARIOUS DOMAINS OF THE MORAL PHENOMENON

(a) THE SCOPE OF THE GIVEN IN THE INVESTIGATION OF VALUES

WHEN we survey the connections of the problems which have been set forth, the interpenetration of aprioristic and aposterioristic knowledge attains in ethics a decisive significance. At all times in the primary consciousness of value, as well as in the philosophical process of knowing it conceptually, aprioristic insight is the fundamental factor. As, however, it is never at hand ready made, but must always be aroused, guided and stimulated to activity, the phenomena which arouse and direct take a prominent place in determining the issue of the procedure. It still remains for us to get a firm hold of these phenomena in their widest extent, by a survey of the various domains in which they are to be found. Here also we must guard against error.

The problem coincides with that of the scope of the given. For every philosophical inquiry this question is one of the most crucial. In most systems the defects are fundamentally mistakes as to what is given; nearly all one-sidedness in points of view is at bottom due to arbitrary limitation as to the scope of the given. Since "critical philosophy" came into being, care has ordinarily been taken to reduce the given to a minimum, to make the basis of presupposition as small as possible, from the very evident feeling that every added factor would be challenged and thereby might contribute to the overthrow of the whole edifice. This tendency led to a selection of the material which was to be presupposed as existent. No fundamental objection can be raised against picking and choosing for the purpose of probing a problem. But in practice the matter assumed another aspect. In reality selection of material was made from entirely different motives, the object being the defence of a position chosen beforehand or of the anticipated system. Thus the selection inevitably became one-sided—a defect which then extended itself over the entire logical construction (for as is the material one starts with, so are the deductions), and the defects avenged themselves on the whole. Problems when suppressed are not removed from the world; they lift up their heads where one is least expecting them. The untenableness which was skilfully evaded in the premises becomes later on appallingly enlarged and spreads over the entire system.

With the historical dying down of the old idealism, the opposite tendency has gradually gained ground: the tendency to include in the given as much as possible, to map out from the beginning as wide a territory as one can. In accepting too much it is not so important to avoid single mistakes—later on they cancel one another of themselves—as to avoid overlooking the preconceptions involved in the principle of selection. The greater evils are due not to positive errors in accepting without discrimination, but to an ignoring of phenomena and a rejection of authentic problems. A narrowing of the field of vision is the inveterate vice of philosophy. The defect in all "isms" —whether rationalism, empiricism, sensualism, materialism, psychologism or logicism—is narrowness in the mapping out of the problem. Everywhere the manifoldness of the phenomena is misjudged and varieties are erroneously treated as all alike.

In ethics it is not otherwise. Eudæmonism and utilitarianism, individualism and ethical socialism, are exactly such one-sided views. They contain errors due to a too narrow understanding of the problem—errors caused by a selection of ethical phenomena which arbitrarily restricts the field of investigation. From the very names of these theories one may distinctively note the special value which they stress as ethical.

To-day ethics, as we have seen, is making its first attempts to draw into the circle of its contemplation the whole universe of values. For a special reason the inclusiveness of ethical phenomena is at the present juncture a prime necessity. Everything depends upon our turning our inspection of values in every accessible direction upon its objects, upon the valuational structures themselves. And as this turning can occur only from the side of given and comprehended phenomena, the whole emphasis rests upon finding and surveying them.

In the domain of theory a limitation of the given has, at least in tendency, a certain justification, because the element of metaphysical construction is far more to the front and, for the most part, dominates everything from the first step. In ethics, on the other hand, which does not become properly metaphysical until the problem of freedom is reached, this conditional claim is lacking. Actually, as regards the main subdivisions of its subject-matter, ethics is merely an exhaustive dealing with phenomena. And as for uncertainty, an erroneously conceived or wrongly placed phenomenon could falsify the arduously sought gradation of values. Consequently it must not be forgotten that our philosophical survey does not take its ideal objects from ethical phenomena given in the realm of fact, but, after turning attention to facts, it beholds its objects immediately and independently of facts.

It does not at all need, therefore, to accept as its material what the accepted facts contain. It remains free in insight despite the real phenomena which confront it. What it sees can always hold its own in contrast to the facts. Its subject-matter is of an ideal nature.

(b) Law and Ethics

Under such circumstances it goes without saying that all departments of mental life, if only they contain any ethical motives, if only they manifest any valuations, preferences, tendencies or acknowledged determinations of a practical nature, must be a significant mine for ethics. Our investigation can dispense with nothing which provides it with material.

But most illuminating for it is anything which besides the primary phenomena embodies also material which has been worked over, mastered by thought, and been stamped with its seal. Since ethical substance finds only very inadequate expression in conversational language, every statement of valuational concepts that is more exact is of service. Hence it follows that a general outlook upon human life is not sufficient to give us our bearings, although in it everything is rooted; the testimony of definitely outlined concepts must be added.

Where moral structures of the communal life show sharply defined concepts, there the greatest amount of preparation has been furnished. It is natural, therefore, to look about first among the departments of science. Now there is only one science of a practical nature which possesses a settled and exact system of concepts—the science of law. A certain justification for taking our bearings from law is indisputable. All law rests upon a fundamental ethical demand, upon a genuine perceived value. All law is an expression of an ethical striving. It regulates human relations, even if these are only outward; it says what ought or ought not to happen, no matter whether or not the form, in which it makes its announcements, gives expression to the Ought. Even the positive law for the time being gives evidence of its relation to value. But this is not the final word. All positive law has a tendency towards ideal law, and this tendency manifests itself in a constant development of accepted law in its ever-living reconstruction through legislation. At all times, where it is a matter *de lege ferenda*, we see in law the activity of the primary consciousness of values.

In this perspective the concepts of legal life attain a high degree of ethical significance. And consequently it can be understood how the theory could have arisen of a thoroughgoing orientation of ethics within the science of law.[1] Therein, to be sure, an all too great approximation of the moral life in general to the legal forms of communal life has played a disconcerting rôle. The fact had been overlooked that morality is something fundamentally different from law, is richer in content, and can and must never lose itself in a code of definitions, not even of ideal definitions. Ethics, in fact, must contain the ultimate foundation of law; in its scale of values it must indicate the place for the value of law in general. But the doing of this can never be the whole of its task. It exhibits an entirely different scope and richness of content. In part its task is in its own way orientational, because it manifests a valuable formal structure which no other secondary aspect assumes. But, in the first place, there are other domains of the moral life which show quite a different and a much richer concrete abundance of phenomena. And, in the second place, all legal life is embedded in the subordinate problem of means. It does not contain the definition of its own highest end, in which alone its determinant value can be discerned.

The "science" of law simply takes over this value as given. It is not its determinative concept that emerges, but merely the concept of the relations and consequences. It is a practical science, in that intermediate sense which does not concern itself at all with its own highest point of view but presupposes it, like any technique and like medicine. But ethics is the science of the highest practical points of view themselves.

Thus it comes about that the science of law, and even the sense of law which exists and lives behind it, can be a guide for ethics only in a very modest degree. They certainly point the way to a real, genuine value, but only to one of many and not at all to one especially dominant. Indeed, taken exactly, they do not lead even to the value itself, but only to the system of its

[1] See H. Cohen, *Ethik des reinen Willens*, for which the parallel of mathematics and logic was decisive.

consequences. It is left to ethics to determine the value as such. And in fact ethics has always approached this value in another spirit and another sense.

(c) RELIGION AND MYTHOLOGY

The older philosophical ethics related itself most elaborately to religion. For centuries, without scrutinizing, it adopted the moral views current in positive religion and was satisfied to be their interpreter.

The ages of such dependence have indeed passed away; but the simple fundamental relation, which could not be lost, has remained. For positive religion, however conditioned it may be by the times, is the great mine of ethical contents, the richest we possess. In this connection one must, of course, never speak of religion by itself. Mythology, which is related and is historically prior to it but is never sharply marked off from it, belongs to the same great group of phenomena. Mythology, indeed, has the advantage over religion proper of a greater variety of content, and often of greater concreteness and plastic differentiation; but at the same time it has the disadvantage of a less intellectual definiteness and conceptual clearness.

Mythology and religion are always supporters of the current morality. They contain the oldest and most trustworthy evidences of the ethical tendency in the human race; they are the most ancient language of the moral consciousness. Within wide reaches of historical development they are even the only bearers of moral ideas. Almost all current morality has first manifested itself in the form of a religious conception of the world. Certainly neither religion nor current custom ever becomes identical with morality itself; but the latter is an essential constituent in each. Whether morality is independent in its essence is another question. Religion itself necessarily denies this independence. According to its mode of thinking, all morality is only a means.

Everything that moves the heart, oppresses it or exalts it, misleads it or guides it to its goal, is somehow expressed in religion and mythology. But the language in which they express it is generally not that of reason—only when religion passes over into dogma does rationalization appear—it is, rather, the language of intuition and picture, of metaphor and symbol, of ideal shaping, even of artistic construction. The mobility and fluidity of such language make of this abundant region a rich mine for ethics. The glowing vividness of its creations is practically inexhaustible. Ethics rightly sees here the living well-spring of its motives. That it has for the most part confined itself to the exploitation of one definite positive religion has been indeed a fatal narrowness. But such narrowness is not necessary, and is not due to the nature of the case. It can be discarded, and will necessarily be discarded in proportion as the survey advances.

From the fact that religion and mythology have been bearers of positive morals, it does not follow that morality absolutely needed these supporters. Rather can their ethical content be entirely removed in principle from the mytho-religious drapery. Whether also in life itself morality can be separated from all religious piety need not be previously settled. This question is irrelevant here. The ethicist will never be able to deny the separability absolutely; for he would then be obliged to deny the morality of irreligious men. That would be a gross presumption. But here we are concerned only with the actual possibility of removing the ethical content, the discerned values themselves, from their mytho-religious matrix.

There exists such a withdrawal not only predominantly in philosophical thinking, but also in life, an actual steady advancing process of discrimination on the part of the human spirit. We of to-day stand in the midst of the process. For the religious apparel does not in any case belong to the essence either of values or of the pure valuational consciousness. The religious man attributes to the divinity everything of which he does not know the source; foremost, consequently, he attributes the moral commandments to it. In so doing he fails to appreciate the autonomous character of the moral values. This view always prevails until the self-sufficing character of moral principles is recognized. Then ethics discards the garments of its infancy and calls to mind its own proper origin.

Here a double relationship reigns. Historically most of our ethical concepts are of mytho-religious origin. But in the order of reality, and for this very reason, the mytho-religious conceptions of morality are of ethical origin. For it is genuine ethical good which from the very beginning lies concealed in them.

It must not be forgotten, indeed, that one must never make a law of this rule. For not all religious concepts of morality prove to be bearers of ethical good. One needs only to think of the notorious notion of the transference of guilt in the concept of "sacrifice." Such views contain no insight into value; they are not valuational concepts. They have nothing to do with any end in itself, with any principle, but only with means in a scheme of salvation. Ethics, on the other hand, has to do only with principles.

(d) PSYCHOLOGY, PEDAGOGY, POLITICS, HISTORY, ART AND ARTISTIC EDUCATION

As compared with religion and mythology the remaining spheres of mental activity are poor in their yield of treasure. Human life in its concrete reality is naturally still far superior to them in moral material. The diversity of the moral consciousness in living morality itself, in its aims and efforts, its active tendencies and under-currents, its approvals and prejudices, in human struggle, passion and joy, in the painful conflicts of life and the evaluation of their solutions, in every manifested disposition, in hate and love, as well as in the ripening of personalities and in the interpretation of their distinctive quality by other personalities—all this variegated abundance is infinitely more than is mirrored in the specifically organized departments of mental life or is brought into form with the impress of their seal.

Psychology, for example, can here render only a certain introductory service; within certain limits it can indeed make clear the mental structures of emotional disposition, passion and volition. But to psychology, as a science of facts, the ideal forms which attain actuality in facts remain alien to the end.

Pedagogy, on the other hand, is of course concerned with these forms. What guides it is the genuine values of discipline in character, like obedience, industry, perseverance, self-denial, responsibility. But, like law, it is more preoccupied with the means of applying them than with the simple comprehension of their structure. It assumes as known what ethics primarily seeks to comprehend.

The life of the State and public morality, and thereby indirectly politics and history, may well cover a wider domain. The structure of the State is as little engulfed in legal matters as is its morality in the legal code. It is more than an institute of law; it is a real entity, with body and soul. It has its own characteristic life above that of individuals, its own laws of development, its own tendencies and perspective. Its Idea inheres in values which have meaning only in and for it, specific communal values. What we in our political consciousness honour in the State, what we love, condemn, strive towards, hope for or welcome with enthusiasm—all this is related to it itself just as the moral qualities and peculiarities of individual persons are related to them. The sole difference is that in the macrocosm of communal life everything appears magnified, objectified, and endowed with greater significance, and thereby is more easily grasped and determined, is more open to discussion. In this fact lay one of Plato's motives, when he attempted to develop his ethics not from the individual but from the State. He was guided, of course, by the questionable presupposition of a thoroughgoing parallelism between the community and the individual. But if one removes this presupposition the domain of the peculiar values of the community as such still remains, a domain which is to be found only in the life and ethical reality of the communal being.

In relation to ethics, art also plays a special rôle. In itself it stands there indifferent to the values of the ethos. But it takes them up into its substance, and gives them palpable form, as it does with everything which it appropriates to itself. In this way it makes perceptible to the senses whatever is generally imperceptible, and it does so in entire concreteness and fulness, without the abstractions of the understanding and its concepts. Art is a language of the ethos, which has not its like. Possibly we should in general know little of the variety and depth of the human ethos, if the poet, the plastic artist, the portrait-painter, did not set them convincingly before us. The poet has been for the people teacher and educator from time immemorial. He has been the sage, the clear-sighted one, seer and singer in one person; he has been the *vates*. For the Greeks, Homer moulded not only their gods but also their men.

In the moral consciousness the unactualized values appear as ideals; but ideals are dead so long as a creative form-giving hand does not set them vividly before the eye—and not only before the bodily eye. The history of the arts contains the history of moral ideas. Art is a second face of man. That it is primarily given to only a few chosen persons does not detract from its universal significance. Uncreative minds it draws after it; it educates and builds up in others a responding genius, opens eye and heart, directs vision to the depths of the eternally valuable and significant, teaches men to behold and participate, where the commonplace mind passes by without seeing. Inevitably the educator seizes upon poetry; he has no stronger means of influencing the young soul. Even peoples—despite all hatred and national misunderstanding—comprehend and honour one another in the arts; in their arts they constrain one another and future generations to reverence. Art is the revelation of the human heart, of its yearning, its ethos, its primal consciousness of values.

Only one thing must not be forgotten here. Art does not

speak in concepts; it does not call things by name. It beholds and forms what it beholds. He who would hear its language, he who would appreciate its contents, must not only understand it, but be able also to translate it into the language of concepts. But that is something different from contemplative enjoyment.

SECTION III
FALSE METHODS OF PHILOSOPHICAL ETHICS

CHAPTER VIII

EGOISM AND ALTRUISM

(a) SELF-PRESERVATION AND SELF-ASSERTION

THE theories of philosophical ethics are peculiarly significant as guides, especially when they are seen to be untenable. Errors are always instructive. The prejudices of empirical psychology are not so widespread in any other department as in ethics. Systematic criticism of these prejudices, however, has thrown light both upon the subject-matter and the method; and it would be helpful to run through the whole of these theories. But this could not be done in a brief space; we can consider only two of the most representative: egoism and eudæmonism, and only the most essential features of each.

The former may be presented as follows. Claims have no meaning unless they can be carried out. This requires some active energy in man to which the claims can appeal, some impulse, some compelling motive. For all human action is "motivated." Now the most general motive must inhere in the essence of the ego, the action of which is under consideration. But the ego shows a fundamental tendency towards itself. In this is to be found the basic motive of all voluntary determination: the self-preservation of the ego, the *suum esse conservare*. It is better expressed by the Stoic phrase, ἑαυτόν τηρεῖν. This means more than "preservation"; it is the tendency to assert oneself.

If self-interest is the highest and only motive, all ethics must be "egoistic," so that the proper meaning of all moral claims must culminate in the maxim: Be a shrewd, far-sighted egoist; discover your real advantage; avoid what is only your apparent gain.

The implication is: all seemingly different motives are in truth only partial manifestations of self-interest. Every other interpretation is a self-deception. Justice and humanity are at bottom not primarily directed to others, but are well thought out egoism. Nothing is easier than to construct out of this simplified scheme of the human ethos a comprehensive genetic theory. Somewhat in this wise: the strong man vanquishes weak men, he uses them for himself; his word is law; but because he makes use of them he must take care of them—in his own interest; their interest is organically fused with his own; his dictation accordingly introduces order, which is acceptable even to those he has subjugated; their egoism is advantageous to his own, as his own is to theirs.

According to this scheme it is possible to explain all human conduct without difficulty. Every kind of altruism, even love, friendship, self-sacrifice, is a disguised egoism. All that is needed is a sufficiently comprehensive understanding of the principle. The advantage of such a theory is the astonishing simplicity and lucidity which it introduces among moral phenomena. It gives a unifying principle, and systematizes the subordinate values, whether these be outward goods or virtues. Moreover, it leads to the easiest waiving of the problem of freedom; for man is then purely a natural being like the animals, and subject to no other natural laws. Egoism accordingly needs no command. It is itself a law of nature. Its morality is the carrying out of an instinct. Finally, it has no need of ethics; there is no such thing. Ethical naturalism resolves itself into a merely theoretical confirmation of facts. No longer is anything commanded; there is nothing that "ought" to be. "Ought to be so" vanishes behind "it is so."

(b) The Truth and Falsehood of the Egoistic Theory

It is easy to see that we are confronted here with an impressive concealment of a problem. Still we must ask: What is right in this theory, and what is erroneous?

There is no denying that it is really to the interest of each individual to seek his own advantage in the advantage of others. Each one is thrown upon the good will of others. Nevertheless, this entire view of life goes counter to the human sense of morality; in all ages it has required a highly distorting psychology to make it plausible.

But this fact is, of course, no disproof of it. It can, however, be disproved. And, indeed, by means of the very same psychology.

Suppose I sacrifice myself for some "good" reason; for instance, suppose that I rescue a child (the old example), that I go to battle as a soldier, that I work day and night to support wife and children honestly. The theory says: in this I am only seeking my own "satisfaction." And it is true that the thought of the end to be attained does really satisfy me; if I omit to do the deed, I experience much greater pain than that caused by the sacrifice. In this way every conscious volition ends in satisfaction.

Something else, however, becomes clear. My satisfaction is not the end which lures me on. I am not thinking of it. The aim of my volition is nothing but a situation, the saving of the child, of my country, my family. My satisfaction is not the object of my will; it is only a psychological by-product of attainment, its emotional aspect. To say "I will something" is the same as saying "I shall be satisfied if I achieve it." The two sentences mean exactly the same. The latter only gives expression to the fact that this emotional tone necessarily adheres to all volition. But for ethics nothing follows from this fact. A commandment never issues from a fact. "Ought" I, as it were, to will that the end I aim at should satisfy me? That has no meaning. Besides, I cannot will otherwise. A commandment to do what will automatically happen, and by necessity, would be absurd. At least the origin of commandments, norms or values is not shown here.

In common speech a sacrificing act is called "altruistic." Language hereby expresses an indisputable antithesis to egoism: the object aimed at is not oneself but another. When the theory declares that in the one case as in the other the ultimate end is always something that "satisfies" myself, the retort must be given that what satisfies me in the sacrificing act is the satisfaction of other persons. This kind of satisfaction of one's self is precisely what we call altruistic. For it the welfare of others is not made a means to one's own pleasure; rather, the delight is in their welfare for its own sake.

But if we modify this theory, if in the will to be good, in the striving for self-respect, we see one's own self-satisfaction and a kind of spiritual self-preservation, the theory is still easier to controvert. Thus modified, it embraces the whole series of moral values in itself and converts the relation to the ego into a mere universal form of subordination to itself. But since along with instinctive self-preservation there is also an alternative in self-respect and self-contempt (which is a form of self-renunciation), then in the decisive instance—in the crucial issue of passing moral judgment upon oneself—the principle breaks down. The question concerning this moral self-affirmation and renunciation is not to be settled by referring it to a general tendency to assert oneself but to a specific kind and form of self-assertion. That is, the explanation is to be found in values and standards of an entirely different sort, in the standards of the quality of one's own conduct. These standards separate what I can respect in myself from what I cannot respect. But in exactly the same way they divorce what I am able to respect in others from what I cannot respect. The reference to self therefore is here an altogether irrelevant point. The object of respect is not oneself as such, but a quality, the dignity of which manifestly exists beyond both self and not-self.

(c) THE METAPHYSIC OF ALTRUISM

In this matter we find ourselves confronted with a metaphysical problem of the greatest difficulty: How is another person brought to one's own consciousness? How is he recognized? Our senses present to us his body only; but this is not what is meant. What is meant is his inward being, the ethos of the man, his personality, that which we love, hate, detest, respect, that which we trust or distrust. We do not "hear and see" one another. Nevertheless, we are acquainted with one another. Under some circumstances we know the personality of others better than we know our own. How has such knowledge come about?

It is natural to argue in this wise: we are directly acquainted with our own personality; every acquaintance with another's must be derived from our own. Of course not without some modification. Deviations are indeed easy to imagine—one wishes even to be different from what one is. Our knowledge of another is then a putting of ourself in his place. Motions, mimicry, words furnish the occasion. Not that we must first draw inferences from them. There is participation, a sympathetic experiencing. The "meaning" of another's gestures precedes the consciousness of our own, just as in general the consciousness of another's consciousness is prior to self-consciousness. Our ego immediately takes sides. An expression of another's suffering causes me to suffer directly with him, an expression of his indignation makes me vibrate in sympathy with him, or, contrariwise, causes me to repulse his indignation just as directly. Cool deliberation comes later. When I understand, my mental attitude has already been completed.

Not until this point do theories divide. Participation may be understood as "sympathy,"[1] wherein one's own analogous acts, of which one need not be conscious beforehand, now come forward, and in some way play the rôle of a conditioning and interpreting factor. Every understanding, then, of another's consciousness arises by way of an analogous experience in one's own consciousness. The force of this view becomes evident in the case of the well-known and all-too-human misunderstandings of another's ethos, due to analogy with one's own, especially in the cases where the interpretation is erroneous. But its weakness lies in its incapacity to explain one's knowledge of a character quite unlike one's own. How radical

[1] Somewhat in Th. Lipps's sense of *Einfühlung*.

this heterogeneity is in the conscious contrasting of personalities needs no comment. The theory fails to interpret the facts.

Or one assumes a moral "sense," an organ for perceiving the character of others. There is said to be an immediate knowledge of another person's sympathy and antipathy, a direct trustworthy sense of his love, respect, reverence, hate, envy and meanness. This phenomenon may be puzzling, but it is not to be denied. An "organ" for perceiving the phenomena of another's consciousness is indeed a highly metaphysical assumption. And if one remembers that there is also a moral experience, that our moral understanding of another person grows with the growth of our own moral life, the assumption may well appear superfluous.

As a rule, extreme theories fall into error through one-sidedness. To carry out rigorously a metaphysic of the moral "sense" is a hazardous undertaking. It can never be verified because it transcends the facts. But one need not carry it to its utmost limit. We need not assert that our sense of another's mental attitude goes beyond our natural and known sources of experience. It cannot function without our eyes and ears. The mediation of the senses embraces the whole range of its activity. But it is not only a matter of the senses. Another capacity, behind the senses, is at work, a capacity which operates in relation to another system of qualities. There is nothing mysterious about this. The æsthetic sense also manifests the same mediation of material furnished by the outward senses. Within this limit the assumption of a special "organ" for perceiving another's character, although mediated physically, is one which is quite inevitable.

It is also not at all necessary to assign the whole contents of sympathetic understanding and participation to the credit of a "moral experience" and to attach this to such an "organ." On the contrary, it can easily be shown that here a wide-reaching apriorism prevails which is always contained in every such "experience." Accordingly, subjectivity as such, the other person's ego-point, which gives the personal impress to every disposition that can be discerned, is undoubtedly not "experienced" (in the strict sense), but is presupposed. Here we can lay our finger upon a psychical a priori. Or should we rather say, upon an ethical a priori?

Actually this apriorism extends farther than one might think. The naïve man is naturally prone to think even of things as personal, in so far as they enter as determinants into his life. A child may strike the table which it has run against. Mythology gives a soul to natural forces, tries to come into touch with them as with friendly or hostile powers. Here apriorism shoots beyond the mark. But it is the same apriorism, whether justifiable or not (whether "objectively valid" or not) —it is the same prejudgment, a judgment prior to conscious judgment, which attributes a soul to the bodily form and sees in it a person.

(d) SELF-APPRAISEMENT THROUGH THE APPRAISEMENT OF OTHERS

Whatever is of aprioristic origin in the highly complex content of moral communal experience—and accordingly whatever could have its basis in the common emotional structure of personal entities in general—has been little examined, and requires a special investigation which in character would stand on the border-line of psychology, epistemology and ethics. From it ethics may await various explanations.

But for the problem which we are now considering, the general view that there exists such apriority is adequate. In practical concrete consciousness, which is always concerned with situations and always embraces as constituents the consciousness of others as well as of self, the morally aprioristic element is ever in reciprocal action with the morally posterioristic element, whether this be something primarily discerned or something conceived on the basis of analogy. And here self-consciousness and the awareness of others always stand in reciprocal dependence. Every experience of one's own self widens one's understanding of others, and every participation in another's life widens the understanding of oneself and intensifies one's own personal experience. Ordinarily there is no less misunderstanding of oneself than of the moral nature of others. In general it is perhaps even greater. On the whole we learn to understand ourselves more in observing others than we learn to understand others in observing ourselves. At a certain height of ethical experience it may be different; but the primary dependence of the understanding is nevertheless the reverse of this; we understand ourselves by observing others.

And if in face of this complex situation one cares to hold by the concept of sympathy—while one perhaps fuses with it the metaphysic of the moral "sense" and of moral apriorism—one cannot avoid setting up, side by side with the appraisement of others, an equally primary and significant appraisement of self through the appraisement of others. The reciprocal action of the two would then constitute the consciousness of the inner moral world in general. But this consciousness is precisely that which is given as a phenomenon; it is the elemental thing; and all analysis of its constituent parts, being an artificial isolation through theory, is an abstraction. The isolated consciousness of oneself is a theoretical artifact. Ethical reality does not know it. And every egoistic theory which is based upon it is equally a forced abstraction. All the insurmountable difficulties of such a theory are fictitious difficulties; they are just as much manufactured as those of an isolated altruism.

The truth does not lie in any such one-sidedness. It is to be sought in the concrete fulness of the moral life which unifies the two partial aspects. From infancy a human being stands within the context of human personalities, grows into it, and in it develops and builds up his whole moral consciousness. The elemental interwovenness of the "I" and the "Thou" is not to be disintegrated. Their unity—however enigmatic—can constitute the only starting-point of theory.

(e) THE FUNDAMENTAL RELATIONSHIP OF "I" AND "THOU," THEIR CONFLICT AND VALUE

Here two points arise which bear upon the relation of egoism and altruism—if one is determined to retain these two misleading expressions.

First, they both have their independent root in man. Originally all spiritual life is at the same time communal and individual. We know consciousness only in the individuation and isolation of the ego and, again, at the same time as embedded in the collectivism which extends beyond the individual. So far as they are not aprioristic, the main features of experience are intersubjective; but they show only the uniformity due to simultaneity and a common origin. The individual, however, in this relatively uniform plurality is at the same time an entity on his own account; he exists for himself with his own meaning and law; and the fulfilment of his nature is possible only through himself alone. Each man stands face to face with every other in the profound identity of humanity, and yet at the same time retains an inextinguishable non-identity. The fundamental phenomenon of "I and Thou" separates, and at the same time binds, men. Unity and separateness are correlative to each other. But their correlation is different from the epistemological correlation of subject and object. Both are subject and both are object. The object of an action, of real conduct, of disposition, and of moral experience is invariably a personal subject. As only a man acts, and never an impersonal thing, so it is only a man towards whom one acts, whatever the intermediate links may be. It is the metaphysical opposition of person to person which first allows the real ethical relationship to arise, from which resolution and action result.

It is ultimately this fundamental relationship of "I and Thou" which makes it impossible theoretically to separate egoism and altruism. These tendencies in man are just as elementally joined, just as correlative, as the persons in the relationship itself. Certainly the relationship is not balanced, but can be transposed and in many ways diversified; and in these transpositions essential differences of value appear. But the correlation continues to exist.

A theory which sees the motive of all active relations between the I and the Thou in the egoistic tendency alone misunderstands the most essential and most characteristic feature of the ethical relationship: the tension between the two tendencies, the reciprocal self-repression and opposition which hold both in suspension. It misunderstands the conflict, which as such does not depress the moral life and weaken it, but permits it to grow, elevates it, and even brings it to the level which is proper to it.

But in the second place: "egoism" in itself is not valueless, it is as little bad—although the altruistic theories so regard it—as it is good. Within its limits it is altogether something valuable. It is valuable in contrast to altruism and as a partial condition of it. It is quite plain that, other things being equal, all participation with others and all sympathy are so much the more active and variegated in proportion as one's own life is so. What a man is not capable of experiencing himself he cannot sympathize with in another. One who has no pride cannot understand an injury to another's pride. One who has never loved, laughs at another's jealousy and longing. One's knowledge of one's Self is and continues to be the basis of the knowledge of another's regard for himself.

This is, however, only an instrumental value of egoism, not the one proper to it. But egoism has its own, and indeed a quite elementary and well-recognized, value in itself. This is nothing else than the justifiable tendency to care for one's own personality. Our life is built upon this tendency, and without it could not continue for a day. Some power must care for one's personality, must protect and preserve it. A man in whom the principle of "everyone for himself" did not dwell as a natural instinct would be an unfit, ill-fated specimen. In itself egoism is something good, although it is certainly not "the good." It might be regarded as the first, the lowest, "virtue," if Nature had not made of it a universal law of the living organism. There is no reason to convert a natural law into a commandment or to make of necessity a virtue. Here is a value, for the realization of which Nature has already provided. It does not on this account cease to be a value. And where degeneracy damages it, our consciousness of the value which belongs to it is distinctly awakened again. We rightly appreciate so-called "healthy egoism" as the basis of every strong personality, not otherwise than we appreciate physical health.

It is conceivable—let it be said without metaphysical boasting—that we here stand in the presence of a universal law of displacement in the valuational consciousness. Perhaps all values pass, in their realization, along the path from commandment to law, from virtue to instinct. Egoism would then be virtue in the stage of fulfilment. And even on that account it need no longer be accepted by contemporary man as a virtue. The perception of value directs itself to a higher plane, when the lower plane has been reached. Perhaps much in our spiritual life may be understood in this way, for example, the oft-cited emergence of the sense of justice out of the egoism of the strong,[1] that blind mimicry of the good which arises in a natural way without being aimed at.

This is, indeed, a thought which one should not carry too far. We cannot base upon it, as has often been attempted, a natural history of values. The good which arises in this way is not good because it emanates from egoism; much rather is the reverse true; because it is good, it emerges. The higher value is not "evolved" out of the lower; its realization is only conditioned through that of the lower. It emerges only in sequence, although occasionally in opposition, to the lower. The lower value remains empty, and has no contents without the higher. Thus its realization advances beyond the lower and beyond itself. It reaches at the same time towards the higher; and the real process, apparently without interruption, passes over into another which has a different direction.

[1] Cf. above, page 120.

Clearly recognizable is an idealistic dependence in the relation of values—that of the lower upon the higher—which rests upon the "actual" dependence of the higher upon the lower. The dependence of the lower upon the higher is purely axiological. It reveals itself everywhere in the actual dependence of the higher upon the lower. Even for egoism and altruism it is a determining factor, since the sense of value tells everyone that the former is the lower and the latter the higher value. Here we have in a nutshell the problem of the gradation of values.

CHAPTER IX

EUDÆMONISM AND UTILITARIANISM

(a) ARISTIPPUS AND EPICURUS

THE customary grouping of eudæmonism and egoism together is a calamitous error. In the human ethos the two of course coincide in many points. But the former in itself is not egoistic and the latter not eudæmonistic. Eudæmonism is concerned not with one's own happiness alone, but equally with that of others; while egoism looks not at all to happiness, nor even to the emotional values connected with it, but solely to self-preservation and self-assertion. To egoism the emotional consequences of the assertive attitude are wholly indifferent. Eudæmonism, however, is concerned with emotional values as such. It therefore demands special treatment.

In all periods of humanistic liberation ethics is eudæmonistic. The various phases through which Greek thought passed after the time of the Sophists were repeated in the seventeenth and eighteenth centuries. They are most instructive.

The extreme doctrine is that of Aristippus: Pleasure is the only good; the highest pleasure is the aim of life, but the most intense is the highest. The further doctrine that bodily pleasure is the more intense is not a valuational judgment; it is only a psychological proposition—one of many which the main doctrine leaves open.

Of all doctrines, that of Aristippus is the most vulnerable. It overlooks the fact that pleasure has no absolute degree, that it is always relative to pain and comes under the law of contrast, that we cannot strive directly for it but only for that which (we suppose) occasions it, but that the occasion by no means under all circumstances possesses the same hedonistic value. In short, the doctrine overlooks the very complex psychology of the balance between pleasure and pain. Just as little does it bear in mind that every pleasure is paid for by its opposite—satiety by hunger, recreation by work, even æsthetic pleasure by the painful irritability of a refined taste. Psychologically the doctrine is an impossibility. Nor can it justify itself ethically.

The Epicurean conception rectifies this error. Not the most intense pleasure, but the most lasting, is the highest, the quiet happiness which pervades a whole life-time. Here the first place is assigned to purely spiritual pleasure. Morality is the cultivation of those noblest human possessions which are always at hand and which one need only learn to acquire and appreciate. Virtue consists in subordinating the lower restless impulses, in developing a sense for the rich fulness of the beauty which surrounds us, in moulding our life into conformity with these ideals: self-control, wisdom, friendship. This is εὐδαιμονία in its clarified meaning, the highest value, the serenity and imperturbability of the spirit. The doctrine of superiority to one's own fate, of the wise man's self-sufficiency, of the insignificance of one's own suffering and death, these are merely corollaries.

An ideal worthy of respect! But what has become of "happiness"? It has ceased to be an emotional value subjectively felt. There still remains only a distant echo of the pleasure-motif. Happiness is here sought in contrast to pleasure proper and in detachment from it. In fact, the whole group of higher values has been introduced unnoticed: inward steadfastness, freedom, nobility of soul, glad and intelligent participation in the multifarious values of life, pure spirituality. In reality these are now accepted as the standards of happiness and unhappiness. "Eudæmonism" has become only the outer vehicle of a complete scale of tacitly recognized values of a higher order.

Involuntarily one asks: Is not this authoritative expression of individual eudæmonism in truth the most clear refutation of it? Do not entirely different ethical values actually, or indeed necessarily, underlie any significant conception of happiness?

(b) The Stoic View

Even the Stoics, whose doctrines were accepted by the strongest minds of later antiquity as a compendium of human wisdom, held fundamentally this same view. The main point of their teaching was likewise the identity of virtue and happiness. They simply stressed virtue still more emphatically. Conduct itself was pre-eminently the valuable thing. Man's emotions were wholly a subordinate matter, an indifferent by-product. Happiness consisted in the consciousness of right conduct. This is the extreme negation of hedonism. Pleasure is an emotion. Emotions are "alogical," they are something lower, something turbulent in man; they are an inner obstacle to that which is better in him, to the logos. Uncontrolled surrender to them is evil; for the higher understanding it is the opposite of pleasure. It is the inner enslavement of man.

Here also happiness is to be found in self-control, self-sufficiency and wisdom (ἐγκράτεια, αὐτάρκεια, σοφία); but nevertheless by these forms of mental attitude was meant something different from what Epicurus meant. To virtue, in which happiness was said to consist, a special quality is attributed, the ἀπάθεια, the absence of desire, as it is generally translated. But the primary meaning is lack of πάθος, freedom from emotion. Here then virtue is no intensified feeling, not even for the abundant values of life; it is not even a wise participation and appropriation, not an inner wealth; but on the contrary a closing of one's self against values which awaken wishes and passions. It is a renunciation of all human goods, a contempt for them, for even the noblest of them. It is in fact a tendency in the opposite direction. Even if it does not quite possess the rudeness of cynicism, it leads to the impoverishment of life, to the stupefaction of the spirit. It involves an atrophy of the very sense of value which the Epicureans cultivated and heightened. The self-sufficiency of the wise man, which needs nothing more, is his rejection of values; it is empty self-control in renunciation. The virtue of the

Stoics is unthankfulness towards life, towards the world and reality. It is the extremest opposite to that great sense of gratitude for an over-abundant life to which Lucretius has given classical expression.

In this kind of eudæmonism the concept of happiness is entirely set aside. In fact its ethical meaning is found in a series of values of a totally different kind, which in themselves have nothing to do either with pleasure or with happiness. On this point the general renunciation of value and the contempt for life need not deceive us. They simply are not to be found where the Epicurean sought for them, not in the diversified fulness of the real. The Stoic also is acquainted with a sublime realm of the perfect; it is the realm of the logos, which is the law, the meaning and the soul of the world. He knows himself to be one with the logos. In comparison with it the human seems to him to be without value. The values which constitute his happiness are life in the logos, the absolute strength, the freedom and sublimity of the human spirit, as compared with the futility, the folly and the disintegration of his nature when devoted to commonplace affairs, to the actualities of the passing moment and in pursuit of happiness. But even here the fundamental value is a genuine, envisaged greatness of soul, the ideal of the wise man.

(c) CHRISTIANITY AND NEO-PLATONISM

Even Christianity is not free from eudæmonism. The belief in another world introduces it. However little this belief may be Christian in origin, early Christianity absorbed it, and with it a considerable part of an inveterate other-worldliness. Eternal reward and eternal punishment await man in another life. What he sows here, he will reap there. Blessedness is prepared for the good man. In comparison with it the sufferings of time disappear, but with them also the values of this world. The devaluation of this world is the reverse side of the teleology of the Beyond. Even the goodness of man in this life finds its value only in the immortality of the soul and in preparation for eternal life.

One may turn and twist this doctrine as one pleases, one may regard it as an outward, historically conditioned form which does not reach the heart of Christian ethics, the morality of neighbour-love; but no one can deny that it is deeply characteristic of the whole Christian view of the world and runs through all its principal ideas and can be entirely removed from it only by distorting it. But just as little can one deny that its fundamental structure is eudæmonistic; it is a eudæmonism of the Beyond. Indeed one may assert still more: it is an individualistic eudæmonism—irrespective of the social tendency in the ethics of primitive Christianity. The individual is not to care for saving his neighbour's soul but primarily and always only his own—"Work out your own salvation with fear and trembling." Since the morality of love for one's neighbour concerns itself with the goods of this world and with human conduct in this world, there is no inconsequence here. While man on earth is caring for his neighbour, he is at the same time caring for his own soul's salvation. If he were to reverse this relation and to care primarily for the salvation of his neighbour's soul, then his chief concern would be, not his own, but his neighbour's love for his neighbour. The altruism of this world is at the same time egoism as regards the Beyond. Here is the point in which the Christian must necessarily be an egoist and a eudæmonist, on the basis of his religious metaphysic of the Beyond.

This is no external accompaniment of Christian ethics. It inheres in the essence of the matter. Man is answerable before God for his own action, but only for his own. The conduct of his fellow-man is withdrawn from his volition. Accordingly he can care only for his own salvation. It is at the same time evident that this is not an especially Christian dogma, but that every system of earthly morals which refers to a Beyond must show the same tendency. On this point one does not need in any way to overlook the profound thought of joint responsibility. But this thought has another origin; it belongs to another stratum of Christian philosophy and, historically as well as in content, stands altogether unrelated to the former. Moreover, as regards joint responsibility, other-worldly eudæmonism as such remains unaltered. It simply lacks the individualistic and egoistic note.

Eudæmonism is reflected most clearly in Christian asceticism, anchoritism and martyrdom. To lay up treasure for oneself in heaven is for the Christian in fact the supreme concern, and is not by any means a mere figure of speech. Even St. Paul's justification by faith, which opposes all salvation by works and every human merit, does not change the matter. Whether it be due to grace or merit, the same glory of the Beyond is the thing yearned for.

Neo-Platonism, together with the tendencies of later antiquity which are kindred to it, shows throughout the same strain of other-worldly eudæmonism. The thought of Plotinus is through and through marked by the great yearning for the "ascent." The "return" to the "One" is eudæmonia in the most daring, and at the same time the most literal, sense of the word. And because this return is not only the basic tendency in human morality, but is also a universal, cosmic and metaphysical tendency of all Being, we have here in the teleology of the ascent a eudæmonism which is projected into the cosmos and is hypostasized. From this source it has been carried over into the Christian mysticism of the Middle Ages.

There is no need to prove that behind the eudæmonistic position there are concealed everywhere other and incomparably higher values. Everyone understands that love for one's neighbour is in itself a moral value, that it is independent of all the blessedness of the Beyond, and that other-worldliness is only a traditional form of thought which was deeply rooted in the age, a thought which the age clothed with eudæmonistic meaning. Likewise it is easy to see that in the valuational concept of salvation itself is hidden something different from mere happiness: deliverance from sin, attainment of innocence, purity, likeness to God, union with God. These last-named values are no longer moral: they are distinctively religious values. So much the more illuminating is it as to the nature of eudæmonism, that it can take these also up into itself and can build up a vehicle for them. That the pleasure-element here again comes more forcibly into the foreground should not lead us astray. Still less should we regard, as the kernel of this eudæmonism, the gross sensualities with which the phantasy of a strong but crudely religious emotion has adorned heaven and hell. The Christian is not a Stoic. The passions of the soul are for him not despicable. For him the highest values are objects of the highest passion, of the most glowing desire, of the purest pleasure. The quality of this pleasure is a reflection from its object. He accepts it as salvation. The objective abundance of values which it contains and which gives it its distinctive quality does not lower it to the level of hedonism.

(d) THE SOCIAL EUDÆMONISM OF MODERN TIMES

The present age scarcely knows a new form of individualistic eudæmonism. But with the appearance of the modern problems of the community and the State and of law, it has brought forth a social eudæmonism. This signifies a thoroughly articulated practical ideal on an altruistic basis. No longer does the happiness of the individual person constitute its content, but the welfare of all. Or, as the fuller formula runs: the aim is the greatest possible happiness of the greatest possible number.

Here the whole realm of moral phenomena is centred, with greater consistency than in the systems of ancient times, upon happiness and even directly upon a striving for happiness. Only in this striving have communal and legal sentiment and civic virtue of every kind any significance. Even the State is a means towards this highest end, and all its arrangements, regulations and laws must serve it. The happiness of the majority is the standard by which every existing institution is measured. Concerning everything the question is, whether it is useful for this end.

And here a remarkable feature appears: there are so many and varied kinds of utility, one's gaze is drawn to so many detailed phenomena and problems, that one loses sight of the whole, of the final end. In this way utilitarianism arises. One attends only to the useful, one has forgotten that it should be useful "for something." Life becomes a searching for means, without any consciousness of the distinctive end in view. Indeed, concepts ultimately become so dislocated, that one regards "the useful," "use" itself, as the highest end, as though there were any sense in setting up the "useful in itself," as though "use" were not precisely the concept of a means towards something valuable in itself.

This displacement of ideas is not merely theoretical. It is carried out in concrete life, and there it has the import of a dislocation of the valuational consciousness, and, indeed, of a passing over into negation and emptiness. Man transforms himself into a slave of utility, but he no longer knows for whose use things are done. He has lost the sense for the value which stood behind everything and gave it a significance. He stands without ideas in a disenchanted world; no lofty point of view lifts him above the commonplace, everything has disappeared in the colourless grey of utility. The "enlightenment" which has led to this kind of morality is in truth a complete veiling of the realm of values. Its spiritual guide, healthy commonsense, is too crude a faculty of perception. It cannot see moral values.

Social eudæmonism, therefore, in its most essential characteristics stands upon an entirely different ground from the ancient forms of eudæmonism. Unlike them, it is not a vehicle for a highly developed consciousness of value, it is not a form of living vision which lacked only a philosophical expression for its true values. It is rather a cramping and impoverishment of the sense of value; and in its extreme form it is, as regards values, pure nihilism. It is a turning away of the mind from the realm of values altogether—and finally even from that of happiness. Thus it leads ultimately to a misunderstanding of eudæmonism itself, and to its own obliteration.

CHAPTER X

CRITICISM AND THE ETHICAL SIGNIFICANCE OF EUDÆMONISM

(a) THE NATURAL LIMIT OF UTILITARIANISM

To criticize utilitarianism philosophically is an easy game. All its preposterous consequences have their root in the banal confusion of the good and the useful.

The useful is never the good in the ethical sense. Language of course adds to the confusion of the concepts. For we say that a thing is "good for something." But this is not the moral meaning of the good. The latter reveals itself only when one inquires after that "for which" anything is good. If one traces this "for which" back to what is no longer good for anything else but is good in itself, one has reached the good in the other sense, which contains its ethical meaning. The morally good is the good in itself. Therefore not to be good for something else is of its very essence. According to its nature, it is never the useful.

The point of view of utility is by no means on that account to be contemned. It is necessary in life as it is in morality. It controls the practice of means, wherever in life something is done for the attainment of ends. Utility is the exact concept of a mediating value, the necessary correlate of a self-value. Its essence consists in this, that it is always related to prior self-values, and that everything which in this sense is of value is so only as a means to these self-values. Utility is on principle excluded from the realm of values proper and primal. Yet it is on that account as little valueless as is the actualization of those values which through it become real.

All concrete morality, which really grapples with practical life and does not remain suspended in theory and idealistic dreams, has therefore a necessary strain of utilitarianism in it:

it must be a morality of means. The Socratic ethics had this strain not less than modern social ethics. For this there is an inherent necessity. But the character of the contents of morality itself is not determined thereby. This character inheres in the values proper, to which the whole structure of the useful, as means, is related. And these values proper can be as varied as is the point of view which at any time selects them. When they change, the significance of the useful changes also.

It is a totally different matter whether anything is useful for law and public order or for agreeableness, for personal well-being or for education and mental improvement, for power and honour or for fidelity and friendship. Here for the first time the paths of morality divide. But Utility, as such, is everywhere the same. It is a universal category of practice, the form of the relation between means and end. Therefore it is absurd to transform utility into utilitarianism. Thereby one converts the means into the end, the derived into the principle, a meaningless commonplace into the content of life.

(b) The Right and the Limit of the Ethics of Consequences

For ethics to criticize eudæmonism is not so easy a game. Eudæmonism has no doubt been repeatedly and satisfactorily controverted—not only by means of philosophical theory, but also through the developments of living morality itself. Nevertheless, every eudæmonism which has hitherto existed has finally resolved itself into other values or has been unmasked as futile and confused.

But we are not concerned simply to refute it, but to extract its kernel of justifiability, the valuable thought within it. For this purpose we need to disregard every misunderstanding and falsification of value which in varying degree at all times has clung to it.

In the first place, the same objection may be brought against it as against egoism.

The pursuit of happiness, which in some way accompanies all human striving, is a natural tendency. What is striven for hovers before everyone as a good, and the good again as somehow a source of happiness. In this sense therefore eudæmonism would be nothing less than a general psychological form of striving, indeed perhaps of the appreciation of value in general.

This point however is not in dispute; what is questioned is the raising of the value of happiness to the highest position. If this is done seriously, one must conclude: The happy man is the good man, the unhappy man the bad man. The paradoxes of the Stoics actually approached near to this position.

Nevertheless, our moral consciousness shrinks from it. It would be necessary to judge human life and conduct entirely according to consequences. The inner reasons, the dispositions, the motives, the quality of the conduct as such would be indifferent. This evidently contradicts the fact of moral judgment. Consequences can certainly mislead the moral judgment. But by "good and evil" something different is meant. It refers to the purpose, to the inward attitude of mind, to the disposition from which the deed issues. The ethics of consequences does not touch the essence of the matter. Consequences do not depend upon the will alone, but it is the will alone which in an action can be good or bad. Upon it alone therefore depends the moral quality of the person. Nothing is easier in principle than to set up a logical ethics of consequences. Social eudæmonism does this most fully. But it never attains to a moral valuation of the person or even merely of the community.

One cannot of course maintain that consequences do not at all enter into the ethical problem. One can easily go too far in this direction. Certainly consequences do not rest in the hand of man. Nevertheless, man rightly feels responsible for them. He cannot be satisfied with willing the right merely inactively. To stand for it rightly within the limits of his own capacity, to discover means, and indeed to do so according to his best knowledge and with the whole commitment of his personality, is a part of his actual volition. The moral disposition itself does not stand in indifference to consequences; if a man is indifferent, his attitude of mind is no longer a right attitude.

In this sense of the inner relation of disposition and will to the consequences of action, the ethics of consequences is a justifiable constituent in every genuine morality. But only in this sense. And this sense never justifies a moral judgment as to an action according to its actual results. Herein is found a first and insurmountable limit to eudæmonism.

(c) The Reappearance of Suppressed Values

Is it really true that the will, when it is directed to something valuable, has happiness in view? At this point it is possible in the first place, as was the case with egoism, to reply: The conscious will knows nothing of this. Before it hovers only the situation. Always with it, on this account, the striving for happiness could enter in as an unconscious motive. But the question is whether even then happiness for the sake of happiness would be striven for, or, as it were, for the sake of some other interest. There are many kinds of happiness which the eudæmonist totally refuses. There is a happiness of the dull, undeveloped and degraded consciousness. Possibly stupefaction is in fact the highest happiness—cynicism comes near enough to this view. But we cannot will such happiness; it passes with us as a human degeneracy. And even the cynic could not will it, if his ideal of the wise man did not involve an altogether differently conditioned kind of regal sublimity. In general we distinguish very definitely between happiness and happiness. The happiness of the egoist is not accepted by us as of equal value with that of the altruist, just as in antiquity the happiness of the fool was not counted to be of equal value with that of the wise man. And Epicurus, the despised, teaches: "It is better to be unhappy and rational than to be happy and irrational."

Not all pleasures and not all forms of happiness are of equal value. This proposition lifts eudæmonism off its pivot. If there be a happiness that has no ethical value or is even contrary to all value, then happiness itself is not the standard but something else in it, its quality, its contents. The suppressed moral values revive; they gain dominance, just as if they avenged themselves upon eudæmonism because of its suppression of them.

The historically instructive feature of Epicureanism and Stoicism is this: Happiness in their schemes is in truth something dependent and derivative. It is only a cloak, a drapery— with Epicurus a covering for the noblest treasures of the mind and for the acquisition of these, with the Stoics a covering for strength of spirit and superiority to fate and chance. Nor is Christian salvation anything else than a veil for the highest good to which yearning aspires—for purity, spiritual health, and union with God.

This is naturally not so evident in social eudæmonism, which is confined entirely within a theory of means. But even in it one cannot fail to detect traces of another kind of valuation. Even a utilitarian esteems honesty of acquisition as a good, theft as bad, although both may have the same "happy consequences." In fact, with him order, just relations and loyalty are values in their own right. And even if stupidity should make men happy, he would not desire this "happiness" for the greatest possible number. Here also, although not acknowledged, something else than happiness is the real standard.

(d) The Valuational Illusion in Social Eudæmonism and its Danger

The mask which here conceals the true content of values is not so harmless as at first sight might appear. It has a particularly pernicious effect upon social life. The oppressed man, the labourer, he who is exploited—or he who so regards himself—lives unavoidably under the belief that the man of means is the happier. He imagines that the rich have every-thing which he himself yearns for in vain. In the other con-ditions of life he sees only the hedonic value. That there are in reality other values which are hidden—education, taste, knowledge—and that these are dearly paid for in pain, he does not see. He is not acquainted with the difficulty of mental work and the burden of great responsibilities. Still in his striving for the alleged "happiness" there is something like a higher guidance. For if he succeeds in working his way up to the longed-for kind of life, it is precisely those values, mis-understood by him, in which he will participate. But he is deceived about the dreamed-of "happiness."

So far it may seem that a blessing lies hidden in this decep-tion. But the reverse is the case, if short-sighted social leaders exploit the illusion, in order to hold up before the crowd a general happiness near at hand, and to incite them thereby to action. Such a vision, when it succeeds, is the means of setting the sluggish masses in motion. It appeals to the lower instincts in man, to the crudest sense of values, and liberates passions which afterwards cannot be checked. But the tragedy is that even this arousing of passion rests upon an illusion, upon a $\pi\rho\tilde{\omega}\tau o\nu$ $\psi\epsilon\tilde{\upsilon}\delta o\varsigma$. The one who is aroused is always the victim. What he can at best attain is always something else than what he had dreamed of. And even if it be something of value, it cannot satisfy him, because it is not the "happiness" which had dazzled him and because he cannot see the real value of what he has attained by his efforts.

If an ordinary man is under such an illusion, it is quite natural. If a demagogue makes use of the illusion as a means to his own ends, the means becomes a two-edged sword in his hand; but it is valuable—as seen from his point of view. If, however, the philosopher allows himself to be misled into justifying and sanctioning the illusion, this is due either to unscrupulousness on his part or to the deepest moral ignorance. Nevertheless, the social theories of modern times have trod this fateful course ever since their first appearance: and it must be regarded as the misfortune of the social movement up to our own day, that this kind of sanction has been set upon it and handed down to us. The seed of untruth has sprouted and the fruits of untruth have ripened. Even the ability and earnestness of Fichte, who came forward with another basis for Socialism, with a foundation in the Idea of law, could not succeed against this illusion. Here, as in so many other departments of our moral life, the principal work still remains to be done.

(e) THE INHERENT VALUE OF HAPPINESS AND ITS RELATION TO THE MORAL VALUES PROPER

Eudæmonism is too old and honourable a form of the moral consciousness to allow us, in criticizing it, to forget the really valuable element in it. This is not exhausted by saying that for centuries it has been a trusted vehicle of the genuine, though misunderstood, valuational consciousness. It could never have been this, if the value, selected by it as a guiding star, were not fundamentally a genuine, indisputable value.

To prove this is superfluous. Everyone feels directly the value of happiness as such and the opposite character of unhappiness. That not every form of happiness is of equal worth does not matter. Indeed one may further concede that even pleasure is a value. These values exist; and to turn man away from this self-evident fact by fictitious theory would be a futile undertaking. A genuine valuational consciousness cannot be argued away. But from this fact it does not follow either that all striving is towards happiness or that it ought to be so. In other words, happiness and pleasure are indeed values, but not the only ones and not the highest. The eudæmonistic point of view rightly plays a part in man's moral consciousness, but it has no right to play the leading rôle. The indisputable value of happiness does not justify "eudæmonism," no matter what form it takes, just as little as the indisputable value of pleasure justifies hedonism.

Happiness evidently holds a unique place among the other values. We cannot reckon it as one of the moral values in the stricter sense. It is not a moral quality of a person; and it is neutral as regards good and evil, is anterior to both. We cannot make anyone directly responsible for our happiness and unhappiness. But it is also difficult to reckon happiness among goods—as the word is commonly understood; it is of too general a character and, besides, never inheres in a real carrier of values; it always remains an emotional value. Nevertheless it is essentially related to everything which has the character of a "good," or, more correctly, to the reality and existence, to the possession, of a good.

Perhaps one comes nearest to its essence in defining it as the emotional value accompanying every real conscious possession; it is therefore a necessary emotional reaction to every valuational reality and relation—or, one might say, to every participation in values—and has its own secondary scale of values. Formulas of this kind can fit only approximately the relation which here confronts us. But we may venture upon two suggestions:

First, there is a universal connection of happiness with the whole series of values, from the highest and most spiritual of the moral virtues to the last and most commonplace of external goods—wherein is to be found the inner reason for the extraordinary diversity in the valuational shades of happiness.

And, secondly, the eudæmonistic principle has a peculiar capacity to be a vehicle of genuine moral values, because of the remarkable scope which it gives to the most varied and most contradictory values of human conduct.

Thus we can understand that happiness, although in fact only an accompanying phenomenon, has still in all ages of immature consciousness played the rôle of a universal form of the valuational sense—that is, the rôle of an ethical category. That this rôle does not by right belong to it does not detract from the force of the historical fact. We have examples enough of a similar extension of single categories beyond bounds in the domain of theory. There have been times when the teleological category has dominated the whole concept of nature; to-day science has reduced the sphere of its validity to very narrow limits. But just as there has been a theoretical consciousness which could not see a mere event except as the execution of a purpose, so has there been for perhaps a still longer time a moral consciousness which could not imagine a "good" in any other form than that of a "happiness." And here also a stringent limitation of the category within justifiable boundaries is the correction required. The correction, however, does not mean a rejection of the category, but a bringing forward of the really determining principles which are hidden behind it.

Happiness is not the highest value; it is always relatively subordinate, an accompaniment, as we have seen. But notwithstanding all this it is nevertheless a value proper which, in those higher and lower masses of value which it accompanies as an emotion, never disappears. It is something different from them all. And to its difference is attached a moral claim of a peculiar kind. The happiest man is certainly not the best— no one would contradict this statement; but it is justifiable to add: The best man ought to be the happiest. It is of the essence of moral goodness to be worthy of happiness.

This claim is only a desideratum. But it reveals the distinctive value of happiness. Whether this desideratum may expect fulfilment is not an ethical question. It falls under the religious inquiry: What may we hope? But the claim as such is independent of its fulfilment.

Only in so far as the consciousness of being worthy of happiness is itself already a happiness does the fulfilment attach to the essence of the matter. But here we are anticipating our investigation. For exactly this essence of the matter, the being worthy of happiness, does not inhere in the relation of man to the eudæmonistic value but to the higher, the properly ethical, values.

(f) Striving for Happiness and Capacity for Happiness

Apart from the ultimate question as to what kind of value may be peculiar to happiness and how it is to be graded, there is a series of further ethical questions which are suggested by eudæmonism and make it an extremely ambiguous phenomenon. Here we can only consider the one question, whether striving after happiness is rational.

That it is so is not self-evident nor does it depend alone upon the valuational character of happiness, but also essentially upon the material involved. To strive for external goods is possible only within very narrow limits; but to strive for qualities of character, if one does not possess a predisposition towards them, is altogether impossible. Still more doubtful would be a striving for love. The striving for happiness is closely related to this latter.

Everyone knows what is involved in the search for happiness. The mythological figure of the whimsical Fortuna hits the nail on the head. It is more than a mere figure of speech. It is in the very nature of "happiness" to tease man and to mock him as long as he lives, to lure him on, to mislead him and leave him standing with empty hands. It pursues him jealously so long as he, diverted from it, is pursuing other values. But it escapes from him the moment he snatches at it. It flees beyond his reach if he passionately pursues it. But if he modestly turns away, it flatters him again. If in despair he gives up the struggle, it mocks him behind his back.

If one omits from this characterization the popular poetic hyperbole, there still remains in it a kind of essential law, an inner necessity. Happiness does not depend solely upon the attainable goods of life to which it seems to be attached. It depends at the same time, or rather primarily, upon an inner predisposition, a sensitiveness of the individual himself, his capacity for happiness. But this capacity suffers under the effort to attain happiness. It is greatest where the good involved was least sought for, where it falls unexpectedly into one's lap.

And it is smallest, where it is passionately yearned for and striven after.

To what this decline in the capacity for happiness is properly due is a difficult psychological question. It is conceivable that the anticipation of happiness, the mere Epicurean dwelling upon it before it is there, diminishes it. It never quite equals what was expected. The anticipation has already falsified it, by prejudicing the sense of value against the reality, in favour of some fantastic image. Or is it that the capacity of enjoyment has simply exhausted itself beforehand? However this may be, the striving itself nullifies the eudæmonistic value of the thing striven for, before it has been attained. The attainment becomes illusory through the striving itself, because thereby the thing attained is no longer the same happiness which was striven for.

In other words, happiness allows itself to be yearned for and striven after, but not to be attained by striving. The pursuit of happiness reacts unfavourably upon the capacity for it. At the same time it always vitiates the thing pursued. When the pursuit dominates a man, it sweeps all happiness out of his life, makes him restless and unsteady, and precipitates him into unhappiness. This is the meaning of that alluring and fleeing, that flattery and mockery.

Real happiness always approaches from another side than one expects. It always lies where one is not seeking it. It always comes as a gift and never permits itself to be wrung from life or extorted by threats. It exists in the richness of life which is always there. It opens itself to him who sets his gaze upon this abundance—that is, upon the primary values. It flees from him who is looking out only for pleasant sensations, charmed only by the emotions which accompany all values. Thus his vision for the values themselves is blurred. But he who yearns for them, without coquetting with his sensations, wins the reality.

Is it a curse upon man, an eternal infatuation, that all striving assumes so easily the form of a search for happiness and that every gain in value takes on the guise of happiness? Or is it a part of eternal wisdom and justice which is fulfilled in the fact that all genuine striving after genuine ethical values of itself brings happiness as its own reward, and this the more, the higher in the scale the value is to which the striving is directed? May we believe that in this sense the man who is most worthy of happiness is also in reality the happiest—because he is the one who is the most capable of happiness? Does it not look as though, in its higher meaning, the proposition that the best man is the happiest is still true? And is not eudæmonism, then, in the end rehabilitated?

These are no longer ethical questions. Moreover, man cannot answer them. But an affirmative answer to them—in case it were justified—certainly would not be a justification of eudæmonism. Happiness, as a moral postulate, is an eternal requirement of the human heart; but "eudæmonism," as the morality of striving for it, is a tendency which destroys itself, in that it systematically leads to an incapacity for happiness.

SECTION IV

THE KANTIAN ETHICS

CHAPTER XI

THE SUBJECTIVISM OF THE PRACTICAL REASON

(a) KANT'S DOCTRINE OF THE "SUBJECTIVE" ORIGIN OF THE OUGHT

EVER since Kant it has been customary in considering the essence of the good to start with the phenomenon of the will. It was an important and genuinely critical judgment on his part that the moral quality of an act never inheres in its consequences, not even in the outward act, but in the inner tendency, in the person's disposition, in the attitude of his will. In this sense the proposition holds good, that the predicate "morally good" applies only to the good will.

We may at first ignore the fact that the problem as to the will which here arises does not cover the whole extent of the problem concerning the good. If we consider the question within its limits—which are those concerning what ought to be done—the whole emphasis falls upon the "purpose." In it lies the inner direction of the will. The content and categorial structure of the purpose again refer to that which we call the end. Thus ethics becomes an ethics of ends. And as it is a question regarding the unity of the moral life, we must pass beyond the single variable end to the system of ends and ultimately to the unity of the final end.

We cannot at the beginning disregard the fact that the ethics of ends cannot justify its task, that the highest ends of action do not coincide with the standard of value which the moral judgment applies to action. On that account, behind all ends genuine values are hidden, even if ordinarily not moral values proper. If one however entirely ignores such difficulties, still the question always arises: How is the relation between the will and value to be understood? Value is that which formulates the commandment, the "moral law," the thing that ought to be. The will is that for which the commandment has validity. The good will therefore is "determined" by the law, it is directed towards the law. It therefore receives the commandment from beyond itself; the commandment is not its own. For in regard to the law the will is indeed free to act contrary to it.

So, at first glance, Kant seems to present the matter. But this is not his real meaning. Such a receiving of the law from beyond, a taking over of its authority, would be "heteronomy." Kant draws the opposite conclusion: the moral law must be a law peculiar to the will itself, the expression of its true innermost tendency. The "practical reason" must be autonomous; it must give its law to itself. The metaphysical essence of the will is precisely this legislation.

But here the relation of the Ought to volition is reversed. The Ought does not now determine volition, but volition determines the Ought. The Ought, as the objective reality, shows itself to be something that is subordinate. It is only an expression of a law and at the same time an objectification of pure volition. The will, as the subjective factor, is that which sets up the standard. Accordingly, we are again confronted here with a reference of valuational essence to something else, to something essentially alien to it; being of value (that is, being commanded) is "explained" here by something which is not itself a value. And here, as in the case of eudæmonism, the principle of explanation is an inward tendency of the subject. No one of course will overlook the profound difference between the two theories: in the one case the explanatory factor is a natural instinctive tendency, in the other it is a metaphysical rational tendency. Nevertheless, in principle, the two explanations stand on the same level. Both refer what in itself is objective back to something subjective.

Kant's conception of the Ought in this respect only follows the general trend of his philosophy. According to this, everything which has the character of a principle inheres in the subject. Space and time are "presentations," categories are "concepts of the understanding," the unity of the object has its root in the "synthetic unity of consciousness." Only the manifold, which, taken by itself, is without principles, is given to and not by the mind. The subject, consciousness, universally possesses the superior import; the object is that which is dependent, derived. It receives its determination from the subject.

All principles therefore display throughout the characteristic of being functional, of being spontaneous. Only one who started from such presuppositions in the domain of theory, where the relation of the subject to the object is merely one of understanding, would think of applying the same presuppositions to the domain of practice. Here, as the facts show, the relation of subject to object is reversed: in knowledge, the object determines the subject; but in conduct, the subject reaches actively towards the object, changes it according to its standard and transforms it. Here it is the subject which determines the object.[1] Here, therefore, it is not idealistic theory but the fact which shows the reversal of direction.

Hence it is easy to see why precisely in ethics the Kantian doctrine concerning the spontaneity of the subject receives a kind of confirmation. Undeniably there exists here a type of principle which is not realized in nature. The "moral law" expresses a claim in contrast to the subsisting relationships of human life. If one understands by the word "objectivity" the actual relationships, it may rightly be said that what a law posits as its contents can be given only through the subject to the object—that is, can literally be imposed upon it.

It therefore follows quite logically, as the *Critique of Practical Reason* affirms, that the subject here sets the law; the ground of its determination inheres in it and not in the object. In this way Kant's doctrine of the "legislation" of the will is to be understood. It "determines" what ought to be. For if it derived that from the given relationships, from the world

[1] Cf. Fichte, *Moral Theory*, 1798, Introduction.

of objects, it would cease to be practical and would rank itself under the "categories of the understanding"—that is, under the laws of nature. But as the practical reason is nothing else than the pure will itself, the Ought is necessarily determined by the will, and not vice versâ.

Translated into the language of the valuational problem, however, this means: the will determines or creates the values, not the values the will. The will is, then, not bound to something which in itself has value, but value is nothing else than an expression for that towards which the will is directed. Values are directional concepts of the pure will.

(b) TRANSCENDENTAL SUBJECTIVISM AND THE FREEDOM OF THE WILL

In the domain of theory Kant's subjectivism is just as assailable as any other metaphysical theory. It stands or falls with the point of view of "transcendental idealism." Criticism of this view is an affair of epistemology.[1] Here it must suffice merely to refer to the fact that the state of being conditioned by the standpoint is enough to render the position ambiguous.

But in ethics subjectivism bears a somewhat different stamp. There can be no doubt here as to the determination of the object by the subject. Hence subjectivism in ethics stands nearer to the fact than it does in the domain of theory. Its main root accordingly lay for Kant in ethics. Its chief concern is the freedom of the will. The will evidently is free only in so far as it bears within itself its own ground of determination. Its highest principle accordingly—however much it may take on the form of an imperative—must emanate from the constitution of the subject.

In this consideration there are passed over in silence two

[1] Cf. *Metaphysik der Erkenntnis*, second edition, 1925, Chapter XVII. Cf. *Diesseits von Idealismus und Realismus*, Kantstudien, Volume XXIX, 1924, Section 2.

points which strike one as difficulties the moment they are formulated as definite questions.

The first difficulty concerns freedom. Granting that the solution of the question of freedom in a positive sense is the supreme requirement of ethics—which indeed is by no means proved—is this requirement really met by a transcendental subjectivism of the principle? Can the will, in so far as it is supposed to be free to follow the principle or not, be at the same time itself the originator of the principle? Is it conceivable that it should first give the law and then transgress it? For it must be able to transgress it, since otherwise it would not be free will but would be subjected to the principle as to a natural law. But if the principle be already contained in its essence, how can the will deviate from it?

Of course one may come to the rescue by recognizing, along with the law, alien "anti-moral" impulses which allure the will from the direction proper to it. Then there would exist two kinds of will: the pure one which gives the principle, and the empirical one which side by side with this principle is subjected to other determining factors. But which of the two is then free will? Evidently the one which has before it the unchecked possibility of following either the principle or the alien determinants. Therefore, the empirical will. But this, according to Kant, is precisely the unfree will—and indeed because it is not subject solely to the autonomous law of the will! For Kant the pure will is accepted as free, exactly in so far as it has no other ground of determination than the principle which inheres in its own essence. Consequently Kant's "free" will has in truth, on the basis of these determinations, self-legislation (in the strict sense, "autonomy"), but has no freedom in the proper sense of the word. It is subject to the autonomous principle of its essence exactly as nature is subject to natural law.

In other words, in ethics transcendental subjectivism does not lead to that freedom of the will for the sake of which it was introduced. What would be really requisite therefore is not the autonomy of the will, not the laying down of the principle by the will, but exactly aloofness from the principle, its own activity in face of the principle, scope for and against as regards the principle. Thus it is evident that only this condition of aloofness fits the facts if the principle has some other origin—that is, if it is not rooted in the subject, if there is no autonomy, no self-legislation of the will.

The first point in question accordingly brings us to the unexpected view that transcendental subjectivism is not only not required by the doctrine of the freedom of the will, but stands directly in opposition to it.

That Kant could overlook this embarrassing connection was not due to an actual inconsequence but to the radical error which he had adopted as to the concept of freedom itself. But this too belongs to another part of our investigation.[1]

(c) THE KANTIAN ALTERNATIVE

The second difficulty concerns not the consequence but the presupposition of the Kantian thesis.

If it be granted that the basing of freedom of the will upon the transcendental subjectivity of the Ought were in fact justified, what then justifies the assumption of the governing presupposition itself? It naturally cannot be justified by that which is itself to be proved—the freedom of the will. For that is not a phenomenon given in experience, but is the issue in question. Kant grasped this problem very well: one can lay one's finger upon the moral law; it is an intelligible fact: but one cannot lay one's finger upon freedom; it must be inferred. And indeed it can be inferred only from the moral law. Everything therefore depends upon our conception of the moral law.

What then justifies the assumption of a subjective origin of the moral law? Here again also Kant's reasoning is very lucid. For him there exist only two possibilities: either the

---

[1] Cf. below, Volume III, Chapters LXVII (*f*) and LXXII (*b*), (*c*).

principle issues from the external world, from things, from nature, or it emanates from reason. In the former case it is "empirical"; it lacks universality and independence (autonomy) in contrast to the categories and the laws of nature, and it is besides merely a "hypothetical imperative," not a commandment proper which could be set up in opposition to natural tendencies. But, if it emanates from reason, it is universal, a priori, an unconditional "categorical" imperative—that is, a genuine commandment standing over against all natural laws, independent, autonomous, indeed superior.

This characterization of the two cases we may concede without qualification. Indeed, *mutatis mutandis*, it can easily be transferred from the Kantian requirement of the unitary moral law to the manifoldness of values. These two possibilities fundamentally apply to every value. In every one the alternative between empirical relativism and transcendental apriorism returns again. The Kantian problem therefore sets us in the midst of the fundamental question as to the essence of values—just as it has historically made possible the actual solution.

How Kant settled this problem is self-evident from the meaning of his ethical principle. The principle cannot be empirical, dependent, merely hypothetical. It has indisputably the character of a genuine commandment, unperturbed by the question whether any experience contains a fulfilment of it or not. Consequently it can emanate only from reason. Hence the autonomy of the practical reason and the dependence of the Ought upon the pure will.

(d) THE FALSE INFERENCE IN THE KANTIAN APRIORISM

The whole argumentation has the form of a disjunctive inference in the *modus tollendo ponens*. Only two possibilities exist. The one is proved to be false. Only the other remains. This inference is only right, provided the disjunction in the major premise was complete. The question is therefore: Is the

Kantian alternative a complete disjunction? Do no other possibilities for the principle actually exist than the two according to which it originates either in "nature" or in "reason"? Or, if we transfer the problem to the realm of values: Can a value only be either abstracted from things (natural tendencies) or dictated by a volitional subject?

The answer must be in the negative. It is simply the narrowness of the Kantian attitude which excludes a third possibility—the same narrowness which admits only the function of the "subject" in the problem of the categories, where the empirical as their origin is excluded. As in that case there is the purely speculative assumption that whatever is known a priori is to be referred to "pure perception" and "pure concepts of the understanding," so in this case the assumption is that whatever is evidently aprioristic in the moral consciousness is to be traced back to a legislative "practical" reason. If the alternative simply ran "either a priori or a posteriori," the assumption would hold good and a third possibility would be excluded. From the impossibility of an aposterioristic origin would follow then necessarily the aprioristic character of the principle. But the Kantian alternative "either from nature or from reason" is not identical with this. From it nothing can be disjunctively inferred. The exclusion of one member does not entail the setting up of the other. The concept of the aprioristic does not coincide with that of origin in reason. The alternative is false, the disjunction not complete. But with it the conclusion falls away. It is a false inference.

In fact here lies the pivot of Kantian subjectivism. It is no ordinary subjectivism; it rests ultimately upon the aprioristic wholly. Kant was not in a position to picture to himself an a priori which did not subsist in a function of the subject. What is apparently evident here is that aprioristic insight subsists in fact without there being given to the mind any real individual objects of perception. Just that is its apriority. The subject does not get his insight from the given case.

He therefore, it is inferred, adds it out of himself to the presentation of the object. But in this "out of himself" lies the entire confusion.

Must the subject himself create that which has been added? Must a spontaneous productive function of the subject stand behind the addition? Is not the reverse also possible? May not the content of what the subject discerns a priori be just as objective as what he perceives a posteriori? That the aprioristic contents are not to be extracted from the real ("empirical") objects as such does not in any way derogate from their objectivity. Geometrical relations cannot indeed be derived from things, not even from drawn figures, but are at best illustrated by these; they are none the less on that account something purely objective, something that can be discerned as objects, and they have nothing to do with the functions of consciousness. The relation of cause and effect is never perceptible to sense, not even when the two members of the perception are given; but it is nevertheless an objective relationship, and only as such is it attached to what is perceived. No inference is permissible that it is a relation which holds between functions of consciousness.

And is it otherwise with the categorical imperative? The exacted harmony of the individual will with the Ideal will of all can certainly never be extracted from an empirical will. But from this, does it follow that this requirement is a function, an act, a legislation of reason? Evidently just as little. It also is something purely objective; its content is an ideal objective relation which, precisely as such, hovers before the moral consciousness, independently of the degree of its actualization in real life.

The prejudice which occasioned Kant's misunderstanding of the objectivity of the thing discerned a priori was just this, that with him only the empirical (only what was at the same time presented to sense) was accepted as validly objective.[1]

[1] The remarkable thing is that this prejudice, taken by itself, is anything but an idealistic prejudice. In so far as in it the "Being of

This prejudice ultimately involved all the confusions of idealism. It is responsible for the fact that the whole sphere of ideal objects—which in Platonism was already discovered and was theoretically constructed as a self-existing sphere—became entirely alien to the nineteenth century.

Not only did the ethical problem suffer thereby; the theory of knowledge also and pre-eminently pure logic were falsified by being made subjective, not to speak of æsthetics, the philosophy of law, the philosophy of religion and other departments. All disciplines, of which the object is ideal, were through this prejudice turned upside down. It is no wonder that the sphere of values could not be discovered, although apriorism, which constitutes the key to it, continued to hold sway. Subjectivistic and functionalistic apriorism was itself a confusion, a total misunderstanding of the originally objective character of everything knowable a priori.

But, from all this, ethics can learn that the universality, the apriority and the categorical character of the principle have no need of a subjective origin—even though it be an origin of the highest dignity, an origin in the constitution of practical reason itself. Its only need is an origin which is not to be found in naturalistic objectivity—that is, not in nature or in the world perceived by the senses. From this sphere ethical consciousness must not derive its principle. As regards it, the principle must be autonomous. The moral consciousness must meet the sensible world with another principle. But how the sphere from which it derives the principle is constituted is a question which has nothing to do with the autonomy of the principle in its relation to the empirical. In itself it would indeed be conceivable that the principle emanated from reason. But in this way it cannot be proved.

For the moment also we can of course only assume that it does not admit of proof in any other way—rather that the

the Ideal" is denied on account of its lack of real existence, one might describe it rather as a realistic, and indeed as a naïvely realistic, prejudice.

opposite can be proved. The settlement of the matter depends upon demonstrating that there is a self-existent ideal sphere in which values are native, and that, as the contents of this sphere, values, self-subsistent and dependent upon no experience, are discerned a priori.

But first we must turn our attention to another group of prejudices, from which it is as necessary for us to free ourselves as from transcendental subjectivism.

CHAPTER XII

CRITIQUE OF FORMALISM

(a) THE MEANING OF THE "FORMAL" IN THE CATEGORICAL IMPERATIVE

IN the Kantian ethics the doctrine of Formalism accompanies that of transcendental subjectivism. According to Kant, a genuine moral commandment, a categorical and autonomous imperative, can be only a formal law. It cannot touch upon the "matter" of the will, it cannot prescribe the content—what ought to be willed; it can only give the general form proper to the will. All "material" determination of the will is heteronomous, is derived from things and their relations which, on the ground of natural tendencies and impulses, appear to be worth striving for. A materially determined will is determined empirically—that is, "from outside." Material determination is naturalistic, not rational. It is not determination by the law and by the essence of the good. For the essence of the good is a purely formal quality of the will.

What is evident and of permanent value in this doctrine is, first, the radical rejection of empiricism in ethics, the view that an ethical principle can never be found in the grasping of goods by the will; and, secondly, the rejection of casuistry and of all prescribing of specific ends which can arise only upon the ground of empirically given situations. The positive element in it, therefore, is the exaction of a strict universality, the exclusion of external determinants, and the conviction that goodness is a quality of the will itself, not of the ends it pursues.

Whether these elements of value really depend upon the doctrine of formalism, indeed whether they are promoted by it, is quite another question. That the imperative which lays down the general constitution of a "good will" must be "formal"—that is, must contain no material determination—is by no means clear. Even the most general qualitative determination must always be concrete, even if it does not prescribe the "matter" of the will—that is, its momentary object.

Hence one easily becomes convinced that Kant's categorical imperative itself is in this sense a thoroughly concrete law. The agreement of the empirical will with the ideal will, the attitude (the "maxims") which one can will to be a "universal legislation," is already a concrete determination. Only its extreme generality can mislead us on this point. An imperative which did not command anything as to content would be empty, therefore in reality not an imperative at all.

(b) THE HISTORICAL PREJUDICE IN FAVOUR OF "FORM"

Behind the formalism of the Kantian ethics stands the still more extended formalism of general philosophy—and, again, behind this, reaching back to Aristotle, a very ancient prejudice of traditional metaphysics in favour of pure form.

"Matter and form" is according to this tradition an incomparably valuable antithesis. Matter is indeterminateness, an obscure background of Being, something in itself of lower value, indeed in many ways directly evil. Pure form is the determining, constructive, differentiating principle; it is that which allows measure, beauty, life and everything of value to come into existence. Aristotle set it up as equal to the end (entelechy). And Plotinus again placed the highest principle of form on an equality with the Platonic idea of the good.

This attitude towards it is still influential. It is alive in the scholastic doctrine of universals, not less so than in Descartes' and Leibniz's doctrine of ideas. Transformed into the subjective, it rules entirely the Kantian theory of knowledge. The contrast of form and matter in cognition determines the structure of *The Critique of Pure Reason*. "Matter" is furnished by the senses, all principles on the other hand are "pure form." This holds good for the categories as well as for

intuitive perception, for the schemata as well as for fundamental propositions, for ideas, for imperatives and postulates.
As all these principles have the characteristic of being aprioristic, it follows that for Kant apriority and formal character
unite in a fixed unity. For example, with Kant it is an impossibility that the categories should contain anything material—
a consequence which is astonishing enough in face of the fact
that among his categories such evidently concrete principles
are found, as substance, causality and reciprocal reaction. It
is still more striking, how with him space and time could take
on a purely formal character, where the substratum behind
the structure of laws and relations obtrudes itself still more
forcibly.

It is a special task of the doctrine of categories to provide
a proof that in all these principles essential elements are actually
contained which cannot be merged into the scheme of form,
law and relation.[1] But that the whole teaching rests upon a
mere confusion can be seen without this proof, from the fact
that the contrast of form and matter itself is purely relative,
that everything formed can again be regarded as matter of
a higher formation, and that in the same way every specific
matter can be conceived as formed out of lower material
elements. At best, absolute matter and absolute form can be
accepted in this progression merely as the extremes. And it
is exactly the extremes which definitely fall outside of reflective
and conceptual interpretation. The whole sequence of phenomena—in every department of nature and of the mind—moves
within intermediate members, within the sphere of relativity.

When once we have grasped the metaphysical source of this
prejudice, it is not difficult to free ourselves from it. It is true
that laws, categories, commandments, as compared with the
special instances for which they hold good, are always universal
and in this sense formal. But this formal character is not in
contrast to matter in the sense of content. All principles have

[1] Cf. Hartmann's *Metaphysik der Erkenntnis*, second edition,
pp. 257–266.

matter also in themselves, otherwise they would be without content. And as all principles, so far as they can be known at all, are knowable only a priori, it follows quite evidently that there is such a thing as aprioristic matter.

At this point Scheler's criticism of Formalism applies—a criticism which of course had its predecessors, but which, in its complete universality, could not be made without the implements of Phenomenology. So long as the transcendental-subjectivistic conception of the aprioristic prevailed, the formal character attached itself misleadingly to the aprioristic. It was the objective interpretation of the a priori which first made room for the understanding of the concrete character of principles and thereby for the "material aprioristic," which, as regards value, is the decisive element.

(c) FORMALISM AND APRIORISM

The definitive view is this: The two contrasted pairs "formal-material" and "a priori-a posteriori" have nothing to do with each other.[1] Not everything aprioristic is formal, nor is everything material aposterioristic. The aprioristic is indeed always universally valid, the aposterioristic is not. But universality as such is not something formal. Within the aprioristic—for example, within the system of geometry—there are laws of greater or less range of validity. And the more general, as compared with the more special, are always formal. The more special in comparison are material. This only means that the more special always has the greater richness of content. But all propositions here are in the same way "aprioristic," without distinction as to the richness of content and the range of universality.

Hence for ethics it follows: A principle, like the moral law, or a commandment in general, even a standard, can very well have "matter," without any prejudice to its apriority. A

[1] See Scheler, *Der Formalismus in der Ethik und die materiale Wertethik*, second edition, 1921, p. 48 ff.

"materially determined will" does not need, as Kant thought, to be determined empirically. The impulsion which sets it in motion need not be from without. Material determination is not naturalistic determination. It does not necessarily spring from general existential laws, it does not imply any causal dependency. It does not degrade the human will into a "natural entity." For its origin can be perfectly autonomous, its objectivity purely aprioristic.

What was valuable in the Kantian doctrine, the rejection of ethical empiricism and heteronomy, the discarding of casuistry and of the prescription of special ends, the claim of strict universality of principle and its validity, not as an end but as the standard for the will in relation to its moral quality— all this can be completely retained and carried out without accepting the "formal" character of the principle. If the matter of the principle itself is purely aprioristic, if it does not emanate from goods which are given and desired or from the concrete tendency of a natural instinct, the entire series of requirements is no less fulfilled in it than if its principle were of a purely formal character. In other words, the distinction between form and matter has no bearing upon an autonomous ethical principle. It is only a question of apriority.

In positive terms: Values may be as formal or material as they please, only they must be something self-dependent, they must be independent of all extraneous principles, and the valuational consciousness in regard to them must be aprioristic. If by the aprioristic we do not understand a function, but only the specific way of knowing something objective which, as such, can be as well understood as mistaken, there is no sort of difficulty in regard to the material content of values. In the problem of the apriorical it is subjectivism which favours ethical formalism. If we remove the subjectivism, the formalism loses its underpinning.

CHAPTER XIII

CRITIQUE OF INTELLECTUALISM

(a) INTELLECTUALISM AND APRIORISM

A FURTHER prejudice on the part of the Kantian ethics, which is connected but is not identical with formalism, is its intellectualism. In his preference for "thought," for "understanding," for "reason," Kant is very moderate as compared with his great predecessors, particularly with Leibniz. Indeed, in conscious contrast to Leibniz, he granted to sense-perception an important position of independence and authority. But in the internal dualism, which arose in this way, he let intellectualism take its course. The contrast between sense-perception and understanding, between intuition and thinking, between the sensible and the intelligible, dominates not only his theory of knowledge but the whole Kantian philosophy.

For the systematic basic problems this might have been almost a matter of indifference, if he had not also by implication identified this contrast with that between the aprioristic and aposterioristic. This identification is not logically carried out; the transcendental æsthetic with its conception of "pure beholding" is in antagonism to it; and the doctrine of the schematism is not less so. But in general it is retained: sense-perception, intuitive objectivity, is an aposterioristic knowledge; understanding, thought, reason, is aprioristic knowledge. The above-considered contrast of matter and form plays the mediating rôle. And behind this, again, stands the opposition of objective and subjective—that is, the opposition between that which is given by the object and that which is brought forth by the subject.

That both these latter pairs of opposites in fact coincide neither with each other nor with that between the aprioristic and aposterioristic has already been shown. But that the latter also does not coincide with the contrast between thinking and sense-perception does not of itself follow—although this comparison is mediated for Kant through both the antitheses just mentioned. It must therefore be proved separately.

This proof also has been completed convincingly by Phenomenology.[1] For ethics it is of fundamental importance. For only through it can we at last see clearly in what form valuational insight of an aprioristic-material kind exists originally in the moral consciousness. Clearness on this point is a condition for understanding all that follows.

(b) SENSE-PERCEPTION, OBJECTIVITY AND APOSTERIORITY

The first part of the proof consists in freeing the aposterioristic concept of objectivity from sense-perception. Single objects of the senses, isolated colours, sounds, etc., are never directly "given." If one would bring them as such to consciousness, they must always be first abstracted from the objective complexes which are experienced, through an artificial procedure, through a special psychological method. Perception, not sensation, is the decisive court of appeal, but perception is always something highly complex. Sensation may be an element in it and as a condition it may be appealed to. But only theory can expose it to view.

Now in the complex of perception which alone can be accepted as an unreflective phenomenal object there is always contained an abundance of aprioristic elements—at least a whole series of Kantian categories, but in truth still much besides. Kant with his concept of objectivity (which changes from one of its meanings to the other) has not at all in mind the objectivity of the natural object, but a gnoseological objectivity which is determined through the theoretical contrast to the aprioristic. The given then permits of being set up as equal to the evidence of the senses. But in that case it is not something present and comprehensible as a phenomenon,

[1] Cf. Scheler, pp. 49–67.

upon which a theory could be based, but is itself already a product of theory. The Kantian concept of experience is ambiguous. At one time it refers to natural and scientific knowledge in its entirety—and in this sense it naturally includes the aprioristic—at another time it refers only to that knowledge which is not aprioristic.

In ethics this ambiguity avenges itself. According to Kant every "material" (empirical) determination of the will is of the senses, is bound to pleasure and pain, and is conditioned by an expected pleasure or an avoidance of pain. The value of the desired goods and ultimately the goods themselves are said to be given only mediately through this relation. From the standpoint of natural objects, this is once more a perversion of the phenomenon. For the craving consciousness the carriers of value are given directly together with the accompanying values, for the sake of which they are desired. Only goods as such are craved, but not the pleasure which is involved in their possession. In a secondary degree a consciousness of values can be attached thereto, values which convert the desired objects into objects of value—that is, into "goods"—and make them desirable. And only in a third degree can a knowledge of pleasure and pain follow, "which we trace back as an effect of the goods upon us (whether this effect be regarded as an experienced excitation or whether it be causal)." Sensibility, so far as one sees it in pleasure and pain, is not the final court of appeal but is something secondary, attaching itself to the craving.

What holds good of craving holds good in a heightened degree of every volition proper, which is not a will to possess but a will to attain ends, a will to actualize tasks. What immediately hovers before the willing consciousness is always a task, the aim itself, and indeed something concrete and material. Reflection upon the willing subject and his situation here retreats so much the more into the background, the more intensive and impassioned the volition becomes. The content of the thing willed transports the person willing beyond himself; it causes him to lose himself in the object, in his idea, in his identification with the thing willed.

All regard for pleasure and pain is here entirely secondary. The "materiality," the objectivity and "actuality" of the thing presented to the will have nothing to do with sense-perception or with aposteriority and heteronomous determination.

(c) THOUGHT, UNDERSTANDING AND APRIORITY

The first part of the proof is only a prelude. The emphasis must be laid upon the second. Although sense-perception and aposterioristic determination are not the same, still thought and aprioristic insight might coincide. For the fact that they do not do so, Kant's transcendental æsthetic could serve as a specific proof. Nevertheless, with Kant the intellectualism of the aprioristic is almost a settled principle. Categories are "concepts of the understanding," fundamental propositions are not simply presuppositions of objective knowledge but are principles of a determining "faculty of judgment." Synthesis is a matter of judgment, and the whole question of rational criticism is directed towards synthetical "judgments" a priori—not towards aprioristic knowledge in general. The task is limited from the beginning; or, rather, it is assumed as self-evident that everything aprioristic in experience rests upon a function of judgment, upon a specific intellectual function.

The consequence is that in all complex perception of an object a judgment leading to a synthesis must already have been made, and that therefore, wherever things or events are grasped, thinking has already been active. But in reality not the slightest trace can be found in sense-perception of thinking or judging. That a thing seen in perspective has also a far side is not first inferred, is neither consciously nor unconsciously thought, but is as immediately and intuitively grasped as the front side, which is seen.

"Thinking" first begins when reflection concerning the

exact nature of something not directly comprehended sets in. The same applies to the connections of substance and cause. Where they are not immediately presented they can of course be inferred by judging. But, in the natural attitude of consciousness towards things and their connections, they are in general grasped directly. This does not prevent immediate and intuitive grasping of connections from being aprioristic. Aprioristic knowledge is already contained in all knowledge of things. But it is not on that account an affair of thinking or judging. Rather is aprioristic knowledge inherently intuitive; and the judgment, into the form of which it can be cast when we afterwards extract and isolate it, is in comparison with it something derivative, something external and indifferent which does not change anything in the insight itself.

To sum up: the natural comprehension of the world of things is from the beginning permeated with aprioristic elements; all comprehension is accomplished in categorical structures, and precisely herein consists the apriority of the latter. Kant understood this relation very exactly; in regard to it the expression "the condition of possible experience" is most instructive. Only the intellectualistic interpretation, the introduction of thought, of conception, of judgment, once again renders this great achievement ambiguous. In order to measure the extent of the transcendental conditionality, we must entirely disregard this interpretation.

To disregard it is in the highest degree important for ethics. In Kant's teaching that the categorical imperative is a law of "reason"—in contrast to the natural law of instinct, inclination and desire—is revealed the same intellectualism as is seen in his doctrine of the categories accompanying the disguised subjectivism. The ethical a priori must be just as much rational and just as much in the form of a judgment as the theoretical a priori; for Kant it is inconceivable that a real a priori could exist in any other way.

The psychological presupposition here is that our moral life is permeated with a practical function of thinking and judging, that choice and resolution, rejection and approval, a moral taking of sides concerning actions and persons, rest upon a logical subsumption of the individual case under the moral law which from the beginning is perceived a priori. According to this interpretation an intellectual function of a practical order dominates the moral life. The form in which it penetrates the manifoldness of the situations and conflicts of life is purely logical.

Kant of course did not carry this ethical logicism to the extreme. In the classification of the Practical Reason there is found a significant attempt to give it an emotional character. It is not Kant's opinion that the naïvely moral consciousness possesses explicitly the formula of the imperative, and that with this, as with a yard-stick, consciousness approaches the situations of life. The formula is only the scientific expression of what everyone tacitly and vaguely recognizes, only an expression of what speaks in his conscience; not a knowledge of the moral law but "respect for the moral law" is accepted by him as the determining factor. The logical scheme, however, of subsumption, of the conscious application of a standard, is still retained. And this is the misleading factor in the Kantian ethics; it is this which has obscured the indispensable significance of its apriorism.

(d) The Emotional Apriorism of the Sense of Value

In our concrete moral life there is as little of such a subsuming function of judgment as there is in the natural concrete knowledge of things. Every moral preference is intuitive, is immediately there and is always contained in the grasping of a given circumstance (whether it be a situation or a finished course of conduct). It does not first wait for a judgment of the understanding.

Comprehension of ethical reality—whether it consist of goods, human relations or demands for a personal decision—is always, even for the naïvest consciousness, transfused with valuations, with preferences in accordance with feeling, with strong tensions for and against. All acts which are related to this fulness of life and which grasp reality are at the same time acts which grasp values and which select according to values. But as such they are never purely cognitive acts; they are acts of feeling—not intellectual but emotional. Upon this fact rests the actuality of the real life which encompasses us, the continual state of tension of man throughout life.

On this account the selective stresses of actual conduct are as little "empirical" as the categorical elements in the experience of things. Yet they are not judgments. The consequence is: there is a pure valuational a priori which directly, intuitively, in accordance with feeling, penetrates our practical consciousness, our whole conception of life, and which lends to everything which falls within the range of our vision the mark of value or anti-value. "Even the emotional aspect of the mind—feeling, preference, love, hate, volition—possesses an original aprioristic character which it does not borrow from thought, and which ethics has to accept quite independently of logic. There is an inborn aprioristic *ordre du cœur*, or *logique du cœur*, as Blaise Pascal happily expresses it."[1]

The apriorism of thinking and judging is accompanied by an apriorism of feeling, the intellectual a priori by an emotional a priori which is equally independent and original. The primal consciousness of value is a feeling of value, the primal recognition of a commandment is a feeling of that which unconditionally ought to be, the expression of which is the commandment.

This priority of feeling has nothing to do with empiricism. The valuational hall-marks which it communicates to things and events are not derived from the things and events, not to mention the pleasure and pain which these induce. On the contrary, the marks are impressed by feeling upon the things and events. Herein consist the aprioristic determination of these emotional acts and indirectly the apriority of the marks which the practical consciousness discerns in the real. The

[1] Scheler, as above, p. 59.

apriorism of emotional acts is just as "pure," original, autonomous and "transcendental" an authority as the logical and categorical apriorism in the domain of theory.

But this does not mean that it is also an original, explicitly present consciousness of law. There is just as little of such a consciousness concerning the order of value and of the Ought as there is concerning the existential and cognitive order. Here, as there, a special philosophical method is needed, which discovers these laws and makes their content and their "matter" accessible to consciousness and to the conceptual understanding. Here, as there, such a method is secondary. In ethics it rests upon the primal feeling of value, and can do nothing except draw out from the total emotional phenomenon the aprioristic content which was already within it. The primary seat of the valuational a priori is the valuational feeling itself which pervades our interpretation of reality and our attitude towards life. Only in it is there any original, implicit "moral knowledge," any proper knowledge of good and evil. And the phenomenon of living morality consists in its presence in all human preference, disposition, and attitude of will. But inner transformation, the process of moral development, the ever-advancing revaluation and transvaluation of life, the change in the human view of life, these are to be traced to the extension and the transposition of the primary feeling for values.

The a priori element of worth contained implicitly in living morality belongs therefore in fact—as we have already anticipated [1]—to the given phenomenon, to the situational complex, to the "factum" of ethical reality. And ethics as a science is the logical work of making explicit this implicitly given aprioristic factor and setting upon it the seal of concepts and formulæ.

Even Kant's moral law is in truth nothing else than the secondary logical form impressed upon such a value primarily felt and discerned through an emotional a priori (for example,

[1] Cf. Chapter VI (f).

the voice of conscience). But the morality systematically formulated by this law is not drawn from a consciousness of the law.

The same holds good for all similar philosophical formulations—for example, for all the acknowledged and ancient definitions of the "virtues." Even here, as regards the single virtues, a primarily discerned and felt value of human conduct is meant; but the philosophical formulation is secondary, whether it consist of an Aristotelian μεσότης or of a Stoic εὔλογον.

(e) The Idea of a "Material Ethics of Values"

Not until ethical intellectualism is overthrown can we realize the full import of discarding formalism and subjectivism. If the primal consciousness of value were an explicit consciousness of law, there would still be a certain significance in describing it as a consciousness of form; also one could, conceivably, regard its essence as a function of the subject. But it has now been proved that in the consciousness of value it is exactly the consciousness of law which is secondary, indeed that universally in the essence of value the structure of law is merely a later impress set upon it. The original feeling of value on the other hand is an approval, an affirmation, a preference concerning something wholly concrete; and this content is likewise essentially different from that which is disproved and denied in the same feeling of value.

Accordingly valuational consciousness is necessarily a material and objective consciousness. But this means that even the values themselves originally do not have the character of laws and commandments, not to speak of legislation and dictation on the part of the subject, but are concrete, material and objective, even if not really existing patterns. That moral laws rest upon these patterns, that everything which ought to be is conditioned by them and refers to them, in nowise derogates from their material, objective character.

Valuational structures are ideal objects, beyond all real Being and Not-Being, also beyond the really existing feeling of value, which alone grasps them.

But that they are something which as regards content are material and are not empty, abstract forms, makes them capable by their nature of being actualized—in so far as they are not actualized. Consequently, on account of their concrete nature they are capable of determining the content of laws which have a bearing upon positive moral life. For only positive contents are capable of being commanded and actualized, but empty forms and abstractions never.

This is why ethics—precisely as a consequence of Kantian apriorism—must be a "material ethics of values."

THE ESSENCE OF ETHICAL VALUES

CHAPTER XIV

VALUES AS ESSENCES

(a) PRELIMINARY CONSIDERATION OF ESSENCE

WE can scarcely succeed in understanding the essence of values in its universality, before we have turned our attention to single values and have encountered their fundamental outlines in greater concreteness and vividness. It is apparent from the first that the general essence is nowhere given directly, at least not as such, but always only together with other more special essences. Procedure therefore should rightly start with the examination of individual values—that is, exactly with that which according to the plan of our present investigations will follow in Part II of this book.

Our proposed anticipation of the subject is nevertheless a practical necessity. It is very difficult to understand valuational materials and characteristics, so long as we may not allow even the most elementary and general presuppositions to be accepted. These alone we intend to discuss here, and we will treat even these only in an introductory manner. We shall, in fact, first be able to gain a deeper insight into the essence of values when we have more carefully surveyed the series of particular values and their groups. Not until then can the more important conclusions be drawn.

In ancient times it was seen that there is another realm of being than that of existence, than that of "real" things and of consciousness which is not less "real." Plato named it the realm of the Idea, Aristotle that of the εἶδος, the Scholastics called it the realm of *essentia*. After having been long misunderstood and deprived of its right in modern times through the prevailing subjectivism, this realm has again come into recognition with relative purity in that which Phenomenology calls the realm of essence.

The German word *Wesenheit* is a translation of *essentia*. It means the same thing, if we disregard the various metaphysical presuppositions which have attached themselves to the idea of essence. But on its side *essentia* is a translation, although a very faded one, of the Aristotelian phrase τί ἦν εἶναι, in which the past tense ἦν, understood as timeless, points to the conception of that which in the structural elements is presupposed—that is, of that which in the concrete thing constitutes the actual *prius* and on that account is always contained in it.

For Aristotle, of course, this "essence" possessed a logical structure. It was thought of as the complete series of the determinant elements of a definition, or as the series of the *differentiae*, which, proceeding from the most general, embrace the ever narrower, down to the "last," to the *differentia specifica*. The εἶδος, which thus arises, is then accepted as the formal substance, the complete structure. This logicism was conditioned by the identification of "essence" with "concept," or, more correctly, by the lack of any discrimination between them. It was this that obscured the doctrine of "essence" even in the Middle Ages, and gave support to the attempted metaphysic of conceptual realism. From this it has been necessary for the principle underlying Plato's fundamental thought to free itself again. In Hegel's[1] doctrine of "essence" this deliverance has been accomplished. At the same time it signifies a harking back to the ancient notion of the "ground," which belonged to the meaning of "essence" in Plato's "Idea."

The kind of Being peculiar to the "Idea" is that of an ὄντως ὄν, the kind of Being of that "through which" everything participating in it is just as it is. Characteristically among Plato's ideas are found ethical principles, the ideal "virtue"—those values upon which his ethics was built. This fact is especially illuminating for the theory of value: in their mode of Being, values are Platonic ideas. They belong to that further realm of

[1] Hegel, *The Science of Logic*, Section II.

Being which Plato first discovered, the realm which we can spiritually discern but cannot see or grasp. As to the kind of Being peculiar to ideas we know nothing as yet more definite; it is still to be investigated. But thus much is immediately evident; even for values, and indeed pre-eminently for them, the proposition holds good: they are that "through which" everything which participates in them is exactly as it is—namely valuable. But in present-day conceptual language this means: values are essences.

These words merely bring together what we derived from the criticism of Kant's ethics. Values emanate neither from the things (or real relationships) nor from the percipient. No naturalism and no subjectivism attach to their form of Being. Furthermore, they are not "formal" or empty structures, but possess contents; they are "materials," structures which constitute a specific quality of things, relations or persons according as they attach to them or are lacking. And, in the third place, not only are they never merely "invented"—as one may so often hear—but they are not even capable of being directly grasped by thought; rather are they immediately discerned only by an inner "vision," like Plato's "Ideas." The Platonic notion of "beholding" well fits that which material ethics designates as the "sensing of value," that which is embodied in acts of preference, of approval, of conviction. Man's sensing of values is the annunciation of their Being in the discerning person, and indeed in their peculiar idealistic kind of existence. The apriority of the knowledge of them is no intellectual or reflective apriority, but is emotional, intuitive.

Thus far, then, we see the meaning of "essence." But it must be granted there is very little herein of positive definition. In what follows, the question as to material contents and their intuitive discernibility will at first be set aside, and only the relation of valuational essences on the one hand to the world of real objects, and on the other to the discerning person (including his acts), will be set forth.

(b) GOODS AND THEIR VALUES

Values are not only independent of the things that are valuable (goods), but are actually their prerequisite. They are that whereby things—and in the wider sense real entities and relations of every kind—possess the character of "goods"; that is, they are that through which things are valuable. To use Kant's phrase: Values, in so far as they are connected with actual situations, are "conditions of the possibility" of goods.

On the other hand, it is an indisputable fact that we cannot otherwise discern the values of things than in "goods"; and it is easy to prove this fact empirically. Is it not evident that the values of things are abstracted from the things of value, in other words, that our knowledge of these values is derived from the experience which we have of the goods?

But what is experience of goods? It is that we are acquainted with one thing as agreeable, another as useful, serviceable, advantageous. In this experience a knowledge of the value of the agreeable, of the useful, the serviceable, is presupposed. Here one "experiences" only that the object before one proves itself to be a means to something else, the value of which was already fixed; and this fixity is something felt, not reasoned about, it is such that there is no doubt about it either before or after the "experience." It is something a priori.

In fact, how could things be accepted by anyone as goods, unless independently of their actuality there were an appreciation of them which told him that they possess a value? Surely value does not inhere indiscriminately in all things; there are bad things as well as good. Now, as there is the same kind of Being in things good and bad, the same reality, wherein could anyone discriminate between them, if his sense of value did not inform him? He must possess beforehand the standard; for example, the standard of the pleasant and the unpleasant, and from the start things must fall for him under this standard, they must divide themselves according to it into things pleasant and unpleasant. He must have an elemental feeling which connects all things and relations that come within his range of vision with the value of life, and he thereby separates them into goods and evils. Otherwise, as soon as one asked: Why is this good? There would be an eternal circle of back-reference. If one answers "because it is good for that other thing," the question immediately arises: "And what is that good for?" So on to infinity; and so long as it continues to move only in the sphere of goods, it evidently turns in a circle. It does not come to a rest until one no longer answers with a good but with a value—that is, with what first converts things in general into goods.

The question "What am I working for?" is not answered by such replies as "for money" or "for a livelihood." It is only to be answered by the value of life itself, for the sake of which it is worth while to acquire an income. Or, if it is not the value of life (for the ready retort may be made "Is bare life itself then worth working for?"), it is surely some specific form of life, an ideal, in short a valuable life, with which one can answer the question. But therein is conceded the apriorical reference of work to a value striven for; in this case the reference is to a value higher than that of life itself, a value which alone makes life "valuable" and gives meaning to work. Only here does it become quite evident that appraisement of value precedes experience. For that which is striven for is still unreal, at least not yet "experienced."

If anyone objects that a man may have the experience of value from others who have acquired it by working, the answer must be: he cannot in this way have experienced the worth of that kind of life which is striven for; rather is the reverse true: he must have already had the valuational standard for it, in order to know that that kind of life which others have attained is of value. This feeling must first tell him that it is a valuable thing. For the mere fact that it confronts him as an experienced phenomenon does not involve the further fact that it is worth striving for. Countless kinds of life are encountered by him in experience; but he does not select every one of them as the goal of his own striving. If he is to select, he must already have the point of view from which to select.

Even the extremest example of another's striving could not convince him that there a value lay, unless there were in the example itself an aprioristic presupposition which had been introduced into it without being noticed—namely, the presupposition that the other person's striving also aims at a value proper and is determined by a primary feeling for it. This presupposition continues active even when one's own sense of value is lacking, when one does not know what another is striving for or why he is working, or to what he is devoting his energies. And that peculiar attraction exercised by another's example, its power of suggestion, rests upon this presupposition, which is not a reasoned judgment, but an involuntary and emotional judgment, and which exhibits the anticipatory character of everything genuinely aprioristic.

In a word, none of the various empirical elements which enter here diminish the apriority of the values which dominate the sphere of goods.

It is interesting to note how Plato, in the *Lysis*, clearly grasped this fundamental relationship. He sets it forth in reference to the conception of the φίλον, the narrower meaning of which, the value of love, approaches convincingly near to the larger meaning of the valuable in general. If we look for the essence of a φίλον in something else for the sake of which it is φίλον, it becomes evident that this something else must itself already be a φίλον. If this backward tracing goes on *in infinitum*, if it nowhere comes up against a first, an absolute, then the whole series collapses; it is inconceivable why all those dependent members are φίλα. There must be, then, a πρῶτον φίλον, for the sake of which all the dependent members are φίλα; but the first itself is not φίλον for the sake of anything else. This, then, is the proper, the true, φίλον of which all those are only "reflections" (εἴδωλα). It is the τῷ ὄντι φίλον, the ἀρχή—that is, the beginning and principle—of the whole chain of dependencies.[1]

The decisive concept in this reasoning is that of the "principle" (ἀρχή): a thing can be worthy of love only in relation to an absolute, to a principle. Or, expressed universally, a thing can be valuable only through its relation to a value itself. This must be fixed beforehand. It is the condition of the possibility of there being anything of value and of its being recognized as valuable, as a good—so to speak. Nothing is ever loved, striven for, yearned after, except for the sake of some value immediately discerned (and felt). But, conversely, never is loving, striving, yearning presupposed in the case of a thing that is of value, or in the case of the value itself which is inherent in the thing. That this relationship is irreversible lies in the very constitution of acting, loving, desiring, striving. It is essentially a one-sided dependence. But what is evident in it is the fact that values possess the character of genuine essences, the character of absoluteness, of principles, and that the knowledge which we have of them can be no other than aprioristic knowledge.

(c) VALUATIONAL APRIORITY AND ABSOLUTENESS

The absoluteness of values and the apriority of the knowledge of them are two entirely different propositions and require separate proofs. In the foregoing argument the apriority of the values of goods may be accepted as proved. But their absoluteness contains an element which was not established, indeed, not even touched upon: the kind of Being peculiar to values. This is still to be dealt with. The meaning of absoluteness, so far determined, reaches only to the dependence of goods upon value as an essence, only to their relativity to it. In comparison with the goods the value-aspect under which they fall—indeed, under which they are not otherwise goods at all—is an independent one. But whether it is not on its side again dependent

[1] Plato, *Lysis*, 219c–220b.

upon something else is far from being evident. We must therefore keep the idea of absoluteness distinct from that of apriority.

This distinction brings the meaning of valuational apriority for the first time into the right light. That is to say, the proposition that values are accepted a priori holds good, even if all appraisements of value should be purely subjective and arbitrary. In that case values are "prejudgments," or, more correctly—for there is no question as to "judgments"—they are assumptions, biases of the subject. Then, of course, they would have no empirical content, not even any correlate of experience which would be able to check them. For realities as such contain no standards of values; rather are they always something measurable which offers itself to possible standards. If one leaves this point of view, one immediately falls back again into the Platonic embarrassment of an endless regression. But such a regression is stopped even by a subjective and arbitrary standard, if only it be of another origin than the actual, of which it is to be the standard of measurement.

It is necessary never to forget that in itself everything aprioristic, even the a priori of theoretical knowledge, is under the suspicion of being subjective and arbitrary, and that it is always wise to meet this suspicion by a special proof of its "objective validity." This fact is well known from the Kantian doctrine of the categories, which needed a thoroughgoing "transcendental deduction" in order to secure objectivity for the categories. A priori judgments may always be prejudices; aprioristic presentations or modes of presentation may be assumptions, fictions. In that case they are indeed presentations, but not cognitions. The Kantian proof consists therefore of the exposition of the relation of the categories to objects of another order, to a posterioristic objects.

This is possible in the domain of theory, because categories are laws which inexorably hold good for all real instances of experience. In the domain of ethics the same thing is not possible. For values, although they are most genuinely objective, are never laws of existence, they are not fulfilled in all actualities. The proof of their "objective validity" therefore is not to be found in any agreement with the real. For discrepancy between them and the actual is by no means evidence against them. The danger of subjectivity and of mere fictitiousness is therefore far greater in the case of values than in that of categories.

With the essence of values the determinant factor is this, that, as regards this danger, their apriority is itself beyond question. Even if they be fictitious, they still remain the condition for the appraisement of value, the *prius* of goods, in relation to which things first become goods. Likewise they remain the presupposition of all striving and craving, they are that through which anything is worth striving for. Thus they continue to be also the final point in the Platonic regression. In short, the whole meaning of apriority as such remains intact. They only lack objectivity, universality and necessity.

Here there is accordingly a difference between theoretical and practical insight, as regards the nature of the apriority involved. The theoretical a priori has only the significance of being an element of knowledge; and this significance falls away if objective validity is lacking to the a priori. It is then merely a mode of presentation without agreement with an object, therefore without cognitive value. A practical a priori, on the other hand, has not the significance of being an element of knowledge; it is a determinant factor in life, in the assessment of values, in taking sides, in longing for and rejecting. All these acts, and many more, remain related in exactly the same way to the a priori of values, even if these are only a prejudice of the person concerned. Indeed, we experience this sort of subjective apriority whenever as human beings we encounter human prejudice. As a fact it plays the rôle of the valuational a priori, and all those acts are determined by it. That it has no right to play this part makes no difference here; the notion is due to a misunderstanding of objective values. But wherein objective values can be recognized, how they differ from subjective prejudices, is not given herewith. This is no longer a question of apriority as such, but a question of the kind of Being of values, of their modality, as well as a question as to their cognizability. But apriority itself—that is, independence of experience—is the same here as there.

The apriority of values is even more unconditional, more absolute, than that of the theoretical categories. And it is so for this reason: that here a fixed relation to the actual is lacking, that non-agreement with the empirically given is no criterion which could be cited against the validity of valuations. The apriority of values floats, as it were, in the air. The whole responsibility for the legitimacy and objectivity of the standard of values falls upon the distinctively aprioristic vision of values —that is, in the last resort, upon the sense of value.

To make the discernment of value secure as a thing primary and objective, to establish its claim to genuine evidence, is the task with which we are now confronted. It is not solved by a proof of mere apriority. And, inasmuch as there cannot be for values a "transcendental deduction" in the Kantian sense, the question arises: What can take the place of such a deduction?

(d) WILL, END AND THE MORAL JUDGMENT OF VALUES

The proposition propounded above[1] requires some words of explanation. There it concerned only the relation of values to goods and indirectly to all acts aiming at goods. But not all acts of a practical nature aim at goods. The higher, the distinctively moral, phenomena consist of acts of another kind; they are related to values of another sort, to moral values proper. Values are not only conditions of the possibility of goods, but are also conditions of all ethical phenomena in general.

What holds good of craving must equally hold good of the higher kind of striving, of volitions proper with goals which are not to be found in goods. The object of volition, for the

[1] Subsection (c).

willing consciousness, has the form of a purpose, an end. It is inherent in the nature of an end that its content is of value, or at least is so regarded. It is impossible to adopt anything as an end, without seeking in it a thing that is valuable. The valuational material, of course, need not be clearly known as such. But the volitional and purposive consciousness must nevertheless somehow have a sense of its quality as a value, must be held by it and convinced of it. But this means that the value is already presupposed, and is a conditioning factor. Indeed, it must be an a priori condition. For an end in itself can never be "experienced." It is not an actuality. And as soon as it is actualized it ceases to be an end.

Mutatis mutandis, this holds also for cases of volition which apparently are heteronomous; to take an example, the blind obedience of a child or of a subordinate. The obedient person need not know the ends of the one who commands; he has not a sense of the values which determine the aims—for only in this case is there any pure or blind obedience. For him the content of the thing commanded is an end in itself, the will of the one who gives the order is the ultimate value. Herein as regards the value of the command there may be a valuational displacement. But, nevertheless, the obedience depends indirectly upon this value. For the obedient person believes in it, even without being able to see it. And in this belief again inheres the moral value of the obedience. In general the degree of autonomy and of personal lucidity as to the value plays no part. The authoritative command which is taken up uncritically, and the independently discerned value which determines the end, are both equally a priori—as regards the actualization which for the will has not yet come to hand.

The same holds good for the moral quality of the disposition, as well as for the consciousness of this quality, for the consciousness of good and evil, which is manifested in approval and disapproval. It makes no difference whether we think of the outward conduct—the mere way of acting, the visible behaviour of a person—or directly of the inner attitude, the distinctive moral conduct of the person which lies behind the deed. In both cases the moral judgment of value consists of an application of standards to the actual conduct, and in both cases ethical value constitutes the standard. The sensing of these values is itself therefore always presupposed; it can be only an a priori perception.

And again, the apriority has evidently this significance, that the factor which decides whether a thing is good or evil can by no means be derived from the same sphere of actual ethical conduct as the modes of behaviour upon which judgment is passed. If this factor is not self-dependent, the same circle immediately reappears as in the case of goods, a regression, which, because it remains in the same sphere, necessarily arrives finally at its own starting point. But in this way a moral judgment would be illusory.

(e) EXAMPLE AND IMITATION

Here one may object: Not every moral rejection or acceptance rests upon an independent sense of value. There is also in fact an orientation of the moral judgment which is based upon the living example of another. In practical life this plays so important a part that one might rather ask whether without it anyone could succeed at all in judging of values.

It is well known that in education nothing is so directly effective and decisive as example. But the adult also reaches out towards concrete patterns. The Christian from the beginning has seen his moral exemplar in the figure of Jesus as the Evangelists draw it. He conceives of his own morality as an "imitation" of Christ. He lives his personal life, with the concrete ideal of man before his eyes; to him Jesus is the standard of good and evil—whether the question be concerning his own resolutions or the approval or disapproval of others.

How does this fact tally with the apriority of values? Are

not the valuations of the follower of an exemplar borrowed manifestly from actuality, from experience? Are they not therefore a posteriori in their nature?

To this it must be answered that precedent to any imitation there must be a recognition of the pattern itself. If this be purely an ideal without any actuality, it stands from the first upon a level with the values themselves; like them it is aprioristic and differs from them only in its lifelike concreteness. But if an actual particular man be the pattern—we will disregard the idealization which is always taking place—the question must be asked: Why do I choose exactly this one and not some other as my model? It cannot be an accident that I choose precisely this one; that the Stoic chooses Zeno or Socrates, the Christian the figure of Jesus. The choice has a very definite ground; it is impossible for us to take any chance figure as our exemplar. We can only accept a model which has definite moral qualities, meets specific requirements—in short, which satisfies us by its content, its "material."

And what does this satisfaction mean? How do I know what qualities the exemplar must have, what demands it must meet? By what do I know that it is worthy of being a model?

This question permits of only one single answer. The satisfaction which the model gives (its very quality of being a pattern) consists in its agreement with standards which I consciously or unconsciously apply. The setting up of a person as a pattern is already a moral judgment upon the person as a value. The choice takes place from valuational points of view.

It is no objection to these points of view that they do not become clear to me until I see them realized (or only intended) in some man. There are many values which cannot be brought to consciousness except in such concrete form (realized or really intended). Nevertheless, the values themselves are not abstracted from the model, but, conversely, they are presupposed in my consciousness of what a model ought to be.

The moral valuation therefore does not rest upon the actuality of the model, but the choice of the model rests upon the moral judgment as to values. The intuitive, emotionally toned knowledge of what a model ought to be is as such a function of the primary sense of values. Here also the values are the *prius*, the conditioning factor. The consciousness of what is worthy of imitation is nothing except a form of the aprioristic consciousness of value.

As a test that such is the situation as regards models, the fact may be cited that there are also negative examples. It is a difficult question to decide, which is the stronger stimulus for the awakening of the moral consciousness: a good or an evil (a deterrent) example. In any case it is a fact that generally a bad example can work for good. That it can also tempt one to evil does not prejudice the fact. It depends on whether anyone has sympathy with that value which in the negative example is violated. If he has not, if on that account a lower value, which is perhaps fulfilled in the example, rules him the more powerfully, then the conduct of the other will "impress" him, will satisfy him, and the negative example will become for him a positive one.

But if his sense of value shows him what the other's conduct sins against, this obscurely felt value will be lifted up into consciousness through the violation of it. The act of indignation, the up-rushing sentiment against the reprehensible, exposes the concrete value to view, forces it into the light of knowledge, and with it at the same time its specific quality. Nothing so strongly rouses the sense of justice as the occurrence of some injustice; nothing excites the love of humanity, like a brutal egoism.

But in every case the sense of value is itself the presupposition. It can never be engendered by a bad example, but it can always be awakened, if it was already there. An attitude of aversion is actually a choice made from the standpoint of value. This therefore is the aprioristic condition which makes it possible for a bad example to have a good effect.

(f) ETHICAL IDEALIZATION AND VALUATIONAL CONSCIOUSNESS

And, finally, the fact is not to be forgotten—thus far we have not considered it—that a positive example is never something taken wholly from actual experience. We project the pattern upon a real person, or we idealize the person, and thus he becomes our exemplar.

Naturally in this case there is no consciousness of the boundary between the actual and the ideal. One adorns the actual person with qualities which he does not possess, one averts one's gaze from his deficiencies and sees him in a fictitious glory of perfection. The actual may be so overgrown with ideals projected upon it that a critical eye can scarcely recognize it underneath them. But discrepancies between reality and the ideal are of no importance. So far as imitation is concerned, all that counts is the ideal picture. How far the real person, in whom one sees the ideal, corresponds to it, is a matter of indifference.

But exactly this indifference to the actual as regards the content and power of the ideal, is the strongest proof of the apriority of the evaluating sense, in the phenomenon of "exemplars." Values here show themselves to be not only something which selects but also something which is essentially a creative *prius*. The values mould, determine, produce the pattern; they are that factor in its ideality which lives and moves, just as they are also the secret of the pattern's power to guide man.

The dependence which is here disclosed might be described as the universal law concerning the essence of the exemplar and concerning ethical idealization in general. It asserts that the dependence of the ideal upon the value which is primarily discerned and felt is irreversible, and indeed is independent of the more or less empirical character of the occasion which incites to idealization. This irreversibility is quite in accord with the fact that one becomes conscious of values in the opposite direction. To the naïve mind the objectivity of the pattern precedes the distinct consciousness of the value, just as the objectivity of goods precedes the distinct consciousness of the values adhering to the things. The order of knowing is the reverse of the order of being. But the order of being, as such, never reverses.

. This fundamental law is of the greatest importance in the domain of ethical phenomena. The living values of all moral systems find their most effective, most satisfactory embodiment in concrete ideals, whether these be only free creations of the phantasy or be borrowed from living examples. Every kind of reverence for heroes is concrete living morality. It is the historic form of the current consciousness of value. And indeed it is not, as it were, a falsified consciousness, but is on the contrary the purest and most genuine which man possesses. Much rather do the conceptual understandings, which historically are always secondary, contain the falsification and accretions.— Into them reflection has entered as a distorting factor. From this fact the investigation of values must draw the natural inferences.

(g) ACCOUNTABILITY, RESPONSIBILITY, AND THE CONSCIOUSNESS OF GUILT

The deeper one forces one's way into the heart of ethical phenomena, so much the more evident become the apriority and the all-dominating character of values as essences. Determination of will, purpose and the setting up of ends, moral approval and disapproval, do not constitute the innermost circle. The moral consciousness does not confine itself to the weighing of actions and dispositions; it also imputes the discerned moral qualities to the person. It not only judges, it also condemns. It metes out guilt and responsibility to the doer, and this without discrimination as to whether it be oneself or another person. It holds that the doer himself is to be judged by the deed, the bearer of a disposition to be marked by its value or anti-value. The moral consciousness turns, incorruptible and relentless, against one's own ego; it permits the ego in its sense of guilt to renounce itself, to consume itself in remorse and despair. Or it leads the ego to conversion, to a change of heart, and a moral renewal of its own nature.

In these phenomena the relation of value and reality is deepened. The consciousness of one's own worthlessness encounters the consciousness of one's own reality. The sense of value here proves its autonomy in one's own selfhood. In the most sensitive point of personal self-consciousness it proves to a certain degree its own legitimacy as a power, against which the natural interest of the ego, self-preservation, self-assertion, self-affirmation, cannot advance. The real individual person with his own acts, not only real but capable of being experienced as real—the empirical person—sees himself set over against an Idea of personality, which has the power to condemn him. The ego finds itself split into an empirical and a moral, an aprioristic, ego. And the empirical bows down before the aprioristic, acknowledges its right to rule and bears the guilt which the other imputes, as an oppressive consciousness. The empirical ego takes upon itself the responsibility which the other lays upon it, and whatever in itself does not agree with the other it charges against itself as a failure.

If the apriority of values is anywhere perceptible, it is so here. For the idea of the moral self is built up out of purely valuational materials and consists of these. The moral man sees this his morally super-empirical essence, his inner determination, his Idea, to be his own proper Self. In accordance with its intentions he tries to live, that is, to form his empirical being. Upon it rests the moral consciousness of himself, of his own value, justified and felt to be justified, his self-respect as a man. And with the consciousness of the failure of his ideal essence, his self-respect forsakes him. The inner standard of that sense of value, which accompanies all his steps in life, indeed all his most secret impulses, constitutes his essence as a moral personality. Moral personality therefore does not exist, if there be no pure a priori of values.

Here we encounter the same irreversible relation of dependence: the person does not make the values, but the values make the person. For example, the autonomy of the person presupposes the values; he is a function of them—although certainly not of them alone. Hence it is a radical misunderstanding when one conceives of values as a function of the moral consciousness. That conception leads to the regression which moves eternally in a circle.

(h) CONSCIENCE AND THE ETHICAL A PRIORI

Anyone who has not yet made himself familiar with the thought of valuational apriorism inevitably raises against this kind of argument the objection that a previous consciousness of value is needed, in order to feel responsibility and have the sense of guilt. Does not everyone carry within himself a factor which points out the way, that is, "conscience"? Conscience is the inner "voice," which declares what is good and bad in one's own conduct, which warns, challenges or guides. Conscience in fact plays the part assigned to values; in it is to be found the moral essence. In addition to it there is no need of a valuational a priori.

This objection impressively reveals the character of the phenomenon of conscience. But it is no objection. Self-accusation, responsibility, and the consciousness of guilt constitute the broad phenomenon of conscience. We may, therefore, say that the whole of the above reasoning starts with the phenomenon of conscience and is wholly based upon its actual existence. But from this it does not follow that the a priori of values is superfluous. Admittedly, there is no aprioristic consciousness of them alongside of conscience, at least not in relation to one's own self. But, so much the more there is such a thing in conscience itself; that which we call conscience is at bottom just this primal consciousness of value, which is found in the feeling of every person.

What else, in fact, can we mean by "conscience"? Everyone understands by it an inner court of disapproval (and approval), a kind of intimation as to good and evil, a "voice" which speaks out of the depths of one's own being, uninvited, unexpected, mysterious—and it speaks authoritatively and convincingly—although in opposition to one's own natural self-assertion. Herein lies the admission that this is an a priori "voice." One may, of course, say that one "experiences" inwardly the judicial decree of conscience; and just because one does not utter it spontaneously but receives it uttered, the word experience is not merely metaphorical. Nevertheless, this experience has nothing to do with empiricism. On the contrary, all aprioristic contents, even the theoretical, are "experienced" in the same way—namely, they are found to be present, are discovered, are beheld; and it is not repugnant to sense to speak in this connection of "aprioristic experience." But where the a priori is an emotional one, where it is accessible to knowledge only indirectly, yet is given primarily to feeling, there this inner experience possesses the character of an invasion, of a surprisal—just as feelings in general overtake a man from within.

The well-known way in which "conscience" expresses itself fits most exactly the emotional apriority of the valuational consciousness, the obscure, half-conscious sense of value, which speaks unsummoned and does not reveal its inner content. The so-called "voice of conscience" is a basic form of the primal consciousness of value; it is perhaps the most elemental way in which the sense of value gains currency among men. And the mysteriousness which attaches to this "voice," which pious minds in all ages have interpreted as the working of a higher power, as the Voice of God in man, fits only too closely the concept of the emotional a priori. For it does not speak when one calls to it or inquiringly searches for it. It speaks only when not summoned, according to a law of its own nature, when one is not expecting it. Evidently it is a self-dependent and self-active power in man which is set apart from man's will. It really is the influence of a "higher" power, a voice from another world—from the ideal world of values.

However obscured the relation may be between this world of values and the real world of man's emotional life, it is indisputable that here we touch the point of contact between them. Conscience is the revelation of moral values in actual consciousness, their entrenchment within the reality of human life. It is a primitive form of the sense of value.

But this is possible, only provided that values themselves are an existent *prius*. They are, then, simply the "condition of the possibility" of conscience.

(i) THE ANCIENT CONCEPT OF VIRTUE AS A CONCRETE CONCEPT OF VALUE

The ethics of the Greeks culminates in the doctrine of virtue. According to Aristotle, virtue is the quality peculiar to demeanour (*habitus*, ἕξις). In the Nichomachean Ethics, as in the fragment of the later treatise, there is an elaborated phenomenology of right conduct which attempts by description to fix the content—that is, the "material"—of each virtue. We moderns cannot in every particular follow this richly variegated doctrine of virtue; our sense of value has become different, and for us other values have come into the foreground. But so much the less can there be any doubt that this investigation of the ancients into the essence of virtue, or rather of the separate virtues, is fundamentally a genuine search for values—it is a phenomenology of the moral materials in all their diversity.

If one examines the method of the ancients in close detail, one finds that under the various forms of procedure—even when it is apparently empirical—there is everywhere a kernel of purely aprioristic research. The well-known difference between the Platonic and the Aristotelian procedure, between the pure intuition of the "idea of the good," and the careful detailed work in the fixing of the ἀνθρώπινον ἀγαθόν, cannot constitute a radical contrast. Even Aristotle does not draw the rich contents of his concept of virtue from the empirical, but from the utterances of the moral judgment of values, from praise and blame, from respect and contempt, from love and hate;[1] and his final views are purely idealistic: the measure (the "mean"), energy, the καλόν, the ὡς δεῖ.

The apriorism of virtue is of course expressed more unequivocally in Plato, although it is far less differentiated in its varieties. He says virtues are "Ideas." From the Idea of justice he projects his "State." According to the ideas of wisdom, bravery and moderation, human conduct is distinguished as worthy and unworthy. The idea of man is entirely determined by the ideas of these "virtues"; it is an aprioristic ideal set over against the actual.

This apriorism of virtue is not lost even in Stoicism, despite all its one-sidedness and poverty of content. To "follow nature" never means, not even with the most materialistic minds of the school, to take one's norm from actual experience. It is the inner pursuit of the final essence, wherein nature is identified with the absolute logos. "Nature" is only an expression for the totality of eternal laws not made by man.

It is thus that Plato, Aristotle and the Stoics have remained a model for all later ethics. Even Christian ethics, with all the novelty of its contents, shares fundamentally in their apriorism. In Augustine it shows a more Platonic, in the Scholastics a more Aristotelian, aspect. These are slight differences, which leave the principle untouched. That moral claims are here understood to be the will of God does not make any real difference. The will of God is only the vehicle of the values, just as "nature" is with the Stoics. In the later pantheism both conceptions have been united almost without any friction.

Stated in general terms: for ethics it is a matter of indifference what metaphysical significance is given to the realm of values, what religious or philosophical view is taken as a background, however much the emphasis may be laid by individual thinkers upon the cosmic view. For ethics the only concern is the apriority of the values themselves.

[1] Cf. below, Volume II, Chapter XXIX (d).

This historical perspective is a most instructive witness for the problem of values as essences. We of to-day, with our still very modest beginnings of investigation into concrete values, see ourselves falsely placed in relation to the most recent past of philosophy, to Kant and the Kantian schools of the nineteenth century. For it was Kant who set up the unity of the moral law instead of the concrete variety of the virtues, the formal principle in place of the fulness of content, and subjective legislation in the position held by the objective essence of moral ideas. On account of this contrast, the present-day investigation of values finds very little solid ground under its feet.

Such insecurity is easy to understand; but it is a mistake. The historical heritage is the widest and securest conceivable. It embraces within a definite scheme the entire diversity of the more ancient ethical doctrines. One naturally misunderstands the situation if one considers only the meagre instances in which a definitely outlined concept of values appears (as in the ἀξία of the Stoics), which has not even the necessary breadth of generality. Here the important matter is not the definitely formulated concept but the essential fact. And ever since the Platonic concept of the autonomous self-existent "idea" of virtue, the essential issue remains immovably fixed.

Investigation with clear methodical consciousness of value-essences as such may be immature, but so much the older and worthier of respect is the general investigation of values which is bound to no philosophically formulated concept. For from the ancient concept of virtue and its elaborations in modern times one may learn this: almost all philosophical ethics, although standing only half-way towards the solution of its problems, yet deserving the name of ethical research, has been fundamentally a concrete ethics of values. Kant, on the contrary, and his followers are the exception in the historical succession. They constitute a chasm which separates us from the great traditions of antiquity and of the Middle Ages.

With the concept of concrete aprioristic value-essence, we

consciously take up the earlier traditions again : the old objective apriorism of the ethical "idea" and the old multiplicity of their contents, the "virtues."[1]

[1] How much our age owes the possibility of such a return to Scheler's ethics I need not set forth, after what I have said above. But the fact that his arguments could not have succeeded, except in criticism of the Kantian propositions, must have its explanation in the historical perspective which I have outlined.

CHAPTER XV

THE RELATIVITY AND ABSOLUTENESS OF VALUES

(a) SUBJECTIVITY AND RELATIVITY

THAT things and their relations can be goods or evils; that striving can be directed towards them; that there are volitional ends which themselves are ideal and yet are really determinant for actions; that there is such a thing as approval and disapproval of human conduct; that a conscience speaks directively in the depth of consciousness, accusing, imputing guilt, imposing responsibility—all this is conceivable only on the presupposition that values, as a determining *prius*, control the attitude which man takes up towards life.

In the older ethics the doctrine of goods and virtues was tacitly based upon this thought. One cannot even say that the thought was "unconscious," but only that it was without a critical consciousness of what this *prius* was. The concept of value was lacking.

But it is also lacking in recent ethics. For neither the dependence of the higher upon the lower values nor the apriority which showed itself along the whole series of ethical problems as yet fixes the specific quality of values, as compared with other essences. This definition is still to be sought for.

The suspicion which is cast upon values is that of subjectivity. Is it not true that "goods" have value only for the man who values them, that the moral quality of deeds, dispositions and persons exists only for persons? Do not even guilt and responsibility exist only in idea? If the value of everything that is appraised exists only in human consciousness the inference is natural, that it exists only "for" human consciousness. Values then lack objectivity. If they are relative to the one who discerns them, their mode of being is also relative, and they must be looked upon as a function of the act of valuing. Thus, then, the door is opened to Nietzsche's relativism.

This view is scarcely consistent with the whole series of the phenomena which we have considered. These themselves have an existential character. They by no means subsist only for the one who discerns them, but in themselves. We come upon them and can in no way dispose of them at will; they are not relative to a consciousness of phenomena, but subsist independently of it, and by the philosophical consciousness itself are deemed to be independent of it.

Thus relatedness to a personal subject has an entirely different significance here. The relatedness of goods to man is not at all a matter of thinking; it is not in man's power, so far as anything is for him a good or an evil, to change matters. It is only in his power within certain limits to strive for that which for him "is" a good and to avoid that which for him "is" an evil. His judgment of goods and evils of course varies greatly. Not everything which "is" good or evil for everyone is felt by everyone to be good or evil. But that evidently is only a matter as to the acuteness or dullness of the sense of values. It does not touch the fact that one thing "is good for him" and that another "is bad for him."

(b) The Relativity of Goods to the Subject and the Relational Structure of Concrete Values

The relatedness to a personal subject, which we are now discussing, is not what one means by the relativity of values. It does not bar out the objective character of values but evidently implies it. A person cannot change the fact that a thing is good for him. The fact that it is so is not relative to his estimate of values nor to him as an appraising subject, but to him as a person. Conversely, an estimate of values is relative to the valuableness of the goods for the subject. In this "for," the subject does not play the part of a determiner or giver of values;

his rôle is that of a point of reference in the relation appertaining to the valuational contents. It is the same "for" which is interwoven with so many categorical structures. In the fact that geometrical laws hold good only "for" spatial figures, mechanical laws only "for" real bodies, physiological laws only "for" organisms—in this fact no one sees any relativity as regards the categorical import of these laws. Yet there is just as much reason here for speaking of the relativity of these laws and of their categories to entities of a definite kind. In the same way psychological laws are also relative to psychic beings; but this does not mean that they exist only in the consciousness of these beings, or that they can be made by consciousness or can be abolished by the beings themselves. But, rather, they are laws to which the psychic beings for whom they hold good are unconditionally subjected.

In the same way also the consciousness of goods and evils —so far as it exists—is subject unconditionally to the laws of values and anti-values. A person cannot at will pronounce anything to be of value for anyone which "is" not of value for him. He can of course do that erroneously, but the error avenges itself upon him and undeceives him; or it brings about his ruin. In short, the relatedness of these values to a human subject is not relativity to the subject's opinion of them or to his appraisement of them, but to the subject's existence, including his entire categorial constitution. In this his constitution is the reason why the nature of things and of their relations "is" not a matter of indifference for the subject himself, but has value or anti-value. Yet the appraisement and the opinion are functions of the values and disvalues which are relative to the existent subject and are inherent in things and their relations.

But this means that the relation of goods to a personal subject —for example, their agreeableness—is not at all a relativity of their value as such, but is a relation which is contained in the valuational material and exists before and independently of any consciousness of it, just as the things themselves actually exist to which the value adheres. Relational structure of contents is not relativity as regards values—just as the relational structure of the categories (and they all have some such structure) does not signify their relativity. The difference between relationality and relativity, which is so often effaced, is as essential for a clear understanding in ethics as it is in theoretical philosophy. The opposite of relationality is the substratum, that of relativity is the absolute. There are relative substrata and there are absolute relations. The relation of the value of goods to the subject is an absolute relation which is comprised in the content of their values. The thing and the subject are here objectively drawn into the structure of the valuational materials, as, so to speak, cause and effect are included in the causal nexus. In both cases the binding relation is purely objective, and, as regards any understanding of it, is absolute. Their complete differentiation in this and that particular constitutes no difference. But in both cases the consciousness of the relation is equally relative to the existing relation. And this connection is as little reversible in the one case as in the other.

The existence of the values of goods is consequently not in the least affected by the relation of the goods to the subject. As regards the subject and his sense of value it bears the mark of self-existence. Its absoluteness includes the self-existence of its relevancy. To state the point formally: the existence of the goods for me depends upon the independent existence of the values of the goods. It is included in the nature of the goods.

From all this one may easily anticipate what a serious matter the self-existence of values is. The exact significance of this self-existence must be the next important question for us to consider. But first we must widen the basis of our investigation. For the values of goods are not moral values. But the relational phenomena of these latter, although objective, are of another kind.

(c) The Absoluteness of Moral Values and the Relativity of the Dependent Values of Goods

The higher values, those which in the narrower sense are moral, are exclusively personal and actional values. They adhere, not to things or their relations, but to deeds, to the will, purpose and disposition. Approval and disapproval refer to them only. They alone speak in conscience, in the sense of responsibility, in the consciousness of guilt. In reference to them also it is asked: In what sense can their absoluteness be doubted, notwithstanding their demonstrated apriority? Is there with them also a relativity to the subject which puts their independence in question?

That sort of relativity which existed objectively in the value of goods is here excluded. On the face of it, moral value in the conduct of a person—at least as such—does not exist "for" a subject, whether for one's self or for another. It adheres simply to the person, or to the act of the person, as a quality. Uprightness, innocence, fidelity, trustfulness, energy, self-sacrifice, carry their moral value exclusively in themselves. The moral worth of a person does not consist in its being valuable "for" another person (that is, in its being goods), but solely in its having the quality in question. Virtues have a purer self-existence than the values of goods. In their material there is no essential or necessary "existence for me" which would be included as an objective relation in the structure of its self-existence. Moral values have another kind of autonomy, evidently more absolute. And on this account we might well speak of an "autocracy of virtue," inherent in its very nature; such autocracy being a concept which was of course understood in quite another sense by its formulators, the Stoics.

This circumstance does not exclude relation to a subject in another way. And about this also it is important to be clear, in order to gauge rightly the difference as compared with the value of goods, but above all in order to be convinced that here valuational relativism is still less involved than there.

The type of relatedness with which we are concerned is threefold in direction.

First, every moral value is also a goods-value indirectly, and as such is relative to a subject—that is, it actually exists "for" other persons. The fidelity of one person is a good thing for another towards whom it is practised; trust is a good thing for him to whom it is shown; energy and self-sacrifice for him for whom they are offered. To the beloved he who loves, to the friend a friend, is a good.

But not in being a precious thing to another lies the moral worth of the person who manifests love and friendship, exercises energy, makes sacrifice and keeps faith. It inheres in him himself, even when he brings no benefit to another, even when it is not a "good" "for" anyone; it subsists exclusively as a quality of his own personality, of his own conduct as such. It is fundamentally a different value from that which accompanies it when it is good for another. And the appraisement of it, which the moral judgment makes, is independent of the value set upon the benefit which it confers upon another person.

The relatedness to another person, therefore, is in this case not only not a valuational relativity, but is also not even an inner relation belonging to the objective structure of the concrete value. For it does not concern the ethical quality of the conduct or of the person, but only the accompanying goods-value. Yet not upon this latter but only upon the former is moral judgment passed.

On this point the ancient ethics worked confusion by its characteristic classification of "virtues" under "goods." In the proposition that virtue is the "highest good" (chiefly suggested by the concept of happiness), the superlative degree of the word "highest" involves a recognition of the superiority of virtue as a value. But the superiority is still only one of degree. Virtue appears as a good among goods. Nothing could have so hindered the ethics of the ancients in its free development as this doctrine of the "highest good," which since

Aristotle has for ever been coming up again. But the fact that this doctrine was possible, and that it could hold its own so persistently, has its explanation in the relation which we have been setting forth. The moral values of disposition (of the ἕξις) have also incidentally the character of goods. If we do not distinguish these incidental values from the primary ones of the disposition itself, we naturally cannot escape the error of converting virtues into goods, although, like the ancients, we think chiefly of goods for one's own personality and not for others. For a value, as goods, attaches to moral worth even relatively to oneself.

In characteristic fashion this confusion of concepts by no means led the ancients to a complete misunderstanding of moral values. The special problem concerning these breaks through the inadequate set of concepts and justifies itself. The values of ἕξις assert themselves. But this assertion gives the lie to their subsumption under goods. The incongruity persists.

(d) THE MATERIAL RELATION OF MORAL VALUES TO PERSONS AS OBJECTS

In this matter the second kind of relatedness is connected most intimately with the personal subject and especially with the other subject as a person.

Every moral value is a value of disposition, but all disposition is towards someone. It has a real object, and this is always a person or a community of persons. It has such an object even when the act is purely inward, merely intended, merely a disposition without action, indeed without any utterance. The object is always still a person. We deal with persons, not with things; we are disposed towards persons, not towards things.

Here therefore the relation is one which inheres in the nature of moral conduct in general, of that conduct about the valuational quality of which moral judgments are concerned. This kind of relation to a subject, namely to the other person, is involved in the structure of the ethical contents itself—in distinction from that of the goods-value which accompanies it. The latter value is not the same as that of the moral action.

Nevertheless, there is a relation of dependence between the two kinds of relationality. The outer relation of the goods for the other person rests upon the inner relation of the direction of the act towards him, without the two relations on that account coinciding or the valuational characteristics commingling. For the other person the goods-value of fidelity consists of security, of the ability to entrust himself to the faithful one; but the moral value of the trusted person consists of a spiritual strength, a steadfastness of disposition, a trustworthiness. However correlated the two values may be, they are as values radically different and they never coincide. Likewise is it with the two kinds of relationship. The other person's ability to put himself in the hands of the trusted man concerns the latter's conduct towards him; but the fidelity is an act of the one who is trusted, an act towards the other. And evidently the conduct of the other is conditioned by it. But the point is that the relation of the goods for the other rests upon the inner relation to him which constitutes the moral conduct of the loyal one.

The inner, intentional relatedness conditions the outer relationality of the goods-value which is dependent upon it. But this relationship no more allows the two relations to coincide than the two kinds of value.

(e) THE MATERIAL RELATION OF MORAL VALUES TO THE PERSON AS A SUBJECT

Finally, a third and still more fundamental relation to the subject as a person consists of the connection between a value and the bearer of it.

Values of each specific type are always essentially attached to a definite order of carrier. For instance, one kind, to things; another (that of goods in general), to real substrata (it does not matter whether these be things, real relations or the real conduct of persons, etc.); a third, to living organisms; a fourth kind (moral values), to personal subjects.

Only a being who can will, act, set up ends and pursue them, who can foster dispositions and feel values, is capable of moral conduct, either of a positive or negative kind. Such a being is a moral subject, a person. The moral values or their opposites attach to him, but always to his personality as a whole, in the way that they never attach to merely single acts. The moral person always stands, as it were, behind each of his acts, and is invested with their valuational qualities—however various, indeed however contradictory, these may be in one and the same person. We rightly say this act was noble-minded, that sentiment mean and unworthy. But this never leaves the person himself untouched. He himself is at the same time, together with his acts, noble-minded or mean. All moral imputations attach to the person, he bears guilt and responsibility; judgments of approval and disapproval made by others, as well as condemnation through his own conscience, apply to him as a person. In this way moral values are related to the person as a carrier of values.

This, however, does not mean valuational relativity. It does not imply that the value of a noble-minded disposition and the anti-value of a mean one are dependent upon whether anybody thinks such dispositions really exist. On the contrary, an actual noble-minded disposition is of value, because such disposition is universally a moral value. The relation to the person as a carrier inheres therefore in the nature of the material; the quality in which the matter of the value subsists can be only a quality of acts performed by a personal entity and thereby indirectly to persons as such. Here the relation also is purely material. The substance of the value includes the reference to the person. It can come into evidence only in a person because it has the essential character of an attribute of a person (as its substance), or, in the language of formal logic, because it is a predicate of the person (as its subject). This relationality is a part of the inner relational structure of moral values. The predicate throughout its scope is drawn into this relational structure. But in itself it is absolute.

(f) THE INTERPENETRATION OF RELATIONS AND THE UNDERLYING ABSOLUTENESS OF MORAL VALUES

If, now, we take together the last two types of relation (*d* and *e*), we obtain the basic relational structure of the valuational content.

These materials are related to personal entities in two ways: first, to a person as the subject of moral conduct or action, and thereby at the same time as the bearer of moral value; and, secondly, to a person as the object of the conduct, as the point to which it is directed. The personal entity is always represented twice in the structure of conduct. Moral acts— whether disposition, will or deed—are in their essence transcendent acts: but they are transcendent in another way than cognitive acts. In the first place, they are directed by the subject to the object; and, according to what they intend concerning the object, they are valuable, or the contrary, while their moral worth or unworthiness does not coincide with the worth or worthlessness of what is intended. And, secondly, they always have as their object another person, they pass from person to person. In this lies the metaphysical reason for the fact that universally in these acts qualities of a peculiar kind—moral values—make their appearance. For every one of these acts affects just such a moral subject as the one from which it issues. The same is true when the act is directed to oneself; and this whether actual or merely intentional. In that case one is oneself twice represented in the same act—as subject and as object of the act. And its relation, including its transcendent bearing, exists here as well as in an act towards another person. The fact that a person as an object is affected, that he somehow is at stake, constitutes the ethical importance of the act. And this is reflected in the responsibility of the person who is the subject, as in the qualities which give their peculiar impress to the subject and his acts.

Upon this bipolar structure of deeds, in which the two poles are persons, depends the double relationality of the values to the personal entity as such—to a subject as subject, and to a subject as object, of the acts. But with this the relation is exhausted. It has resolved itself, without a remainder, into the inner relational structure peculiar to the contents itself, which is universally embedded in the essence of personal conduct. This structure is a general one, in which the manifoldness of acts and of their values has unlimited scope.

Herewith the nature of the twofold relation is completely severed from the nature of the values themselves. The ethical dimension of value and anti-value, together with its qualitative differentiation, finds scope only within this general relational structure. But this means that the values themselves are not at all affected by this relation. They are absolute. The structure is nothing but the presupposition of their manifestation; it is their categorial (not their axiological) *conditio sine quâ non*; only when personal entities stand in actional relation to one another can there be any moral value or its opposite. But the values themselves are neither contained in the relation nor, as it were, derivable from it. They come to it from another source—as standards, as something new.

CHAPTER XVI

THE IDEAL SELF-EXISTENCE OF VALUES

(a) THE SELF-EXISTENCE OF VALUES FOR KNOWLEDGE

THE proposition that values are essences has had light thrown upon it from two sides. First, values are a conditioning *prius* of all phenomena of the moral life, in connection with which the apriority of the valuational consciousness constitutes only one partial phenomenon. And, in the second place, they are absolute, as regards the subject who appraises them. It has been shown that all "relativity to the subject" affects only the structure of the content. But the value of the content is not identical with its structure.

The content and the valuational character do not coincide. The "material" is only the concrete structure which has the value. The moral worth of trust is not the trust itself. The latter is only the material—a specific relation between person and person, which can be quite generally described. But the value of trust is not this relation, and indeed is not only not an actual relation between particular persons, but is also not the idea of such a relation in general. The "material" is here simply the idea of trust. It is, taken by itself, purely an ontological structure, not axiological; it is the ideal or essential structure of a specially formed relationship. Its proper valuableness is something altogether different, not capable of being derived from anything else, but entirely capable of being sensed in its own peculiarity and of being exhibited in the valuational feeling. The valuableness is different from any given structure and from every relation, although it inheres in them; it is an *ens sui generis*, an essence of another sort. It is a something which indeed varies with the diversity of the material—for not only is the material essence of trust, for example, different from that of fidelity, but the value of trust is also different from the value of fidelity. And, nevertheless, valuableness is a something which through all differentiations always remains different from the material; a something which builds above it, camps over it, lends to it a glimmer of meaning, a significance of a higher order, an import which for ever remains transcendent to the existential reality; a something which remains on the further side of reality, incomparable, and which always draws it into another sphere of cohesions, into the intelligible order of values.

In a separate analysis of values we shall have occasion later to treat of this order as a specifically axiological and qualitative grade of high rank—in contrast to the structural order of materials. The perspective given here may be accepted as only an anticipation. Its essence depends upon the absoluteness of values, which rightly perdures above every relation of the material.

But the meaning of the "essentiality" of value is not herewith exhausted. Whatever in its mode of being is not relative to a subject, whatever confronts a thinking subject as independent and immovable, whatever sets up before him a self-subsistent regularity and energy of its own which the subject can grasp or miss but cannot get rid of, that has for him the character of self-existence.

Values have self-existence. This proposition is simply the positive formulation of what was given above in our criticism of Kantian subjectivism. Values subsist independently of the consciousness of them. Consciousness can grasp or miss them, but cannot make them or spontaneously decree them. This does not hold true of the material. By his co-operation a subject can very well—within certain limits—produce the material (for example, he can set up a relation of confidence): but he cannot thereby prevent such a material from being of value— or the contrary. Such a material simply "is" so, without any co-operation, and even if it is believed not to be so. Hence, concerning the characteristics which values have, the proposition holds good that they have self-existence.

To values, then, everything applies which, as regards knowledge, is true universally of whatever is self-existent. They are objects of possible valuational discernment, but they do not first come into being in the discerning of them, they are not views—just as little as they are thoughts or presentations. This it is which gives gnoseological weight to the thought of valuational vision and feeling. Knowledge of values is genuine knowledge of Being. In this respect it stands absolutely on a level with every kind of theoretical knowledge. Its object is for the subject just as independent a reality as spatial relations are for geometrical knowledge or things are for knowledge concerning things. The grasping of them, however different it may be in other particulars, is just as much an act which goes out to something beyond itself as every other cognitive act,[1] and the whole difficulty which besets the epistemological problem of transcendence reappears in regard to the knowledge of values. In this "beholding" of them the subject is purely receptive; he surrenders himself to them. He sees himself determined by the object, the self-existent value; but he himself, on his side, determines nothing. The value abides as unaffected by his beholding as does any object of knowledge by the fact that it is known. Spontaneity in ethical conduct, on the contrary, sets in upon the basis of a primary beholding of values. But it is not spontaneity as regards value, but as regards other persons.

Thus far the concept of the self-existence of values is still merely gnoseological. It has no bearing upon their distinctive mode of existence. But ethics is not concerned with the knowledge of values alone, but also with the values themselves. Their mode of existence is therefore still further to be determined.

(b) Ethical Reality and the Ethical Ideal Sphere

Theoretical philosophy knows two essentially different kinds

[1] Cf. *Metaphysik der Erkenntnis*, Chapters LXI and LXXII.

of self-existence: one real and one ideal. The former belongs to all things and events, to everything that is "actual," to whatever has existence; the latter to the structure of pure mathematics and logic, and, over and above these, to the essences of every kind which persist throughout the changes of individual existence and, when distinguished from this, permit of being discerned a priori. Between the two subsists an essential relationship which is profoundly characteristic of the whole realm of Being and of the knowledge of Being: the structure of ideal self-existence reappears in that of the real —not indeed without a remainder and not exhaustive of the latter, but in so far that the aprioristic knowledge of ideal Being at the same time constitutes an inner foundation for all knowledge of the real. So far as it reaches, aprioristic knowledge of reality rests upon this partial agreement of the ideal and real structure of Being.

In the domain of practice, real self-existence has only "ethical reality": it embraces only whatever is real moral conduct, real action, real disposition, real resolution and purpose: but, likewise, whatever is real valuational judgment, consciousness of guilt, feeling of responsibility. Yet in a wider sense everything that is ethically relevant has a place here: the whole realm of goods, from valuable things up to spiritual goods and to the dependent goods of virtue. Real self-existence embraces therefore everything that presupposes an existence of values; but this latter does not itself belong to it.

Values have no self-existence that is real. As principles of action they may participate in determining reality, they may even to a great degree be themselves "actualized"—but for this very reason their essence, their mode of Being, remains merely an ideal mode. As for the distinctive valuational quality of anything, for example, of a specific material, let us say sincerity or love, it makes no kind of difference whether there be persons in whose real conduct it is embodied or not. Indeed the actualization of the material is itself a value; but it is another, a derived one which has its root in the value of the given material. These values as such, in comparison with the actual, always have the character of an "Idea," which indeed, when the actual corresponds with it, lends to this the character of a value, but which with its ideal nature still remains on the other side of actualization. Strictly taken, values themselves are not at all "actualized," but only the materials, to which, whether ideal or real, the value belongs.

The mode of Being peculiar to values is evidently that of an ideal self-existence. The values are originally patterns of an ethical ideal sphere, of a realm with its own structures, its own laws and order. This sphere is connected organically with the theoretical ideal sphere, the logical and the mathematical, as well as with that of pure essences in general. It is a continuation of them. However different their ideal structures may be from values, they share with them the modal character of ideal self-existence.

It is clear that the ideal sphere, although homogeneous in mode of existence, is entirely heterogeneous in content. At the same time it overlies the whole sphere of real Being, not only that of ontological reality, but also that of ethical reality. And it is articulated in accordance with the real sphere. Indeed, it is also easy to see that the ontological ideal and the ethical ideal spheres are not isolated members, but that a vast æsthetical ideal sphere is contiguous, and that there are still further members which introduce still further variations of content. Yet in mode of existence the sphere remains a unity. It is also a unity for knowledge. For its patterns are known in all the departments always and purely a priori—without distinction as to whether the acts, which are vehicles of this knowledge, bear the stamp of intellect or emotion. In this connection, sense of value and logical reasoning stand on the same level. Idealistic knowledge of Being permits of only one mode of knowing, the aprioristic.

(c) IDEAL SELF-EXISTENCE IN GENERAL

As regards the Being of values, the parallel with logical and mathematical objects is extraordinarily instructive. For the self-existence of values, although only of an ideal nature, is in many ways exposed to doubt. One may see grounds for suspicion even in its ideality; and owing to this one proceeds to attack the self-existence of the theoretical ideal forms. Unsophisticated thought is only too prone to look upon real actuality alone as self-existence, but to exclude the ideal from it.

In this presupposition two prejudices are involved.

In the first place actuality and Being are falsely identified —although the circle of the "actual" need not be limited to things. Everything that is not actual then belongs without further ado to Not-Being. And, unless one understands this in the Platonic sense as Being of another kind, one can understand it only to mean absolute nothingness.

Secondly, however, ideality is mistaken for subjectivity— a confusion for which the double meaning of the term "idea" is to blame. When "idea" is taken as the equivalent of "presentation," ideality becomes the mode of Being of whatever subsists only in and for the presentation of a subject; but beyond that it is meaningless. This meaning of "idea" has also degraded the philosophical term "idealism" into subjectivism. With this meaning an ideal sphere can naturally have no self-existence. Under the pressure of this prejudice, logic in the nineteenth century became subjectivistic and finally almost passed over into the psychology of thinking.

That the true meaning of logic and especially mathematics is different from this, that they treat of a system of laws, dependencies and structures which indeed on their side control thinking, but themselves can neither be forms of thought nor be in any way infringed by thinking, is a view which to-day has been regained in its full extent through the criticism of psychologism.[1] Logic and mathematics are objective sciences; the same is true of every study of essences, which Phenomenology has opened up. In these sciences the objects are not less genuine objects than those of the concrete sciences; they are merely not real objects.

The basic thesis, therefore, which is the backbone for all such special points of view, is this: There are ideal objects of knowledge which are just as independent of the knowing subject as real objects are—that is to say, there is such a thing as ideal self-existence.

In the domain of theory this basic thesis is accepted as assured. There the question does not arise as to a metaphysical definition of what ideal self-existence is. It is as impossible to define this as it is impossible to determine metaphysically what real self-existence is. Each must be taken as a fact. It is of little importance in comparison, that something may be said about the relation of the two modes of Being to each other. But the certainty of the phenomenon is clearly revealed by the way the ideal forms present themselves to the knowing consciousness.

It is this consciousness which believes the logical and mathematical forms to be something independent of it. There is a consciousness of the fact that a° does not cease to be equal to 1 when it is not "thought" or "known," but that it "is" equal to 1 always and under all circumstances. It knows that not only in thought does no conclusion result from two negative "judgments," but also that, independently of thinking, two negatives, by the mere form, exclude any positive resultant. This postulated independence of consciousness is the postulated self-existence of the ideal objects. If anyone objects that affirmation is poor evidence, that a man who dreams, or one who is deceived, or who is in error, also believes that the object he beholds is self-existent, the answer is: from a dream there is an awakening, as there is from error and illusion, but from logical and mathematical insight there is no awaking.

[1] Most effectively in Part I of Husserl's *Logische Untersuchungen.*

The "belief" in ideal self-existence stands entirely on the same level as belief in real self-existence. We also cannot prove that things exist, but can only postulate this when we perceive. It is only for a very untrained mind that the degree in the force of conviction is different. And this is because such a mind brings with it a natural predisposition in favour of real objects, while the believing attitude towards ideal objects must be first acquired by a special reversal of interest. But when it is once acquired, the affirmation that the object is independent of consciousness is the same in both cases.

Whoever, therefore, doubts ideal self-existence must also doubt real self-existence. The universal scepticism to which this leads can never indeed be entirely exterminated. But it floats in the air. It is the most precarious of all hypotheses. And as it goes counter to natural comprehension, the burden of proof rests with it.

Perceived reality differs from mere presentation, from the merely supposed object, by the impossibility of voluntarily displacing it, of perceiving it otherwise than just as it is perceived. But the ideal object, which is known a priori, differs in exactly the same way from one which is a "mere thought," from one which could also be thought of as different. Indeed, the Kantian universality and necessity of the a priori are not something psychological, and do not mean that actually everybody sees that $a° = 1$. In fact not everybody can see it, but only the person who has an eye—that is, the mathematical training to see it. Yet whoever has reached the level of such intelligence cannot think as he pleases, but must think that only what in itself "is" $a°$ necessarily and objectively "is" $= 1$.

In the same way no ideal object of a priori insight can be displaced by the subject or made dependent upon him. It offers the same absolute resistance to the will of the subject as any real object of perception. And this resistance "is" its objectivity. In it we have the gnoseological meaning of ideal self-existence.

(d) THE ETHICO-IDEAL SELF-EXISTENCE OF VALUES

This certainty of ideal self-existence in the domain of theory —which subsists without metaphysical interpretation purely as an objective phenomenon and factum—furnishes the analogy according to which we must understand the ethico-ideal self-existence of values. They also are subject to those same misunderstandings and prejudices. Their non-actuality tempts one to assume that they are subjective. But here also we meet the phenomenon of affirmation and an immovability which is raised above all arbitrariness.

The moral judgment of values, which declares that a breach of trust is revolting or that malicious joy in another's misfortune is reprehensible, does not refer to the sensation as revolting or reprehensible. The judgment is rather itself this sensation, or its expression. What it means is something else, an objective revoltingness and reprehensibleness, which is independent of the sensation. It means something objective, something existing in itself. But, of course, a self-existence that is of an ideal nature.

In harmony with this is the conviction, which accompanies every genuine judgment of values, that everyone else must judge in the same way and have the same impression. And here also the universality and necessity, which betray themselves in such a conviction, are not a psychological factum. For, actually, other persons occasionally feel and judge otherwise. And the one judging knows, or may very well know, of the deviation of the judgment of others from his own.

But it is here just as it is with mathematical insight. Not everyone is capable of it; not everyone has the eye, the ethical maturity, the spiritual elevation, for seeing the situation as it is. Nevertheless, the universality, necessity and objectivity of the valuational judgment hold good in idea. For this universality does not at all mean that everyone is capable of the insight in question. It only means that whoever is capable of it—that is, whoever has attained the adequate mentality—must necessarily feel and judge thus and not otherwise. This is a quite commonplace truth. Not everyone, for instance, has sense and understanding for the moral value of a noble-minded act matured in quiet meditation, or of consideration for others practised in a fine way; but everyone who has the understanding for them must judge them as something of value and must respect the personality of the doer.

In this sense—the only one under consideration—moral judgment and the primal moral feeling which underlies it are universal, necessary and objective. In this sense also the value expressing itself in the judgment is independent of the subject who judges. It has as genuine an ideal self-existence as any mathematical law.

The principle that values have an ideal self-existence has a striking significance for ethics. It affirms more than the mere apriority of valuational discernment and the absoluteness of discerned values. It affirms that there is a realm of values subsisting for itself, a genuine κόσμος νοητός which exists beyond reality just as much as beyond consciousness—an ethical ideal sphere, not manufactured, invented or dreamed, but actually existing and capable of being grasped in the phenomenon of the feeling for values—a sphere which perdures side by side with the ethical real and the ethical actual sphere, just as the logical ideal realm exists side by side with the ontological real and the gnoseological positive realm.[1]

(e) VALUATIONAL DELUSION AND BLINDNESS

The doctrine of apriority and that of self-existence are not identical. To see the truth of the former is relatively easy; it was sufficient to understand that standards of value are the

---

[1] In both departments, by the "actual" sphere is understood the phenomenal realm of transcendent acts; therefore, in the department of theory, the realm of cognitive acts; in the department of ethics, the acts of conduct, disposition and will. Cf. the passage on the ideal sphere in *Metaphysik der Erkenntnis*, second edition, Chapter XXVII (c).

presupposition of moral phenomena. But prejudices, arbitrary assumptions, presentations, emotional attitudes can also be a priori. Now values announce themselves primarily as enlistments of emotion. They are therefore exposed to doubt as to their objectivity so much the more, because feelings are less objective than discernments.

The concept of self-existence first raises them above all such doubts. But it itself is rooted in the fact that it is as little possible to summon up arbitrarily a sense of value as it is to construct a mathematical truth arbitrarily. In both cases there is an objectively beheld existent, which presents itself and which the feeling, the intuition, the thought only follows but cannot dominate. We can experience as valuable only what in itself is so. We may of course also be incapable of such an experiencing: but if we are in general capable of it, we can experience the value only as it is in itself, but not as it is not. The sense of value is not less objective than mathematical insight. Its object is only more veiled through the emotional character of the act; it must be especially raised above the act, if we want to become aware of it. But even this later making of it known to ourselves can change nothing in the structure of the object (the value).

The opposite question here forces itself to the front, whether the evidence of the primary discernment of value is not also subject to delusion. And it is natural to believe that, if there is valuational delusion, the self-existence of values becomes again doubtful and gives way to a certain relativity.

That is a great mistake. On the contrary, where there are delusion and error, these consist of non-agreement with the fact. The fact, as something fixed and independent of the truth or error of the knowledge—that is, the fact as something existing in itself—is precisely the presupposition of delusion; otherwise delusion would not be delusion. But the "fact" is in this case the value itself. Accordingly, if anything is proof for the self-existence of values, it is exactly the phenomenon of delusion.

If values were only things posited by the subject, if they consisted of nothing except the act of valuing—that is, of the evaluating sense as such—then every chance enlistment of feeling would be as justifiable as every other. Valuational delusion would then be altogether impossible.

But there are many authenticated delusions as to values, even falsifications which rest upon perversions of the sense of values, as in the manifestations of resentment.[1] These manifestations, as well as their exposure through normal moral feelings, would be an impossibility—that is, they would not be falsifications, if the genuine values which were lacking did not have a self-existence independent of them. It is possible to be mistaken and to be set right only where the object is a fixed one and has its own definite character which is not changed by being understood or misunderstood.

The ordinary kind of delusion as to values is of course purely negative, the incapacity to discriminate, valuational blindness. But this is not delusion proper, but only a defect of the sense of value concerning a definite point. It stands on all fours with the theoretical incapacity of the mathematically untrained and untalented person. There are such things as education and lack of education of the sense of values, talent and lack of talent for the discernment of them. There is such a thing as individual maturity of the power of discrimination in the individual man, and there is a historical maturity in mankind. Whether the latter always means progress must remain undecided; possibly it brings with it a narrowness of the consciousness of values, so that there is always lost on the one side what is gained on the other. Perhaps there is also an enlargement of the field of valuational vision. But the fact is that we always survey only a limited section of the realm of values, while we remain blind to the other sections. That is the reason why the

[1] As in Nietzsche; cf. also Scheler, *Ueber Ressentiment und Moralisches Werturteil*, 1909. Nietzsche is a case in proof. In his statement that there is such a thing as falsification of values, he actually gives the lie to the relativism of values which he proclaims.

historical shifting of our gaze, with its circle of light, on the plane of self-existent values—which is reflected in the multiplicity and transiency of moral systems—is so very instructive for philosophical investigation.[1] And at the same time the reason lies here why this shifting and this variability do not constitute a "transvaluation of values," but a revaluation and reorientation of human life. Values do not change, but our insight into them changes. The insight however changes, because the values themselves and their ideal order do not change with the movements of the mental eye, and because they are objective and self-existent.

(f) The Transference of Attention and the Limits of Valuational Knowledge

The progress of valuational knowledge is different in form from that of theoretical knowledge, even from that of the theoretical knowledge of ideals. The antithesis which arises within the total movement may present similarities in certain respects. But the relation of gain and loss is different; it shows a more stable equilibrium, and yet progress as such is questionable. So far as can be seen, it does not advance to a wider range, the survey does not expand—it is possible that these tendencies are due to the later philosophical views as to value—it gives rather the impression of a planless wandering about. Every movement the law of which we do not know gives the impression of planlessness. We do not know the law in accordance with which the axiological field of vision moves. That does not prove that it is without regularity. A metaphysic of the human ethos, which would grasp the real manifestations and their changes in history, would need to survey this regularity as well as the realm of value itself.

Here only a general perspective may be given.

In all departments of genuine existential knowledge— whether as to the reality or ideality of the object—there is

[1] Cf. Chapter VI (a).

the phenomenon of the two gnoseological limits, which are inscribed upon the existent: 1, the momentary limit of knowledge, or the movable limit of *objectification*; and 2, the absolute limit of knowability or rationality.[1] Beyond the former, Being is only transobjective; beyond the latter, it is also irrational (not in the sense of being alogical, but of being beyond intelligence).

That the former limit exists in valuational knowledge also, we learn from the phenomenon of the narrowness of the field of vision and the momentary restriction of insight into values. That the latter, the absolute limit also exists cannot be learned except from a special analysis of values. But the relation of the two limits is here not the same as it is with theoretical knowledge. At least, in the primary discernment of values the limit of objectification does not move unequivocally towards the limit of rationality, but the whole momentary sphere which is included in it, the halo of ethical ideal objects, moves about, together with the centre, within the boundary of the rational: it wanders away at the same time from the realm of the valuational manifold which is generally discernible.

The moving glance of secondary discernment, which historically in the stages of this wandering gathers up the material, relinquishes the total view. The task of philosophical ethics, in contrast to positive living morality, hereby acquires an unequivocally characteristic mark. Its disadvantage in being derivative and dependent has the converse advantage that, in being subsequent and taking a synoptical view, it, on account of its range, sees something entirely new and unique: the connections, the graded order, the relations and regularities which run throughout the realm of values. It is precisely the stages in the moving about which for it are not lost. In philosophical ethics they are caught up and correlated. Its tendency is towards the systematization of values.

The relative limit of the philosophical knowledge of values

[1] Cf. *Metaphysik der Erkenntnis,* second edition, Chapters XXVII and XXVIII.

is therefore not the same as that of the primary view. It is wider, it is not confined to the narrow field of the primary insight. Its radius is greater. But as it generally occurs only when the original view has already preceded, and as, even when it pushes spontaneously forward to make new discoveries, it can only do this by disarranging the direction of the primary discernment, it can evidently move only within the boundaries which are generally accessible. This means, however, that the second and absolute limit of valuational knowledge is the same for it as for the primary perception. Philosophical investigation can only grasp what can be grasped by the living moral sense as to values.

CHAPTER XVII

VALUES AS PRINCIPLES

(a) RELATION OF VALUES TO REALITY

EVERY kind of ideal Being has some sort of connection with the real, whether this consists of agreement or disagreement. In connection with our problems, the logical ideal structures, including the mathematical and all discernible essences, have their significance in this—that they are at the same time to a great extent structures of real Being. Upon their agreement with the real rests the ontological importance of logic, mathematics and the theoretical analysis of essence. The limit beyond which this agreement does not exist does not detract from its importance. Real Being has still other structures and other substrata. They do not concern the world of ideal Being· as such, which on its side also possesses structures which do not appear in the real and which to it are as indifferent as it is to the ideal. In short, the ranges of the ideal and real structures interpenetrate, while they are in part coincident and in part mutually exclusive, and every connection between the two realms of Being applies only to the sphere of coincidence. It consists simply in the agreement, in identity of structure —a fact which from of old has given occasion for far-reaching conclusions. The non-coincident parts of the two spheres stand there unrelated, they have nothing in common —a fact which has the same right to respect in the metaphysics of Being, although it is not conspicuous and has been hitherto almost entirely overlooked, as in that of knowledge.

In the ethical domain this relation becomes transposed. Here also there is a certain agreement of the ideal and real, just as there are limits to the agreement. But the limits of agreement are here not the limits of connection. The connection subsists in full actuality above and beyond them. Ethical ideal self-existence is not indifferent to the ethical reality which contradicts it; it fixes the contradiction as a relation of opposition and strain, and denies the real which contradicts it, however well-founded this may be ontologically; it stamps it as contrary to value and sets against it the Idea of its own proper structure. The moral consciousness feels this opposition in the form of an "Ought-to-Be."

The self-existence of values subsists independently of their own actualization. But this independence does not signify indifference to actuality and non-actuality. We feel this immediately when we mistake the one territory for the other, taking the values of things as indifferent to attitudes of minds, the values of dispositions as indifferent towards things: but the values of things are not indifferent to things, nor are the values of dispositions to dispositions. Within the sphere of the forms to which as vehicles they are connected, values are not indifferent or inert towards what is in antagonism to them; rather do they have a quite peculiar way of denying them. This denial has nothing to do with theoretical negation. It does not at all question the reality of the thing denied; it is more a refusal to recognize it despite its reality, it is in tendency a nullification. Likewise in the affirmation of values that are unreal there is a tendency, a producing, an impulsion towards actualization. As merely ideal forms, values of course have no power to cause this impulsion and that nullification to prevail. But the actuality of the relationship quite evidently exists even beyond the limit of agreement. Indeed, the relation gains its full actuality in and through the realm of disagreement: here only exists a relation of tension and tendency. And it is easy to foresee that, where a real power is seized by it and is committed to the ideal tendency, this relation forthwith must be transformed into a real relation, and the ideal tendency into an actual one—that is, in the moulding of the actual.

(b) Values as Principles of the Ideal Ethical Sphere

Ideal self-existence, as such, is not a Being of principles. Every ideal sphere has much rather its own special principles, its own highest laws, axioms or categories. For example, logical and mathematical Being. But in the same way real self-existence has its own special principles. Existential categories of the real are themselves real categories. Their mode of Being is nothing else than this, that they are determining forms, laws or "categories of the real." In the same way knowledge, as a special sphere of the relation of the real to a subject of possible objects, has its special principles, which, as those of knowledge, are not the same as the real or the ideal principles of Being.

This of course does not mean that these three realms of principles would lack agreement. On the contrary, it is evident that there can be a priori knowledge of the real—that is, of its principles—as there can be of the ideal, but only in so far as the two-sided categories of Being coincide in content with those of knowledge. In so far as ideal and real Being are rational, this identity must subsist.

This doctrine of identity—the fundamental thesis of theoretical philosophy—is naturally a restricted one; and indeed, as the question concerns the interpenetration of three spheres, their restriction is also different in a threefold way. The common territory of the ideal and real categories does not coincide with that of the real and cognitive categories; and the territory common to the real and cognitive again does not coincide with that of the cognitive and ideal categories. Ideal and cognitive categories, for example, coincide to a much wider extent than do the latter with those of the real. In agreement with this is the more restricted irrationality of ideal Being, and the more extensive of the real. It is natural to think that in the department of theory the centre of gravity of the entire relationship of principles rests in the real. For here we have that excess of categorial definiteness which in relation to knowledge gives overwhelming excess of weight to the object. The knowing subject only represents, and that only approximately. But the object remains entirely unmodified by the subject.

In the ethical domain the situation is different. Values are also principles. Even in them we could recognize the character of "conditions of possibility," namely, those of the ethical phenomenon. Accordingly, we might expect that they are immediately ethical principles of reality, or at least of acts, for the phenomena belong to ethical reality and actuality.

This, however, is contradicted by the fact that these phenomena by no means thoroughly meet the demand of the values, that they challenge it on one side just as much as they satisfy it on the other. The material content of values in every connection detaches itself from the real as something beyond, something purely ideal. Its fulfilment in the real is at the same time something merely accidental, in any case not something necessitated by the content as a principle. To this is to be added the fact that valuational discernment always and under all circumstances regards the content as something independent of reality and of actualization. This independence is just as essential a constituent of its absoluteness as is its independence of the subject and of his opinion. Values are primarily and throughout *ideal* self-existents; and in so far as they are principles, they are from beginning to end only principles of the ethical *ideal* sphere.

This is by no means a tautology. Ideal Being and the Being of principles even here are not the same. The sphere of values is not exhausted by its own independent values proper. It embraces derivative values, and these likewise are purely ideal essences and subsist independently of reality and non-reality (for example, the whole sphere of mediating values, of the useful, the dependence of which upon the proper values themselves is an ideal relation of essences). But they are not principles. Genuine, proper values, however, are *principles* of the ethical ideal sphere.

(c) Values as Principles of the Actual Ethical Sphere

Now, if the character of values as principles were exhausted in the circumstance that they are principles of the ethical ideal sphere, all properly practical, actual significance would be stripped from them—that is, they would not be ethical principles at all. The ethos of man has actional character; it is no ideal form, not an essence. The essence of values, therefore, cannot evaporate in essentiality. It belongs to their essence as principles of the ethos that they transcend the sphere of essentialities and of ideal self-existence and seize hold on the fluctuating world of moral acts. They must be principles of the actual ethical sphere also.

How this transcendence proceeds is a metaphysical question, which at this point we can ignore. The fact is that it does proceed. There is a valuational consciousness—the primary discernment—and this is *determinant* for every moral judgment, every accountability, for the sense of responsibility and for the consciousness of guilt. The phenomenon of conscience is clear evidence for the actuality of values. Still clearer is it for the transcendent acts proper, the qualities of which are the object of valuational judgment for disposition, will and deed. Purpose, resolution, end, are necessarily determined by value. Indeed commonly there are other values which determine the end—the values of goods and circumstances; but these are not less actual, and they are not matters of indifference for the moral quality of transcendent acts, in which they are involved.

The whole sphere of ethical acts is penetrated by valuational points of view. The determination issuing from the values as principles is their presupposition throughout. Yet of the relation of transcendent acts to the moral values proper it holds good only conditionally, since disposition and will can resist values. But for the appraisement of values and for the acts related to it they are the condition of possibility. In this

way, therefore, values are as a fact at the same time principles
of the actual ethical sphere. And herein consists their specific
actuality.

But of course this is true of them in a sense very different
from that which holds in the ideal sphere. In the latter, values
are inviolable, supreme determinants, decisive powers, to
which there is no resistance, and to which everything is subject,
as in the theoretical spheres everything is subject to the categories. Without exaggeration one might say: values are categories of the ideal ethical sphere. But one cannot say: they
are categories of the actual ethical sphere. Here their rôle is
of another kind, and thereby their difference from the categories
appears. Here they are no longer inviolable determinants nor
absolutely ruling powers. Here not everything is subordinate
to them; the acts of the subject do not accommodate themselves to them unresistingly; they have their own actional
laws, determinants of another kind. Desire shows a certain
natural regularity in its connection with goods—at least in so
far as a sense of their value is present. The higher forms of
desire, however, manifest a much greater freedom towards
the higher values, although these are distinctly felt or are
known even in their detail. The will can counteract the
consciousness of value. The same holds good of inner conduct,
of the disposition.

One might think that at least the valuational judgment
(including the phenomena of conscience) would be ruled unconditionally by values. But this is so only within the limits
of the momentary consciousness. It, however, is restricted by
its narrowness of vision; it marks out only a fragment from the
realm of values. And only the values which fall within this
section are momentarily "actual"—that is, are determinant for
the judgment, "speak" in conscience and decide the inner
attitude of the man to life.

Ethical values are therefore only conditionally, and not
once for all, principles of the moral consciousness and its acts.
And the additional conditions which convert them into prin-

ciples do not lie in the realm of values, not even in the ideal sphere, but in the different law of the moral consciousness. This law is the function of a choice of values. It constitutes the basic difference between values and categories.

In one way, values are weaker in influence than categories. They do not rule unconditionally; without help they do not shape to their form the phenomena for which they hold good; of themselves they have not the strength to execute themselves in the actual sphere; they are thrown back upon an outside power which enters in. But this power is not always there; and, when it is there, it belongs to the actional realm.

In another way, they are stronger than categories. Categories rule the existent without check. The phenomena which are under them possess no laws of their own besides them. They are the only ruling powers in their own realm. Values, on the other hand, so far as they are at all actualized, must be carried out against a stable structure already present; they find in it an obstacle, passive indeed and inert, but nevertheless rigid and immovable. And, in so far as they succeed, they build upon the categorial stabilities of acts a new and higher formation which rises in the same way over these as over a material object. In another and more special sense they are creative principles. They can transform Not-Being into Being. The *generatio ex nihilo*, which is otherwise an impossibility in all realms of Being, here is possible.

All moral values have a tendency towards creative achievement. It inheres in the essence of them all, to be principles of the ethical sphere of action. That they are not always so is not their fault—or only negatively, in so far as categorial determinative power is lacking in them—but is due to the actional sphere itself. This basic relation between valuational principles and moral consciousness constitutes the special essence of the ethical phenomenon. If the acts of the subject were under the control of values as under categories, the law of which must be blindly followed, their essence would not be fundamentally different from that of a natural process; the values themselves would be throughout existential categories, simply, as it were, of a higher order, a rectilineal continuation of the ontological domain of the categories. That would involve the suspension of the ethical phenomenon as an actual sphere of a peculiar, non-ontological kind. We then could not say that values belong primarily to the ideal sphere; they would then be actualized just as primarily in the real acts of the moral subject. Will and disposition would then throughout render account to all values, and such a thing as being bad or being good would be excluded. And the opposition, the tension, between the real conduct of a person and the Idea of right conduct, in which lies its peculiar reality, would be annulled.

(d) Values as Principles of the Real Ethical Sphere

The possibility of conduct contrary to values gives to them, as principles of action, their specific quality of actuality. That quality becomes manifest in the fact that even in the case of disagreement the connection is not broken (as with the categories), but continues in full force and is even solidified in a tension *sui generis*. In metaphysical language, it is the tension between two different sorts of principle, it is the coexistence of ontological and axiological determinism in one world. This one world, the theatre of tension, strife and ever-new solutions, is pre-eminently the actional sphere of the moral consciousness; but subordinately it is the world of reality in general. For to this latter belongs the moral consciousness, which is drawn into the real world as a member of it and there expresses itself in transcendent acts.

Here we touch upon the third, and metaphysically decisive, characteristic of values as principles. They are also principles of the actual, of the real ethical sphere. Indirectly, through the actional sphere, they succeed in moulding the real—in line with the ontological categories. They achieve this of course only within a restricted area, since the radius of human activity, when measured by the temporal and spatial dimensions of the world, is narrow.

But the extent of the cosmos is quite an irrelevant matter; our whole concern is with quality, with grades in the scale of categorial formation itself. Here, in the smallest circle, a world of structures, which has not its like in nature, is unfolded, a cosmos within the cosmos, embedded in the real ontological whole, carried by it, dependent in a thousand ways upon its universal connections, and yet structurally superior, autonomous, with its own laws, not borrowed from elsewhere.

The real ethical world is not that only of the moral subject with his acts, it is also that of his living creations and his self-perpetuating works. For the individual subject is not alone, he has no existence in isolation. Every community carries in itself forms which are produced from valuational points of view—extending from ephemeral momentary situations to permanent communal customs, from the most personal emotional relations to historical life peculiar to nations and their constitutions.

All that has been said concerning the ethical sphere of action applies, *mutatis mutandis*, to the realm of ethical reality. Values have a conditionally determinative relation to it also. In it, too, they are not necessarily decisive, they do not fulfil themselves without resistance. They are always only in a restricted sense principles of the real ethical sphere, according to the ethos of the time, which within the scope of its own vision selects them according to laws which are unlike those of the realm of values. Also the conditionality of the principles is here greater, for the actional sphere is the mediating factor. In life the realization of values takes a route which is not accidental, along the consciousness of value, along disposition, will and deed. Only where a personal entity with its striving for a discerned value is at hand, can a value be productively realized. But if we add the mediation of the positive sphere as a further conditioning factor, if we include it in the way in which values generally arrive at being ontological, of actualizing principles, the proposition is essentially valid here, that values—despite their inability to execute themselves— nevertheless in their own way are stronger in force of efficiency than are the categories of Being, in that they, in the theatre of the world, oppose the force of the categories. In so far as in them, as values, there exists a tendency towards the real, it is this tendency to shape in higher fashion the categorial world already formed, supplementing this by their highest structures, personal entities, and building it up according to their own pattern, the pattern of the ideal essences.

(e) Teleological Metaphysics and the Ethical Phenomenon of Values

In following the above considerations one finds step by step traces of the fact that, behind the whole relation of the spheres and grades of values, a swarm of metaphysical problems springs up. How far these can be pursued, where thought may encounter the ever-pervasive limits of rationality, is not a question for ethics, but for metaphysics, to settle.

The relation of ontological to axiological determination is —although not under this heading—an old point of dispute. And many thinkers, with a correct feeling for the puzzling categorial superiority of values to principles of Being, have given precedence in their systems to values. Pre-eminently Plato, in that he raised the idea of the good to the apex of the realm of ideas, allowed values to rise "above Existence in strength and dignity"; likewise, Aristotle in the principle of the νοῦς as the highest perfection and of the ἄριστον; so, too, the Stoics in the twofold concept of the logos as the primal principle both of morality and of the cosmos; in the same way, the masters of scholasticism, in so far as they accepted the *ens realissimum* and the *ens perfectissimum* as identical. But even Kant with his primacy of the practical reason gave precedence to values, as well as did Fichte and Hegel, who established on this basis a teleological dialectic of universal reason. Everywhere, except with difference of form, the axiological principle is made the foundation of the whole.

This metaphysic of value, however impressive it may seem to us, nevertheless does violence to the problem of value, and ultimately to ethics. Indeed, it is a failure to recognize man's place in the cosmos. If there be a universal and real teleology of values in the world, then all reality from beginning to end conforms to valuational principles and is based upon them as constitutive. But in that case values are ontological categories and, as such, are entirely actualized. And man with his sphere of action is altogether eliminated. He is superfluous. The values prevail without his consciousness of them, and without his contributing to reality. The world-process then is universally an unfoldment of the valuable and before the tribunal of values is its own justification. Viewed as a whole it is perfect, it is the living theodicy.

Such a theodicy may be a metaphysical need of the human mind, but it has no ethical justification. The justification of evil in the world is from the start a perversion. Evil cannot be justified and ought not to be. To give value to that which is contrary to value is a falsification of it. So long as in the real there exists that which is contrary to value, we have a living proof of the fact that ethical values are not merely categories of existence, but prevail only in a very conditional manner. But the fact that the actional sphere of ethical consciousness plays here a mediating rôle must just as clearly be inferred from the circumstance that volition and action are conscious of value. It is only possible for man to have a task in the world, however restricted it may be, provided there are values which without his co-operation remain unactualized. But upon such a task depend the unique position and the dignity of man in the world, his difference from other entities which do not participate in the creative process.

Here the theory of value touches upon a fundamental metaphysical problem. In terms of the relation of "spheres," the situation may be thus defined: In the theoretical realm it is the ideal sphere which mediates between the actual and the real, but in the practical realm the actual mediates between the ideal and the real. In the former the original determinations rest in the ontologically real, and their transmission to the subject is knowledge of the real: in the latter the original determinations rest in the ideal essences, and their transference to reality pertains to the subject who beholds, wills and executes values, and, what is more, it pertains to every preference, although purely inward, for one value as compared with another.

The naïve view always regards the world anthropocentrically; everything in it turns upon man, who is the essential kernel of the whole. The critical and scientific view sets up the antithesis: man in comparison with the whole is a speck of dust, an ephemeral, a negligible, phenomenon. Ethics synthesizes these extremes; the cosmic insignificance of man is not the last word; besides the ontological there is still an axiological determination of the world, and, in this, man plays an integrating rôle. In this his insignificance is overborne —without a reintroduction of anthropocentric megalomania. Man, a vanishing quantity in the universe, is still in his own way stronger than it: he is the vehicle of a higher principle, he is the creator of a reality which possesses significance and value, he transmits to the real world a higher worth. Nature is bound down to its own laws; man alone carries in himself a higher law, whereby he—or more correctly the law through him— creates in the world, or from Non-Being brings forth into Being, that which was prefigured in its ideality.

We may name this rehabilitation of man the miracle of the ethical phenomenon; it is the sublime in him, that which verily lifts him above his own mere existence in the world. Kant's saying in regard to "the moral law within me," which for sublimity holds the balance with the "starry heavens above me," gives expression to the real sentiment of ethical self-consciousness.

But so much the more is it incumbent upon us to hold the metaphysic of this great vision within strictly critical limits. It gives neither ontological priority to axiology nor primacy to the practical reason. All that it really justifies is an axiological primacy of the ideal sphere, in contrast to the ontological primacy of the real sphere.

SECTION VI
THE ESSENCE OF THE OUGHT

CHAPTER XVIII

THE RELATION OF VALUE AND THE OUGHT

(a) THE IDEAL OUGHT-TO-BE

IN the characteristics of values as principles, which we have just been considering, the concept of Ought is distinctly contained. It adheres to the essence of ethical values and makes itself felt even where it is not brought into the foreground. It can be especially detected where valuational materials which are not realized are in question, materials from whose mode of existence the opposition to reality and the tension between the spheres cannot be separated. To them belongs somehow the tendency to reality, although in themselves they are purely ideal essences, and although it is impossible to understand how such a tendency could be compatible with their ideality.

This difficulty can be met only by a modal analysis of the Ought. For the moment, independently of it, the relation of value and the Ought is to be determined.

There is something absurd in the thought that a value is a thing that ought to be only in so far as its matter is unreal. That a man ought to be honest, straightforward, trustworthy, is something which does not cease to be because somebody actually is so. The man ought to be even as he then is. That is by no means a statement without significance; it is also not a tautology. We may reverse the sentence and say: "he is just as he ought to be." Thus it expresses a valuational judgment which is sensible and perfectly clear. And this judgment has the form of an Ought. Hence it follows that the Ought belongs to the essence of the value and must be already contained in its ideal mode of existence.

Ought in this sense is not Ought-to-Do, which refers to a volitional subject. It is only an ideal or pure Ought-to-Be. Because something is in itself a value, it does not follow that someone ought to do it; it does mean, however, that it Ought to "Be," and unconditionally—irrespective of its actuality or even of its possibility. Accordingly, there is sense in saying that universal peace among nations ought to "be." That has a meaning, not in so far as peace is actual or possible, but in so far as it is in itself valuable. Yet it would be senseless to say that a single individual ought to bring peace about. Conversely, it holds true of goods provided by nature that they ought to be just as they are; yet with them there is no place for an Ought-to-Do. A place for that is not possible until someone is in need of the goods and someone can acquire them by effort. Consequently Ought-to-Do is always conditioned by Ought-to-Be, but Ought-to-Do is not attached to every Ought-to-Be. I ought to do what ought to be, in so far as it "is" not, and in so far as to make it actual is in my power. This double "in so far as" separates these two kinds of Ought. Between goods and moral qualities there is in this respect no difference. The ideal Ought-to-Be inheres necessarily in them, but Ought-to-Do does not.

The Being of values, as ideal, is indifferent to real Being and Non-Being. Their ideal Ought-to-Be subsists independently of the reality or unreality of their matter. And, again, their ideal Being is also not indifferent to real Being and Non-Being. The ideal Ought-to-Be includes the tendency towards reality; it sanctions reality when it exists, and intends it when it does not exist. It transcends ideality.

This antinomy inheres in the essence of values themselves. It announces the inadequacy of ontological modalities for their peculiar kind of Being; it is an exact expression of their essence as principles which are ideal and yet are at the same time drawn towards reality. This double nature is the ideal Ought-to-Be in them: it is the idea of their being directed to the sphere of the real, the idea of their categorial transcendence and of their breaking forth out of the ideal into the real.

In this sense value and the ideal Ought-to-Be are indissolubly bound together. They are not on that account identical. The

Ought signifies direction towards something, the value signifies the something itself to which the direction points. The goal conditions the direction, but the direction towards it conditions the mode of being of the goal. Value and the ideal Ought-to-Be stand in strict correlation, in reciprocal conditionality. The ideal Ought-to-Be is the mode of being of value, its proper modality, which is never lost in the structure of the matter. But the value is the content of the Ought; it is the categorial structure, the existential mode of which is that of the ideal Ought-to-Be. In the older—of course inexact—conceptual language, one could say: The ideal Ought-to-Be is the formal condition of the value, the value is the material condition of the Ought-to-Be. The correlation is balanced, not like substance and attribute, but like substance and relation. On neither side is there a greater weight. The relation is stable, poised.

(b) THE POSITIVE OUGHT-TO-BE

The positive Ought-to-Be can be clearly distinguished from the ideal Ought-to-Be. It occurs where the ideal finds itself in opposition to reality, where the self-existent values are unreal.

This kind of Ought adheres to the structural non-agreement of the spheres, to the tension between them. The tension is precisely the actuality. For the real is indeed indifferent to the disparateness of the ideal as such; it has in itself no sympathy with it, no tendency towards it: but the ideal is not indifferent to the real; in it something presses beyond its own sphere into the real—irrespective of the possibility and impossibility of actualization. Nevertheless, the positive Ought-to-Be is indeed not an Ought-to-Do, nor does it necessarily draw any such thing towards it; for not everything that is not, but ought to be, comes into the domain of striving. But it is just as fundamentally distinct from the ideal Ought-to-Be; it does not adhere to value as such, it is added thereto. In the positive Ought-to-Be, for example, the ideal Ought-to-Be of the value is only one element; the other and equally essential factor in it is the opposition of the spheres. It therefore stands midway between the ideal Ought-to-Be and the Ought-to-Do proper.

The positive Ought-to-Be accordingly presupposes in a given situation the Non-Being of what ought to be. Hence it is only possible within a real self-existent world—that is, it presupposes this real self-existent world, together with its real determinations which deviate from the constitution of what ought to be. It has, as condition, the whole ontological system. First, against this, in its isolation and indifference to values in general, the positive Ought-to-Be is contrasted in its own kind of Being, as something unfulfilled. For the fulfilment can take place, if anywhere, only in exactly this real, indifferent, self-contained world. But the disparateness and the resistance first make what-ought-to-be non-existent and thereby make the Ought-to-Be itself positive. Tendency itself is first possible, where there is something which resists it. Without such a something, it fulfils itself unchecked; therefore there is no tendency.

In this stage of the problem ontology and ethics become sharply separated through their fundamental modalities: To-Be and Ought-to-Be. But in so far as the latter is something positive, subsisting only in opposition and in a state of tension, the correlation of the two is not in balance. The excess is on the side of existence. The Ought as positive is dependent upon existence, not indeed upon the special structure or the content of the existent, but upon the presence of a real existent in general. But the existent is not dependent upon the Ought: the same actual world can be there, even if no Ought-to-Be exists, and even if there is no tendency thrusting itself into the real world. A real world at rest, moved indeed, but only moved ontologically and in its movement closed within itself, without a tendency towards anything, without striving or activity towards an end, is very well possible. And it is actual, so long as there is no entity in it, which beholds values and is capable of tendency.

This does not contradict the qualitative superiority of

values as principles, over existential categories. Within the existent the Ought-to-Be is active, the Ought-to-Be which proceeds from values and becomes positive through the resistance of the existent, a thing which the categories never could achieve. Dependence and superiority are not in antagonism to each other. In the graded realm of principles it is precisely the dependent which is always and necessarily at the same time the superior: the higher principle is always the more complex, more conditioned and in this sense the weaker; but the lower is always the more unconditioned and more general, more elemental, and in this sense the stronger, but at the same time the poorer. The higher cannot dispense with the lower nor break through it; it can construct nothing by violence against the lower determination, but upon the lower as a basis and upon its structures it may well form another and higher edifice. In this alone consists its superiority.

This and no other superiority is possessed by values in their passage out of the ideal into the real world. The whole ontological formation of the latter stands over against this act of transcendency. And this opposition is at the same time an obstacle and a condition to the mode of Being of the positive Ought-to-Be in its relation to the real.

(c) RANGE OF TENSION, DEGREE OF ACTUALITY AND THE ETHICAL DIMENSION OF THE OUGHT-TO-BE

In itself the real world is neither a value nor in antagonism to value. It is neither wholly as it ought to be, nor wholly as it ought not to be. Single values may be completely actualized in it, others altogether non-existent. But in it, on the whole, what ought to be is always in part real and in part unreal. It stands half-way up the scale of values. The good floats in it midway between Being and Non-Being; and man, as the only real carrier of the good who comes in question, stands midway between good and evil, being wholly neither, participating in both. The Platonic image of Eros in its relation to the eternal

Ideas is the image of man in his relation to the ethical values —to the mode of Being of the moral essence, as it exists in the real world.

For the positive character of the Ought-to-Be, this position of its content, between Being and Non-Being, is essential. Its positive character itself, as intermediate, increases in proportion to the distance of the existent from what ought-to-be. The range of the tension between man-as-he-is and man-as-he-ought-to-be determines the degree of positivity. The ideal Ought-to-Be, on the other hand, the pure validity of value, does not affect it. As against this the range of tension is something general and indeterminate. It presupposes in the ideal the fixed point of relation. The other point which rests in the real is movable, it is the shifting opposite of value in its transcendent relation to actuality.

This relation again evidently presupposes a dimension in which the capacity to shift plays a part. Ontologically it is simply one among many other qualitative dimensions which are valuationally indifferent. There are interesting attempts to determine it as such—for example, Aristotle's attempt to understand it as a mean dimension between the extremes of too much and too little.[1] Here theoretical thought has wide scope. For the problem of the Ought, such attempts are indifferent; they do not touch the ethical essence of the dimension. This rests only in the nature of the Ought-to-Be itself as a direction or tendency towards something. The dimension of the Ought is primarily the purely axiological dimension between value and disvalue. And the fundamental law of the Ought-to-Be consists in this, that its direction within this bipolarity always points unequivocally to the positive pole, the value. If one adds that the real, the value of which is in question, always stands between the two poles, one derives from this law, as a consequence, that on any momentary level the "good" is always that which lies higher on the upward curve towards

[1] On Aristotle's theory of the μεσότης, cf. below, Chapter XLVIII (a).

the value, the "bad" is that which lies further down towards the disvalue. Good and bad, when seen from the point of view of the real, are directional opposites on the ethical dimension of the Ought-to-Be.

This is not a definition of good and evil. It is only the minimum which may pass current concerning them, even in more precise definitions of them.

(d) PLURALITY OF DIMENSIONS AND VARIETY OF VALUES

The essence of the Ought-dimension with its polarity of value and disvalue is identical for every Ought. But only in its universal structure. It differs materially with the content of the Ought. And this content pertains to values.

So far as there is a variety of ethical values, and so far as every value has its own independent Ought-to-Be, we obtain variety in the dimensions of the Ought. How these stand to one another is not to be learned from the essence of the Ought, for this is one and the same in all. If the system of the dimensions is to be learned at all, it is only from the system of values. For direction and situation are determined by the ideal pole of every dimension. Only the inner connection of the valuational materials can here furnish an explanation.

However much these dimensions may intersect, they cannot in any case coincide. And thence it follows for the real which moves within them, that it can include, at the same time, different levels of height in different dimensions, and therewith, at the same time, different ranges of tension and different positive gradations of the Ought-to-Be; and, indeed, so much the more, the more values there are, for which there is a potential carrier.

But this variety of directions and of grades of actuality by no means signifies a plurality of the Ought-to-Be itself. The Ought-to-Be is only a modality, and in the first place a tendency. Both of these are only in the singular. The variety of both lies exclusively in the contents. The plural therefore is an affair of the values; there is only one Ought-to-Be. This is one of the historic reasons why a strict valuational concept could not be developed, so long as ethics believed in the concrete unity of a principle. Here the concept of the Ought was sufficient.

It became inadequate as soon as the variety in the ethical sphere of principles itself was discovered.

CHAPTER XIX

POSITION OF THE OUGHT TOWARDS THE SUBJECT

(a) THE POLE OF THE OUGHT-TO-BE IN REAL EXISTENCE

ONE thing must be borne in mind. The positive Ought-to-Be does not lie within the ideal realm. It issues thence, but extends into the real; and in so far as it is a determining factor there, its activity is a real creating, a bringing forth.

One must not interpret this phenomenon too narrowly. It by no means consists only of a volitional determination through values, not to mention the actional efficacy of the will. It already exists in every affirmation and denial of values, in every preference and participation. Every one of these acts is real conduct. Ethical actuality is made up of these inner factors —in situations, in personal relationships, in the tendencies of public life. Everywhere mutual exclusiveness of the realms is abrogated. Ideal patterns show themselves as real powers. They attain actuality.

If, now, the positive Ought-to-Be makes itself felt so effectively in the real, although it emanates from an entirely different region, if it penetrates into the blind process of the cosmos, there must be in the existent a point of support for the Ought, like the point of contact for a physical force, the Archimedean point at which an ideal power can move the real and itself become a real power. For this it is not enough, as many theories maintain, that the Ought and the existent should be over-arched by an existence of a higher order, that there should be an "existence of the Ought." In such a "higher" existence there is presupposed a metaphysical unity of ideal and real self-existence, of which we know nothing; accordingly what we are looking for is assumed. Here we must keep much closer to the phenomenon, follow its structure and grapple with its inherent difficulties.

In the stream of real existence, in fluctuating reality itself, there must be a point of support, upon which the Ought-to-Be impinges. There must be a something or other within the real course of the world which is added to the world as a member of it and is dependent upon its universal conditions: it must come under the laws of the real world, share completely in the world's existential mode of coming into being and vanishing, it must be a thing that passes away like the world's other forms. And yet it must at the same time be able to be a carrier of the imperishable, the ideal; it must in this one connection be more than the other forms, distinguished from all other reality by an essential feature, able to act in a manner different from the rest of the real world. In short, there must be a real self-existent which can serve as the originating point of a real tendency in the stream of Being; there must be a form capable of intent in the midst of blind events, itself brought forth and borne along by them and yet, amidst them, powerful in self-activity.

An origin of the Ought in the real world must not be sought for in the carrier of the Ought, for the Ought originates beyond existence; the carrier is only the point of its manifestation in the real, the point of its metaphysical transformation from a merely ideal into a real power.

(b) The Rôle of the Subject in the Metaphysic of the Ought

The subject is such a pole of the positive Ought-to-Be in the realm of the real.

The subject—not as a metaphysical subject in general, but as empirical, actual, just as we know it in man—fulfils in every particular the specified conditions. And indeed only the subject does this. In this he stands alone. He is not himself something that ought to be, he is a real existent among others. He is wholly under the laws of actuality, shares in its comings and goings, and is at the same time different from every other being—by virtue of his inner world, consciousness, which has its own code of laws. He is in metaphysical connection with the world of values, he senses their ideal self-existence. And he possesses spontaneous self-activity, capacity to direct events. The subject is the only real entity in which the positive Ought-to-Be can be transformed into a real tendency.

The metaphysic of the Ought is exactly this, that in its unfoldment in real existence, in its actuality, it is necessarily directed to a real subject. Herein it is radically different from the Being of ontological principles, which in their actuality are directed to no mediating element, but are direct and unchecked determinants. Being, understood ontologically, stands on the other side of subject and object, and embraces them both; in it they are on the same level; but the Ought stands even on the other side of existence, it embraces both Being and Non-Being, and it is positive when its content is non-existent. In so far as the Ought enters into Being, and in so far as the positive Ought-to-Be becomes an existent, it can be this only as it at the same time seizes hold of something already existent, and points it to that to which its own direction points. It seizes upon the subject. For this alone permits of being grasped hold of by the ideal power of values. The rest of existence is dull and dead to the call of the ideal. It does not "hear" it, it lacks intuitive rationality.

Over against the world of existence, in which he is embedded, only the subject, sensitive to value, possesses the presage of consciousness; only he knows. He is "the mirror of Being," he is that point in existence in which existence is reflected in itself. In him arises the counter-world of the self-existent world, the realm of representation. The inner aspect of this realm is the theoretical consciousness. Being, as such, needs no counter-world. It can subsist without consciousness, it does not need to be known to a subject. Its becoming an object to a subject—so far as this happens—makes no change in it.

It simply adds the Being of knowledge to its own total constitution. Being, therefore, is indifferent as regards the knowing subject; only the knowing subject is not indifferent as regards Being. If for a subject Being were nothing else than an object, the reverse would of course hold true. But that is not so in the phenomenon of knowledge, which is an idealistic construction. Being lies outside of the relation between subject and object.

But for the Ought the subject has a greater significance. Its incorporation into the coherence, its function there, is a radically different one. The ideal Ought-to-Be is of course as indifferent to the subject as it is to existence; it subsists just as independently of him. But the positive Ought-to-Be is not indifferent; for its unfoldment in the existing world does depend upon the subject.

All principles have it in common, as an essential feature, that they are valid "for" something, for a specific kind of existence. Even values have significance "for" something. This "for" expresses their relatedness to a special kind of carrier.[1] But they are still further valid "for someone"—as existential principles never are; and this second "for" is their relatedness to the value-sensing subject. It does not attach to the ideal validity of values, but to their positive validity. It is an expression of the fact that the Ought which issues from the value is not attached directly to its carrier, but to a mediating element in the real, to the subject, to whose judgment it leaves the decision as to whether the realization of values is to be carried out or not. We can see clearly the actional sphere of the subject, whose mediating position between the ideal and the real sphere reappears in this relation.

Unlike the categories, the Ought cannot directly determine the real, which it aims at determining. But rather does the real —provided that it is not already, so to speak, what it ought to be—remain throughout untouched by the Ought. What in it ought to be, continues, in spite of the actuality of the Ought,

[1] Cf. Chapter XV (e).

to be entirely non-existent. The positive Ought-to-Be could determine nothing at all unless there were an entity with a capacity for directing events, the direction of which could be guided towards its own aims (the valuational matter) and to which it could communicate its own purely ideal tendency. The Ought has no existential energy emanating from itself; it needs something else which offers to it its own existential energy to be directed by the Ought. The Ought needs this alien energy of an existing entity, because the entity thrusts its ontological determination against the resistance of the real.

The Ought—and ultimately the value—therefore, of course, determines the real also; not unconditionally, however, and not directly, but only by the roundabout route through the practical subject, through the medium which senses values and is capable of directing events. The real determination, which issues from the moral values, is an indirect, interrupted determination, and on that account is also conditioned by the point of interruption.

(c) OUGHT-TO-BE AND OUGHT-TO-DO, THE METAPHYSICAL WEAKNESS OF THE PRINCIPLE AND THE STRENGTH OF THE SUBJECT

As regards the Ought, consciousness is not a knowing but an active striving, a willing, a doing. Knowledge is, of course, a factor in it, but is subordinate. Only an active subject—that is, one capable of independent action—can be immediately determined by the Ought in the direction of further determination of an object. The real determination has the form of action, doing, conduct, and so far as it is merely inward, that of a mental attitude, a disposition, a tendency. Here the Ought-to-Be of the object is transformed into the Ought-to-Do of the subject. This transformation is the breaking through of the actualizing determination of the real which issues from the value. The relation of the Ought-to-Be to the Ought-to-Do is the reverse side of the essential reference of this determination to the subject. The overrunning brings it about that the values determine only indirectly and conditionally in the real world what they specifically intend in the positive Ought-to-Be. The activity of the subject is inserted in between; only for it are the values valid immediately as determinants. But even this activity they by no means determine unconditionally.

In a certain way the positive Ought-to-Be determines only "at second-hand." One fundamental feature of the moral subject is that he is the administrator of the Ought in the world of real existence. He is not an absolutely faithful administrator of this metaphysical good; he can betray it. Whether he recognizes the positive Ought-to-Be as for him a universally valid Ought-to-Do, and whether he then commits himself to it with his whole might, always rests with him and depends upon his constitution. The entire self-regulation of the subject is inserted into the metaphysical nexus between the principle and the real to which it is applicable. The weakness of this nexus is the subordination of the Ought to the existential principle: the determining power of the Ought depends upon an intermediate element which it does not itself dominate, which is under an entirely different determination, and, whenever it recognizes the demand of the Ought, has the freedom to follow or not to follow.

But this weakness of the principle is at the same time the strength of the subject; it is his qualitative greatness, his position of power in the world. The practical agent is differently placed in it from the purely knowing agent. He is not only a mirroring surface, something existing for himself in the real world, and picturing the world's formations; he moulds, transforms and builds up: he is a world-creator in little. What he forms and builds up does not emanate from him himself, it is not his creation; it is something he has overheard from another world, to which he is responsively sensitive. But what he senses has no compulsion over him. It is only a good entrusted to him, the metaphysical import of which he feels as a claim laid upon him. Nevertheless, the claim is not a coercion. The essential feature of the moral subject is this, that, in regard to the values which he feels and their claim upon him, he has the same mobility, the same range of activity, as in regard to the real world. This range is limited simply by the fact that with his sense of value he recognizes at the same time the values which he feels as standing above him and his action, and he knows that a violation of them (within the range of his will) falls upon his own head. But this is not a realistic limitation.

The attitude of the subject to the Ought is the central point in the ethical problem. The fact that it primarily touches only the narrower problem of the Ought-to-Do, while leaving on one side the wider problem of the appreciation of values, makes no difference. Every attitude of mind, even the appreciation of the fulness of values, is an inner action. But upon the Ought the fundamental ethical problem is concentrated in a peculiar way. The actual may very well be valuable, even without any mediation by the subject. As regards him the valuable may have arisen accidentally out of blind ontological necessity. But such a mode of origin excludes all essential dependence upon values as principles. On the other hand, the Ought is the essential binding force in them, the tendency towards values. Actual existence therefore can very well contain values, but it cannot contain the Ought. Also it cannot take up the tendency towards them, unless one of its own entities shows itself capable of so doing—that is, capable of taking values up through the Ought. A personal subject is an entity which is capable of this tendency—and, so far as we can know, it is the only such entity in the world. It alone can introduce the Ought into existence.

The subject as a practical agent is the unresting point in the world, in which the world loses its ontological equilibrium. He introduces something above himself, he adds a weight through himself. But the added weight does not originate with him; the unstable equilibrium is due to the ideal principle which forces its way into the indifference of the real, in that it gains a power over one of the world's entities. The subject as a practical agent is the intersecting point between two heterogeneous determinations or powers; at the same time it is the battlefield where these powers clash with each other within the one real world. Hence the restlessness in the nature of the subject, his continual confronting of decisions. Thus it comes about that the Ought, although it is not rooted in the subject, but confronts him as a positive claim, nevertheless, as a positive tendency in the real, can attach itself only to a subject, and can determine reality only through a subject.

(d) Value and End, the Ought and the Will

As ideal essences, values are self-existent and need no authorization from a subject. But in the real world this self-existence does not suffice. Here for the actualization of the Ought-to-Be, issuing from values, there is need of authorization. A real subject must affirm them in contrast to what already "is." The affirmation must therefore be a setting apart above the existing, an anticipation prior to the process of realization. The form of such an assertion is the end. It is not the subjective form of the act as such, but the objective form of the content. Nevertheless it has in it the element of a tendency towards the content; and in this sense it remains linked to the act, bound to the subject.

In the actional sphere of the real subject, the end corresponds to what the value, behind it, is in the ideal self-existent sphere. Not every value with its material becomes the content of an end set up. For not every value is the aim of a positive Ought, and certainly not of an Ought-to-Do directed to a subject. Only the latter here comes in question. But within this limit the end is related to the will, as value is to the Ought. It is the affirmation of the value by the practical subject. Only a practical subject can set up ends—that is, transform felt and discerned values into ends of his volition. Consciousness, foresight, resolution, activity, commonly constitute the condition of this act. In the first of these factors the valuational consciousness is included. For the subject can convert into an end only something felt to be of value. In his valuational feeling he may err; then the end set up will lack real value. Also in his setting up of an end he can depreciate a value which by right should be felt to be higher; he can neglect it and prefer a lower value to it. But he cannot set up and pursue as an end what he does not at all feel to be a value.

Furthermore, it belongs to the essence of the realization of the Ought in asserting ends that only the subject himself can set up his aim. He alone is capable of tendency, for him alone the assertion has meaning. The setting up of the end is reflexive: it is from a subject for a subject. Of course a subject can establish ends for other subjects, but only within the limits of his active power to lead others willingly to the end— that is, to induce them to set up the end for themselves. The establishing of the end is here merely doubled, and in both subjects is reflexive.

(e) THE APPEARANCE OF SUBJECTIVITY IN THE OUGHT AND THE AXIOLOGICAL DETERMINATION

In view of this situation there always exists room for the question whether an element of subjectivity does not attach to value and the Ought. The subject must mediate them in the real world, and indeed in a twofold way, once in setting up the end and then in action, in the execution which, again, the subject carries out. The metaphysical intercalation of the subject into the nexus of determination shows itself in this way as something entirely concrete, something known to everyone, but precisely as something which is generally supposed to be subjective.

The fundamental misunderstanding here is that one does not see the values behind the ends of the subject, the Ought behind the will. One sees only what obtrudes itself in the appearance—that is, the real tendencies issuing from the subject. And one ascribes them either to the subject himself as the primal author or to the confluence of real causes in him. In both cases one overlooks the fact that no subject can aim at anything which is not somehow a value in itself and felt by him to be a value. But the positive Ought-to-Be attaches to this valuable entity, as such, in so far as the real world does not fulfil its requirement. This "Being," however, is the ideal self-existence of the values.

As to the double intercalation of the subject into the nexus, this does not signify the projection of the entire nexus into the subjective, into the realm, so to speak, of mere presentation. Rather is the subject as a real entity intercalated; and the acts which set up the nexus, the sensing of value, the affirmation of the end, the will, the action, are nothing but real acts. Their subjectivity is not a deficiency of self-existence, but simply a specific form of their real self-existence. Universally, the subject and his acts are not "subjective"; only the content of consciousness is subjective, in so far as nothing self-existent corresponds to it. The subject himself and his acts, however, are anything but a content of consciousness—they cannot be classed with things which have nothing self-existent corresponding to them. They are much rather purely self-existent, indeed a real self-existence. They may become objects of conscious presentation or not; their being so presented adds nothing to them. In fact, as a rule they do not appear in the naïve moral consciousness. The willing and active subject has an immediate consciousness only of the end—and with it the means—but no consciousness of the setting up of the end as such.

The acts of the real subject, which are here under consideration, are so little in a position to degrade value and the Ought into something subjective that the opposite is much more true: the tension introduced into the nexus of the axiological determination of the real lifts above all doubt, above every base suspicion of subjectivity, the true reality of the value and of the Ought so far as any doubt arises. For this nexus is ontological, and what is involved in it has full ontological import. As principles, values are perfectly analogous to existential categories; their determination of the real—so far as it occurs at all—is ontological determination. Only it is conditional and indirect determination. This fact derogates from its strength to execute itself, but does not detract from its mode of being. Much rather it elevates to the same mode everything which is counted among the conditions of this determination. But among these conditions must be included the mediating acts of the moral subject.

Value and the Ought are in themselves neither subjective nor objective. Like the existential categories, they subsist on the other side of subject and object. That they, furthermore, subsist beyond Being and Non-Being separates them, of course, from the categories. But it does not bring them into the subjective, it does not set them on a level with cognitive categories which actually determine only the forms of consciousness. The Ought is not analogous to knowledge, as in a certain sense the will is, but analogous to Being. It is an Ought-to-Be. Knowledge, although a transcendent act, flows into the subject. It is of existential origin, subjectively conditioned, and of objective validity. But the Ought is of ideal origin, is subjectively conditioned in its fulfilment, and is of existentially real (super-objective) validity. The cognitive form remains a form of consciousness; it does not again transcend the bounds of consciousness after it has once arisen in the transcendent act. But the Ought returns into Being. For it the subject is only a point on its journey. The Ought crosses the boundary of consciousness twice: when it enters, in the knowledge of value; and when it issues forth, in the deed. Both these acts, and all others which lie between them, belong to the metaphysical nexus of the determination of the real through values and share in the self-existence of the real.

(f) SUBJECT AND PERSON

Thus far, as regards the Ought-to-Be, the conditionality of its actualization through the subject has been considered in one aspect only. But this conditionality has another aspect. The existential determination issuing from values does not pass through the subject without modifying him. It gives him a dignity of a peculiar kind—personality, which is as much a categorial novelty as it is a valuational mark. A moral subject, who of all real entities stands alone *en rapport* with the ideal world of values and who alone has the metaphysical tendency to communicate them to reality which lacks them—only such a subject is a "person." The essence of personality, for instance, does not attach to the acts which the subject brings to the service of values. Neither the discernment of values nor the activity, the setting up of an end, the will, transforms the subject into a person. There are two special elements—both distinctively ethical—which contribute the decisive mark. But both refer to the relation of the subject to the values.

One is this: that the values do not coerce the subject, but, even when they are discerned, impose only a claim upon him, while leaving him free. The fact, therefore, that it is in his power to take hold on value or not and to place his own acts in its service or not gives to him a kind of equality with the great metaphysical powers of existence—ideal as well as real —at least in principle; in this way he is an independent factor, a proper ultimate of existence along with these other powers. It is this which has been called moral freedom. A personal entity is a "free" entity. It contains its own principle, its own autonomy—together with the autonomy of nature which is in it and the autonomy of values which is also in it. To this point is attached, of course, a long series of metaphysical difficulties. At present it is only possible to describe how the phenomenon of the moral subject includes freedom. The justification of it must be reserved for another investigation.

But the second element of personality is found in the

valuational marks which the subject retains in his acts. These
are not identical with those found in the object of acts. Moral
values do not inhere in the ends, as such, which are set up,
but in the acts directed towards them, and ultimately in the
subject of the acts. They have indeed in themselves an Ought-
to-Be, ideal as well as actual, but never directly an Ought-
to-Do. They can and should determine the choice of ends,
but they do not furnish the matter of the ends. The moral
value of a loving person attaches exclusively to his loving
conduct; but this is not the object of his volition, it is not
the content to which his inner disposition is directed, but is
its moral constitution. The ends of his volition, on the other
hand, are to be found in the person who is loved, or in the
goods which for him are of value. But the moral worth of the
love is altogether different from the value of the things which
are good for the other, or from the worth of the other person
himself. It inheres in the personality of the one who loves.
Who does a good to another wills a good for that other; he does
not will to be good himself; rather "is" he good, in that he
wills the good for the other.

Action, will, disposition—even up to the innermost and
purely emotional attitude of mind—are the carriers of moral
values proper; and thereby the subject can come into consideration. These values are "relative" to the person as their carrier.
For as their carrier the subject is a "person." However different
these values may be from those which constitute the matter
of the will and the content of the ends, they stand in the
closest relation with them; for exactly that conduct has moral
value which is a commitment of the person to ends directed
and selected by the moral feeling for values. The commitment
of the person is the correlate in reflex of the setting up of the
end which yokes the subject as the moving power to his own
tendencies. The subject himself sets up his ends. There are
always two acts disposed one after the other and equally
transcendent; the act which initiates and that which executes.
And each independently of the other has range of freedom.

For each the person is accounted responsible. Each is attributed to him and for each he is blamed in case of failure. And just on this account the person is in these acts the carrier of good and evil, but at the same time this means that he is the carrier of the whole differentiated scale of moral values and dis-values. Only in a personal subject as a responsible and account-able being can these inhere.

(g) PERSONALITY CONDITIONED BY VALUE AND THE OUGHT

Thus the two elements of personality—freedom and the carrying of moral values—are deeply embedded in each other. Together they constitute a unified metaphysical feature of a personal being. And as in each the presupposition is the ideal Ought-to-Be of values, the metaphysic of the Ought is shown to be at the same time the metaphysic of personality.

The fundamental relationship which prevails here is no one-sided dependence, as it may perhaps have appeared hitherto. Not alone is the determination of the real by values dependent upon the moral subject on account of his rôle as mediator; but also, conversely, the moral subject is on his side at the same time, and rightly, conditioned by the self-existence of the values and by the positive Ought-to-Be, the mediation of which falls to him. Only through the intrusion of values as determining powers into his actional sphere does the subject become that which he morally is, a person: a personal being is metaphysically possible only at the boundary line between ideal and real determination—that is, at the point of their reciprocal impact, their opposition and their union, only at the connecting point of two worlds, the ontological and the axiological. The intermediate position between the two, the non-merging of either into the other, as well as participation in both, is the condition of personality.

It is no new thought that a moral being has a double nature and is an entity having two strata. In this sense the Kantian ethics distinguished between man's "natural" and his "rational" character. If by reason one understands the discernment of values, the distinction touches the essence of the matter. Only one thing remains to be added: the ultimate import concerns not so much the difference between the two strata as the positive relation, the stratification, of the two determinations in one being; in short, the form of their unity. To grasp this peculiarity in its structure transcends the limits of human understanding—just as, in every possible conception of the moral freedom of the person, there remains something wholly irrational. Just this unity, nevertheless, the personal essence, is something which cannot be resolved into its two constituents; it is a categorial novelty, an irrational remainder.

If the part played by the subject were exhausted in automatically mediating the axiological determination, he would himself be merely an ontological entity—categorially higher, indeed, than others, but still to be classed under natural laws; and moral values and disvalues could not be manifested in him. What first gives personality to the subject is the circumstance that his mediation is not automatic, that he can just as well mediate as not mediate, and that he consequently bears the responsibility for what constitutes his conduct in ethical reality, and for what makes him a person. For in his practical conduct, outward or inward, he is always the carrier of moral values and disvalues. He is himself at the same time an ontological and an axiological entity, a real self-existing being, and at the same time possessing in himself the higher, the distinctively moral values or their opposites.

But this means that personality as an essential structure is not only existential (as the subject is), but also valuational—that is, his valuational content is *sui generis*. It is the substantial basic value, in which moral values as attributes are manifested. The power to carry moral values is the moral essence in man—it is something which is still on this side of everything distinctively good and evil. This basic value is the axiological condition of all higher values, moral or personal. It is the same conditioning relation as that between the universal value of the living organism and the special biological values and disvalues, which can be manifested only as attributes of a living being. The substantial value, as compared with the attributes, is indeed lower, but precisely on that account it conditions the attributive values.

This is the reason why man's moral nature, his personality, can never be determined simply from the ontological point of view. It is not a purely ontological nature, but is axiological as well. Man is a valuational entity. Hence values are not determined by the moral subject to whom they are "relative," but the subject is determined; in his fundamental nature he is definable only by his relation to values—by the way in which he is the unique bearer of moral values.

CHAPTER XX

THE OUGHT AND THE FINALISTIC NEXUS

(a) CATEGORIAL ANALYSIS OF VALUE AND THE OUGHT

VALUES are principles. They stand, although conditionally, on a level with existential categories. The peculiarity of their contrasted nature does not prevent them from being analogous to the categories.

They must, however, have a definite categorial conformation, which permits of being analysed. And since they are higher principles, which are erected upon the structure of lower ones, these latter must be contained in them and, with definite modification, must reappear in them. A whole group of such structural elements we have already met with in our analysis of value and the Ought. For instance, the opposition, or polarity, of value and disvalue, the valuational dimension extending between them, the variation in the range of tension holding between them and the real, as well as the unbroken continuum of the displaceability of the real in relation to valuational dimension. The series of stages in this displacement is, again, not homogeneous, like the mathematical series, but is qualitatively differentiated; it is not static, like spatial dimension, but is dynamic, like the flow of time in which it actually moves; it does not advance indifferently like the causal process, but mounts unmistakably, accompanied by the irreversible direction of the Ought-to-Be towards value; it is a progressive realization, an ascent directed to an end; but it is not a blind, not an accidental adaptation to an end, not ontologically necessitated as organic entities are, but is a purposed, foreseeing, predetermined tendency to a goal, in which the end, and ultimately the value itself, is the formative power.

These categorial elements all concern the essence of value itself less than that of the Ought-to-Be which adheres to it, or than that of the real determination which issues from it. This is no accident. The Ought as a structure is relatively comprehensible and definable, the value itself is not. Single valuational materials are capable of being described, the consciousness of them can be defined in its actional character (sometimes specifically), but the valuational essence as such, which is behind, remains floating in a certain incomprehensibility. It is marked by a strain of the irrational. In it this strain is greater than in the valuational materials, because the existential principles can be approximately grasped by means of their gradational connection, while with the value itself something new begins.

However near to each other categories and values may be metaphysically, a chasm yawns between them. For our understanding, the series does not close. Whether they are not in themselves closed we of course cannot know; for the human consciousness does not grasp all principles. In any case, for our comprehension the series is not closed. But that is a matter which would require categorial analysis.

One must keep therefore to what is conceivable; one must keep to the Ought, although into it the essence of value does not merge.

One comes nearer to the kernel of the matter when one considers the relational categories. Even Plato saw something substantial in moral values (in the "ideas" of the virtues). But neither he nor anyone later has exhausted this thought, so far as ethics is concerned. For with them substance was only formal substance. There is, however, in values something which does not resolve itself into form, law or relation; there is something of the nature of a substratum, something material. Now this material in them is linked with a power of a peculiar kind which is inherent in them. Values are genuine "first movers," in the Aristotelian sense; from them proceed creative energy, productivity, fashioning, actualization. Value is the power which stands behind the energy of the Ought-to-Be. In the presence of the valuational principle the existent loses its equilibrium, it falls into motion and it tends to something beyond itself. Value is its centre of gravity, the "first entelechy" of its movement.

This Aristotelian concept of substance—which is at bottom a concept of ends—has shown itself to be, for nature, a doubtful foundation. But it fits ethical phenomena precisely enough. In ethics there is the assumption of a point aimed at and the assumption refers to the substantial essence of the principle. Value is at the same time power and a directional point. As something substantial it does not impel the process from behind and push it forward, but draws it to itself. It is a point of attraction which the Ought-to-Be indicates and towards which the real tendency in the pursuit of the Ought-to-Be proceeds.

(b) PRIMARY AND SECONDARY DETERMINATION

Here on every hand one is surrounded by the teleology of values in ethical reality. It corresponds to what in nature is the causal nexus. Like that it is a nexus, a type of determination of the real. But it is a different type, higher and more complex. It is the kind which is peculiar to the realization of what ought to be.

Herein a qualification must be noted at the outset. The realization of what ought to be is a determination which is broken into two members: the point of disruption is the personal subject. The first member—we might call it the primary determination—is that of the subject by the value; it consists of the discerning, the sensing, the beholding of the value. This, which leads initially from ideal to real Being (since the sensing of value is a real act), is naturally not finalistic. It belongs to a type still more general but metaphysically not more closely analysable—a type which is on the one hand nearly related in structure to the cognitive relation (since valuational intuition and even the primary feeling of value are a kind of comprehending), but is on the other hand a relation of dominating and conditioning, such as subsists generally between all principles and the field in which they prevail.

The second member is only the subsidiary and further determination, which proceeds merely from the willing and acting subject when he discerns a value. It lies wholly within the real; in it the transformation of the ideal into the actual (the valuational consciousness) is already presupposed. It issues from the real subject and, where an outward action ensues, it extends to something else that is real, but only to an inner disposition, to the shaping of the personal subject himself. As regards the reality of the determination there is no difference between the inner and the outer life of the subject. The psycho-physical problem of course depends upon this double aspect. But both sides lie within the same reality; the physical and the psychic processes flow in the same time, only spatiality divides them.

The subsidiary determination is the one that is finalistic. It is a wide domain which the finalistic nexus controls. All acts proceeding from person to person carry this nexus in themselves as a categorial form. Such are all striving, willing, acting, all wishing, longing, hoping, all the unspoken and uncomprehended tendencies within the mere attitude of mind. For to this belong not alone the conscious setting up and pursuit of ends; every activity of the subject has essentially the structure of this nexus. All practical intention is finalistic.

(c) THE FINALISTIC NEXUS AS A THREEFOLD PROCESS

Here also, as in the causal nexus, there prevails a thorough dependence of member upon member, an ordered sequence. But in this sequence the structure of the dependence is totally different from that existing in the occurrences of nature. In the causal series the later is throughout determined by the earlier; the dependence follows the direction of the time-process, it flows straight forward in the temporal sequence. In the finalistic series the earlier is just as completely determined by the later, the dependence flows counter to the flow of time; as regards time it is a backward movement. Here everything is directed by the final member, the end. In this sense the finalistic nexus is the reverse of the causal. The relation of end and means is substituted for that of cause and effect.

The dynamic of the causal series is that of a blind forward push, wherein the direction of the process is always merely the resultant of indifferent factors; the dynamic of the finalistic series is the attraction issuing from the final end. The prior existence of the end is the condition of the whole.

Nevertheless this description is incomplete. Although the prior existence of the end is the condition of the whole, the mode of existence peculiar to this condition must be borne in mind. How does the end exist before its actualization? It can exist only as an end set up, an end set up in anticipation; and only a consciousness is capable of setting it up in anticipation. The positing of the end is accordingly the first link with the still non-existing future, a link anticipating and disregarding the process.

A second link is added. The process peculiar to a real occurrence, even if it be finalistically determined—that is, bound to an end—flows through time and shares in the direction from earlier to later. In it the "means" are real causes which step by step bring about the thing aimed at. In the achievement of an end the process of actual happenings is therefore, despite the finalistic determination, a causal process. It differs from other causal processes only by the already prior determination (sometimes, a choice) of the means from the point of view of the end. But the way in which the means as a series achieve the end is causal, in that the later member is throughout the end of the earlier. The finalistic nexus presupposes the causal nexus; in this stage of its fulfilment, of its realization, it is causal. The lower form of determination is caught up into the higher and more complex, it is a constituent part of the latter—in accordance with the general law of categorial gradation, by which the lower category is always a presupposition and categorial factor of the higher. The higher cannot exist without the lower, but the lower can exist without the higher.

If we include in the whole of the finalistic nexus both the setting up of the end and the actualization, this whole no longer appears simply as a reversal of the causal nexus, but as a determinational form of a much higher type. As the backward determination from the end to the means constitutes the distinguishing characteristic of the finalistic process as such, we could describe this together with the causal process as a circular course: first, the backward determination from end to means, and then the forward advance from means to end. But even this is not adequate; for the first condition of the whole, the setting up of the end itself, is not yet contained in it. If this also be included, we have in the finalistic nexus three links between the starting- and the finishing-point of the process:

1. The setting up of the end by the subject, an over-leaping of the time-process, an anticipation only possible to consciousness and a taking of one's stand regardless of the order of time.

2. The return determination (distinctive of the finalistic process) of the means by the end, beginning with the means nearest to the end and so backward to the first means—the present one—which is close to the subject; where the link just ahead (in the backward process) has as its end the subsequent one (next preceding in the backward process) and is determined (sometimes, chosen) by it.

3. The actualization of the end, its real attainment through the series of means, wherein the relation of means and end which was reversed in the backward process is changed into a straightforward continuous relation of cause and effect.

(d) FORWARD AND BACKWARD DETERMINATION IN THE FINALISTIC NEXUS

Only the last stage in this three-level relation has the character of a real process in the course of the world. On this account it has a full causal structure; issuing from the subject, it is an incursion of action into the real course of cosmic events: hence it can have no other categorial form than the causal form. The last member of the second stratum is the first of the third, the first means which it is in the power of the subject to lay hold of, and from which all the further effects of the final end proceed. The dependence of the finalistic series upon the causal series of the third level is of the greatest importance for the understanding of the whole: only thus is a coherence of the two types of determination in the one real world possible. The finalistic determination inserts itself without opposition into the causal, precisely because the course of its own actualization is itself causal. Or, to invert the expression: The intervention of any entity which pursues ends in the world in which it exists is only possible in a world causally determined. This goes directly counter to the prevailing opinion, which looks to indeterminism for the greatest scope for action. The reverse is true: In a world without law and determinism, where everything was by chance, an agent who pursued ends could not hold his own at all; but this signifies that in it action, the actualization of ends, would be an impossibility, because the agent could never foresee what causes, as means, would induce the desired effect.

The first and third links of the finalistic nexus move in the direction of the time process. But only the third exists in it and flows within it. The first overleaps it, anticipates the future and thereby sets the future determinantly before the present. The second process alone moves backward. This also does not exist on the level of actual events; it is determinant for real events only through the subject's activity, to which it shows the way. But it exists only in consciousness, as does the setting up of the end. Just as only a consciousness can freely overleap the time-process, so can only a consciousness return from the future back to the present—from a final end to the first means which is within the power of the subject.

The whole, therefore, is not a simple circular course. The first half of the circle—if we may keep to the metaphor—is run through twice, the other only once. The first two stages of the nexus constitute a closed circle, both, however, on this side of actuality, purely as an affair of consciousness, as an objective structure of consciousness. They lead ideally from the subject in his objective and present world to the end as a thing of the future, and back again from this over the series of means to the subject in his actual present circumstance. And only now does the actual stage of the nexus set in, the stage in which that same series of means in reverse order is passed through in the real process as a causal sequence.

One easily sees that it is the second stage of the nexus which gives the peculiar impress to its finalistic character. To it is due the determination of the earlier by the later, so characteristic of ends. It also renders the finalistic nexus capable of being a form for the actualization of what ought to be. For in the Ought-to-Be the point aimed at is given, but the real tendency towards that point is a pre-requisite. Only finalistic determination can render the Ought competent in the real world.

(e) DUPLICATION AND IDENTITY OF THE END

The two other levels of the finalistic nexus, which encircle the backward determination, both run from the subject to the end. But in very different ways. The first, as a mere anticipation through consciousness, without reflection upon the intermediate members (the means), runs to an end merely set up and unreal. But the other, as a real and actualizing process

—led by reflection upon the means—runs to the achieved and real end.

In the finalistic nexus, therefore, the end appears duplicated. First as set up and unreal, as a predetermination before the process. As such it is essentially a determinant, the centre of gravity of the process. But the second time as an actualized and accomplished end, as a result of the causal course that has been run (the third level), and at the same time as a result of the whole three-level structure of finalistic determination. The two kinds of end are to be distinguished, according to Aristotle, as the "first entelechy" and the entelechy simply— only that both with him refer to every occurring process and not specifically to the ethical problem. In the former meaning, the end is determined by a principle (the value), it is the thing of value posited by consciousness; in the second sense the end is the Real determined by the principle—through the indirect way of consciousness. In the finalistic nexus the former is the first conditioning factor, the other the last thing conditioned. The whole range of human striving and achieving lies enclosed between the one and the other.

And yet, in another sense, they are identical and are rightly called the same end (as by Aristotle the same entelechy). For they are distinguishable in the finalistic nexus only by this, that in it they are different stages in their mode of existence. They differ as a thing set up in consciousness and the same thing as a real self-existent. But as concerns their matter they are identical. For this is in itself indifferent to the difference of modality and the stages of the nexus.

In this identity of content is rooted the appearance of a circular course in the finalistic process. If we ignore the modal difference, the end set up is not actually different from the end actualized. And, furthermore, on this rests the apparently purely causal course of the finalistic series in concrete occurrence. For if we look only to the real process (the third level), we have before us only the causal series. That this in its individual peculiarity could never have come about if the effect had not been an antecedent and the cause a consequent, could not be inferred simply from the third process. This is the *pons asinorum* of ethical naturalism, which thinks to be able to explain everything by the law of cause and effect. In the same way one overlooks the fact that the circular process is never wholly closed. In concrete cases the end attained deviates very considerably from the end aimed at. In this way there exists of course a material non-identity. But this is not due to the nature of the finalistic nexus but to the defect of the subject who is not master of it.

The subject is twice drawn into the nexus, in as much as the first and the third stages both emanate from him. He can set up the end only reflectively, only for himself (the subject). He sets it up with his own activity, his willing and acting. In the positing of this end he is drawn into the actualization as its starting-point. Thereby he is twice represented in the nexus, and each time with different functions: once as affirming (discerning values and foreseeing), and again as willing and acting.

However different these two functions in the finalistic nexus may be, their identity is dominant: the identity of the subject himself as the unit of these functions (the acts)—that is, as the personal entity. And here also the circular course is practically never complete; in concrete cases it never closes exactly. The subject, to whom the claim involved in setting up the end applies, is no longer in his empirical intentions the same as the one who set up the end; only in a qualified way does he represent in his volition the end affirmed by him. He does not unconditionally and steadfastly identify himself with the subject who affirmed the end. If the possibility of such empirical inconsistency did not exist, the way to hell would not be paved with good intentions. But even this well-known phenomenon is not grounded in the essence of the finalistic nexus, but in the moral inconsequence and weakness of the subject, in his incapacity to commit himself wholly to his own ethical intentions. There is a break, a split in his personality, a self-betrayal.

(f) MAN'S PROVIDENCE AND PREDESTINATION

The part which the subject plays in the finalistic nexus corresponds exactly with the position which he holds in regard to the positive Ought-to-Be. This correspondence is rooted in an inner necessity. A teleology which did not refer to values—that is, of which the ends were not materially determined by values—would in itself indeed be conceivable, although we do not meet with it as a fact. But if one sets aside realization that is accidental (that is, not led by values), then an actualization of what ought to be, which takes a different way from that of finalistic determination, is not possible. For it the finalistic nexus is the essential form. Thus it is clear that the position of the subject is one and the same in both circumstances.

The real dynamic of the finalistic series corresponds to the ideal dynamic of the Ought-to-Be. It is not a blind, crude coercion, like that of the causal sequence, which pushes forward in time, indifferent to its results. It "sees" at the same time. And not only at the same time. As a fact, it "foresees"; it anticipates the final point and thereby predestines the whole series by the direction it takes. In it the whole is prior to the part; while in the causal series, which step by step integrates itself, the whole comes only at the last.

In this anticipation there is a twofold meaning: foresight and predetermination—providence and predestination. Both are concerns of the subject as a setter-up of ends. In both inheres the basic character of man as a moral personality. For it is precisely these anticipatory acts, whereby he is the carrier of moral values and disvalues. And it is just here that we get a metaphysical insight into the nature of man. For providence and predestination are the attributes of divinity, whose wisdom, power and overruling control of the world they are said to express. Mythological and religious thought has always attributed all power to God, as it has also understood values to be his commandments. Ethics may allow free play to the metaphysics of faith so long as this does not encroach upon its own domain. But just as it needed to restore to values the ideal self-existence which is peculiar to them, so it must also restore to man what is man's.

There may or there may not be a providence of the Almighty —no one knows and no one will ever prove it—but this we know, that there is a human providence. And, likewise, a human foreordination. Imperfect, limited it may be, and for ever fragmentary, far from attaining to the ideal of an infinite providence; but it has the advantage of being not merely an ideal but a fact, a tangible phenomenon in human life. The setting up of ends by man is a fact. Ethics does and must do what in the eyes of the pious may be blasphemy; it gives to man an attribute of Divinity. To him it restores what he, mistaking his own nature, discarded and ascribed to Divinity. Or, to express it differently, it allows Divinity to step down from its cosmic throne and dwell in the will of man. The metaphysical heritage of God falls to man.

In philosophical language, teleology is the peculiarity of human nature. Whether it is found elsewhere in the world, we do not know; for it is possible only in a conscious entity capable of knowing and striving. But whether, besides men, there are other beings with such a capacity is a matter of purely speculative assumption. In man alone do we meet a setting up of ends, as well as a providence and foreordination, the capacity of striving and of actualizing a thing predetermined. For a philosophy which modestly and without preconception follows phenomena, there exists only in consciousness the category of ends as a constitutive principle—that is, the setting up and pursuit of ends, not merely conformity to ends, which can accidentally exist; perhaps this category exists in higher natures, if such there be, but certainly not in lower. The lower forms can be drawn (as means) into the finalistic nexus of the higher. But taken by themselves they are entirely without purpose, alien to it and indifferent. Precisely on account of this indifference, because they have no purpose of their own, they are in a position to take part, as means, in a nexus which in itself has no reference to them.

CHAPTER XXI

THE TELEOLOGY OF VALUES AND THE METAPHYSIC OF MAN

(a) TELEOLOGY, NATURAL AND COSMIC

THE great majority of philosophies have converted purpose, as a category, into a universally ontological, and especially into a naturalistic, category. Herein they have followed mythical thought, which sees in every striking phenomenon of nature the working of purposive powers, and, then, cannot abstain from interpreting the whole of nature, according to the analogy of one's own personality, as animated, as foreseeing and striving.

Philosophy of course does not do this unintentionally, as myth does, but as an explanation of apparent and actual adaptation to ends. The domain to which teleological metaphysics lies nearest and where it has asserted itself longest is that of organic nature. It was early recognized that in regard to manifestations of living matter the causal explanation fails. The thought is always justified that here a different kind of determination sets in—perhaps in the form of other, higher, more specific biological categories. But that the category in question should be precisely that of the finalistic nexus, which in reality we meet with only in a willing and acting consciousness, is an arbitrary assumption of this sort of metaphysics. Involuntarily one seized upon a known type of determination, without taking into account the possibility that, besides the two known types, there may be an indefinite number of unknown ones.

The Aristotelian philosophy, which gave to cosmic teleology its classic form, was rooted in a metaphysic of organic nature. From that it transferred the thought to the whole of inorganic nature, to motion itself; and it ultimately included everything in one single teleological cosmic principle, in the pure energy of the "first mover." This cosmic principle must necessarily assume the form of reason, since teleological processes can issue only from an entity which is capable of setting up and pursuing ends. Accordingly, divine, absolute reason assumed the leadership of the whole.

As regards inorganic nature, a criticism of this view arose at the inception of modern natural science. As regards organic nature, Kant's *Critique of Judgment* first proved it to be untenable. As regards the cosmos universally, a thorough criticism of it has not yet been made. Probably it cannot be given in general, because the theory is too far removed from the phenomena to have a firm foothold anywhere. In general metaphysics, teleology has only the character of fiction and is not to be taken seriously by philosophical science.

The Kantian analysis of the teleological problem has the merit of having shown exactly wherein lies the predisposition in the human mind to interpret natural phenomena teleologically. There are natural structures, the adaptation of which for the existence of other structures (for instance, the adaptation of organs for the organism) is an essential feature of them. They actually function "as if" they had been produced for a definite purpose. This "as if" is as little an arbitrary point of view as is the belief in the phenomenon of adaptation. But from the two can never be inferred the actual presence of purpose as the creative principle or of origination due to purposive activity. From the phenomenon of adaptation purposive activity can never be inferred. Yet every causal course of events can be interpreted, without self-contradiction, as a finalistic process. The phenomena exhibit only the third stage of the nexus (the causal process), and so it is easy to construct behind every causal occurrence the two preceding stages of the finalistic nexus, the setting up of an end and the backward-flowing determination of the means by the end. The phenomena as such do not oppose this interpretation, they defencelessly yield to any or every interpretation if only it does not contradict them. But the interpretation can be as little proved as disproved by the phenomena. Viewed critically, it remains a mere "as if." It may be given the significance of a methodological working hypothesis. But even then it has no claim to any bearing on the matter in hand, its only significance is the subordinate one of being a principle of investigation.

That there is such a thing as an unpurposed beginning of an adaptation which serves a purpose, or, as Kant called it, "adaptation to an end without an end" (he should have said: without purposive activity), is a very simple thought, indeed self-evident. Besides, it has been verified in countless phenomena which for centuries could only be accounted for teleologically. It has become a commonplace of present-day science, even in biology. Nevertheless, what occasions a continual exposure of the cosmic concept to teleological falsification is, first, the great complexity of ontological determination (whether causal or non-causal) and our ignorance of it, its inaccessibility to our understanding; secondly, the astonishing easiness with which purpose, as a principle, deludes us into thinking we understand, even where the situation is most intricate—, the old belief in the *simplex sigillum veri* still holds sway—, and, thirdly, the wide-reaching analogy which actually holds good, as regards the outward structure, between conscious purposive activity and merely accidental adaptation to an end.

(*b*) PHILOSOPHICAL ANTHROPOMORPHISM AND THE PRIMACY
OF AXIOLOGICAL DETERMINATION

It is evident that this liability to false interpretation is greatest in general metaphysics, where it is most confusing. Here the embarrassment is added, that man has a natural proclivity to subordinate ontological to axiological points of view, to conceive of the world-process at large as an actualization of what is valuable in itself. This conception necessarily involves a universal world-teleology.

But the consequence is, that one tacitly accepts what no human thought can justify: a consciousness which sets up ends, foresees and preordains and is in control of the real guidance of the process, an active subject, a personal entity on a large scale. If the world-process be a purposive activity, "someone" must stand behind it who is purposively active within it. Teleological metaphysics leads inevitably up to a personal Creator—that is, to that assumption which more than any other is beyond all verification.

When more closely scrutinized, this teleological concept of a personal Creator is seen to be in every particular a faithful copy of man, only raised to the absolute. Foresight and predetermination are conceived as augmented, infinite, perfect (*mens infinita, ratio perfecta*). The infinite personal Creator, as the vehicle of cosmic ends, is in everything the projection of a human and personal entity into the superhuman and cosmic.

It is not otherwise possible: every teleology of nature, of Being and of the world is necessarily anthropomorphism. It does not on that account need to stand on the level of mythology. Philosophical anthropomorphism can even avoid the distinctive concept of an infinite person, it can satisfy itself with the hypostasization of cosmic ends axiologically postulated, but otherwise existing without any vehicle and at the same time floating in the air—although in all this, taken strictly, there lurks from the beginning an inconsequence. Even so, the humanization is not lacking. It is found not only in the expressed concept of an infinite person, but in teleology itself, in providence and predestination. It is easy to see that all the finer, perhaps even the significant, distinctions—like those between theism and pantheism—are for the question in hand entirely beside the point. Teleology is always teleology.

But, finally, this metaphysic has its root in a universal primacy of values (or of value) as compared with existential categories. Axiological determination is set before the ontological. The form of axiological determination in the realm of reality is necessarily teleologic, since the positive Ought-to-Be, which issues from values, previously determines the very goals of the processes. But such a metaphysical primacy of axiological determination means a perfect determination, in which man is deprived of all range for any determination emanating from himself. The finalistic nexus does not determine in the same way as the causal nexus; it previously fixes the goals, therefore the results of all the processes. In the face of such a fixation there is no place for a finite being like man, embedded in the cosmic process itself. He is handed over unconditionally, in a bondage not of his choosing, to fixed cosmic ends. This bondage prevails throughout him and his acts—however much his acts may appear to him, in his ignorance of cosmic teleology, to be of his own free determination.

(c) The Nullification of Man and the Inversion of the Fundamental Law of Categories

For ethics this view—most consistently carried out by pantheism—is nothing short of catastrophic.

Here man is lifted metaphysically above all responsibility and accountability; conscience and the sense of guilt are delusions. In the world-process he may be a carrier, even an actualizer, of certain values. But his conveyership of these is here not different from that of other entities and things. The actualization which proceeds from him is not his work, but that of a teleological process carried on through him, and yet not in the first place willed and chosen by him. The possibility of freedom and responsibility is removed, and with it that of conveying moral values, which is impossible except for a free being who is capable of responsibility. As a moral being, as a person, he is annihilated, he stands on a level with natural entities. His nature, axiologically autonomous, and his teleology are destroyed in the cosmic primacy of axiological determination and in the cosmic teleology. In a world, determined axiologically throughout, a moral being is an impossibility. A thorough cosmic teleology utterly nullifies ethics. It is a theory of predestination—whether theistic, pantheistic or atheistic—and leaves fatalism as the only standpoint for man.[1]

Inferences of this sort are of course very seldom drawn. Ethics, however, is not to be corrupted by any philosophy. Somewhere along the line theory will break the chain of consequences and adapt itself to compromises. It is these implications which have obscured a matter in itself clear. The simple fact is that the phenomenon of the moral consciousness of man as a personal being is incompatible with cosmic teleology. A choice must be made between a teleology of nature and existence in general and a teleology of man. The alternative is a genuine and complete disjunction; we cannot resolve it either into a "both-and" or add to it a third possible case. On one side of the alternative stands a theory; on the other, a phenomenon. To a fantastic mind the theory may be of greater importance; to a philosopher the phenomenon is under all circumstances of greater weight. He must give up teleological metaphysics in favour of the ethical phenomenon.

In face of this fact one cannot refrain from asking: Wherein lies the special error of teleologism, the final ground of its discordance? Cosmic teleology is a theory closed within itself; how, then, can it contradict any phenomenon? The answer is: The self-consistency of a theory is never a proof of its tenability. Only its harmony with all the phenomena which it directly or indirectly touches can give it a footing. But here we have an entire group of phenomena—phenomena distinctively ethical—which contradict the theory. Besides this general proof, only a thorough doctrine of the categories can answer the question. Here the decision therefore can only be hinted at—on the basis of the indicated analysis of purpose as a category.

Every teleological view of the world rests upon the primacy,

---

[1] That the opposite is continually reasserted by representatives of such a metaphysics (for example, by pantheists) is a fact which betrays their way of thinking. They lack not only philosophical coherence, but every trace of serious categorial analysis.

outlined above, of values, as compared with ontological categories. This primacy is at the same time a superiority of the Ought-to-Be over the existent. And this superiority is a questionable thesis. According to it, the lower, simpler and more general principles are made dependent upon the higher, more complex and specific. But this is an inversion of the general categorial law, according to which in the gradation of the categories the lower always constitute the presuppositions of the higher, the lower are the categorial conditions or elements of the higher. Every higher category unifies the lower ones in a new way and is a higher formation which rises over them as over a material. The novelty in it is this formation itself. But thence it follows that the lower categories are always the more independent, the more unconditioned, and even subsist for themselves without the higher, and that the higher are always conditioned by them, are dependent upon them and exist only under them as their presupposition—indeed, that the new formation can become active only within the range which the lower categories leave undetermined. Against a lower a higher principle cannot enter, it cannot suspend the action of the lower; it can form a higher structure only upon a lower and with it as a building-stone. In short, the lower categories are the stronger, the higher are the weaker.

Teleological metaphysics strikes against this law. It is the inversion of the law. In it the higher principle (value, the Ought, the telos) is given precedence to the lower, the latter is made dependent upon the former. The causal nexus of nature is made dependent upon the finalistic nexus, although it is the presupposition of the latter, as the analysis of the latter has shown. The whole coherence of the world is understood according to the analogy of man and his acts. The principle of purposive activity, which we are acquainted with in personal entities and which in them has its native home, is widened and is surreptitiously carried over into real structures of every kind. The teleology of man, justifiable in its own place, is translated into a universal teleologism. This naturally shares the weakness of all transcending of limits, of all philosophical "isms."

The consequence is, that the uniqueness of man in his cosmic position is lost sight of. If the whole world is essentially like him, there remains for him no categorial distinction, no prerogative, no superiority. But upon this prerogative rests the whole ethical problem. The causal nexus (the lower form of determination) would not be taken from him; for it contains no predetermination, which would be fixed and could not be changed; the causal nexus is at the disposal of every power which is in a position to enter it as a partial cause. The finalistic nexus—the higher, the more specific form of determination—is not at the disposal of every power. If converted into a world-principle, it would dispossess man of his right.

The metaphysical humanization of the Absolute is the moral annulment of man.

(d) ETHICS AND ONTOLOGY, MAN AND NATURE

To deprive man of his prerogative is an ominous proceeding. One thereby surrenders the single point in the world at which there is really verifiable axiological determination, a constitutive teleology. In the human being we have all the conditions together which are requisite. Whether there exists elsewhere in the world anything of the kind, no one can know.

One can imagine a being capable of purpose as much as one may wish—a certain obscurity hides the inner conditions—but the capacity to foresee and foreordain, which alone renders possible the setting up of ends and the selection of means, can exist only in a real consciousness of a special grade. The finalistic nexus of course falls into the temporal dimension, but in its second stage it does not coincide with the temporal succession, but flows in the opposite direction. Now, to turn time back upon itself is an impossibility; the lower category—time in its irreversibility—is the stronger. Only a form in itself timeless can move freely against the temporal current, can forestall it and return against it. Thought, the content of consciousness, can do this. Of course the conscious act cannot. This also is subject to time. But its objective content is not identical with it. Only consciousness can furnish the ontological mode for the anticipation needed in the finalistic nexus and for the reversal of temporal succession.

Ethics with its cluster of problems is the natural advocate of man in the realm of metaphysics. It defends him against being degraded by high-flying speculation, against the surrender of his special rights to the Creator or to the world. It rehabilitates him cosmically and metaphysically. For this it needs no speculative device. It can simply hold fast to its own phenomena. It stands nearer to the facts than general metaphysics does. Metaphysics must heed ethics; not ethics, metaphysics. The position of ethics is the stronger.

The total determination of ethical reality is embedded in the universal ontological determination. It must contain the universal type of the latter, but must rise above it. It can never be exclusively finalistic, but only a blend of causal and finalistic. It can be that, because the finalistic nexus, in its third stage which is itself causal, is superimposed without resistance upon the universal type of causal determination. But the blend does not consist alone in the fact that the actualization of the end occurs causally, but in the fact that there is always an abundance of causal factors which are not determined by an end, as means, and which therefore act quite indifferently and mechanically. The finalistic nexus is actually always woven into the already existing network of causal determination. The finalistic series, thus admitted into the causal nexus, is and remains an alien body in the world-event —despite its externally causal structure (in its third stage)— just as its result in existence remains an alien body, although it shares in the real mode of being. The alien nature of its origin, the uniqueness of its determining principle, remains intact throughout its intervention.

And even by virtue of this difference in its nature it takes a dominating position. Within its own range in existence it is, among the many ontological constituents, the one which gives to the total result the decisive turn. The superiority in the world, which it confers upon man, is not that of greater determining power; by its cosmic littleness and dependence man's determining power is incomparably weaker than the causal nexus which dominates everything from beginning to end—it is a vanishing drop of real purposive activity in the sea of ontological causality which is purposively indifferent. But it is a seeing, a foreseeing, a conscious predetermining; thus it draws into its service the blind happening, into which it penetrates. From among naturalistic forms it selects, as means, what will serve its ends.

Providence and fore-ordination are the attributes of Divinity, which give to man his position of power. Finalistic determination is actually capable of turning the wide stream of causal determination, of directing it to given ends. The power of the higher over the lower form is the categorial reverse side of its peculiar weakness and dependence. This phenomenon—one might call it the miracle of ethical existence—is nothing else than the simple consequence of the categorial law as to the indirect relation subsisting between the height and the strength of categorial formations. But naturally it exists only where the distance of the higher from the lower, in spite of all dependence, is preserved. If we wipe out the distance, if we invert the fundamental law, if we universalize the higher type of determination, we surrender the central phenomenon. Nature, if it were structurally like man, if it were also like him teleologically and axiologically, would leave no room for man. His axiology and teleology would not find at hand any existential processes for him to guide, there would be none which were not already appropriated teleologically; he would find no processes, the stages of which could serve him as available means to ends.

(e) HUMAN TELEOLOGY AND "CHANCE"

The teleology of man is not otherwise possible than in the form of higher determination, raising itself upon a world already determined ontologically throughout. The metaphysical condition of its existence is the twofoldness of determinations and their stratification in one world. It is like the art of the sailor, who, when there is no wind, is himself unable to sail, but who, when the wind is up, by the mere guiding of the sails and rudder can give the ship any course—even indirectly against the wind. Man allows natural forces to work for him; he harnesses them as means to his ends. For his own mechanical energy is slight. His mastery over natural power rests singly in his teleology, which he possesses beforehand.

The finalistic series, taken in itself, is always an incomplete determination. The causal factors, indifferent to the end, the factors with which this series is involved in real life, partly escape man's anticipation. His foresight is not only limited in range, it is also in itself discontinuous. Hence his predetermination also is always more or less uncertain. The result may go counter to it. Human purpose can mistake its goal, as human knowledge can mistake its object. Then the result is one that was not willed; it is non-teleological, accidental.

The conception of chance which comes up in this connection is the only justifiable conception of it, the only one really corresponding to the facts. The metaphysical and ontological concept of it is a false one. In existence there is only necessity. What really is has its sufficient grounds for being just as it is—indeed not only mechanical causes but ontological grounds. Behind it as its determinant stands the whole of connected Being, including the system of its principles. Here one may speak of accident only subjectively and in an inexact sense, as referring to that the grounds for which we do not discern. Ontologically there is no chance, unless it be in reference to the whole as such. But here an entirely different sort of metaphysical problem enters in, which has nothing, except the name, in common with the accidental (the contingent) as something undetermined.

The true meaning of the accidental is not the opposite of something caused, and certainly not of something determined and necessitated in general, but of something aimed at, purposed, striven for—and therefore indirectly of what ought to be and of what has value. Accident is from beginning to end a teleological concept. Ever since ancient times it has been native to teleological systems. In so far as these systems are metaphysically wrong, chance as a metaphysical concept is not at all justifiable.

But it has a rightful place where teleology actually and indisputably exists, in the life of man, in ethical reality. It is involved in the point of view of a being who is purposively active. And indeed it signifies exactly the limit to his purposive activity, which is that of his foresight and predetermination. The accidental is what is not foreseen, the palpable evidence of deficiency in human prevision. It exists only for the teleology of man. And precisely on that account it plays so large a rôle in the practical life of men; for here all perspectives are teleological. But ontologically it does not exist at all, not even for man. For ontologically he is just as thoroughly determined as everything else.

SECTION VII
METAPHYSICAL PERSPECTIVES

CHAPTER XXII

TELEOLOGICAL ACTION AND REACTION

(a) The Interlacing of Causality and Finality

THE ethical problem of teleology is no more confined to a lineal series of ends than the ontological problem of causality is to a lineal series of causes. As the latter spreads out into a system of sequences, into causal action and reaction, and in reality always appears only as a constituent part of such a system, so the finalistic series spreads out into a similar serial system and *in concreto* never consists otherwise than in such a system. Only the interlacing is here more complex because the determination of ethical reality is a blend of causes and ends.

Primarily it is an interlacing of the final series with the existing causal series; and it is possible on the basis of the causal structure of the third stage of the finalistic nexus. The finalistic series so fits itself into the causal totality, into the bundle of crossing ranks, of which the real consists, as to divert the total resultant. Its introduction is always at the same time the beginning of a competition. The finalistic determination struggles for the upper hand, for its own control of the causal series. If it succeeds, the mastery is a directing of the total process to the previously fixed end, the actualization of the value by the forces of the causal series which is indifferent to the value.

Man is from the start yoked to this texture, outwardly and inwardly. As an ontological being (a natural entity) he is throughout determined. To this is added his axiological determination. As a being who senses values and is actively directed towards them, man is the teleological being among causal entities—once more inwardly, and as yet on this side of action; for both kinds of determination meet within his own twofold nature. In every inclination, disposition and mental attitude both are contained and possibly are in conflict with each other. For only conditionally is the axiological determination ever master of the ontological.

(b) THE COMMUNITY OF CONVERGENT AND DIVERGENT PURPOSES

But, secondly, there is an interlacing of the finalistic trains among themselves. And this is again essentially different from the ontological interlacing of the causal trains.

The latter join one another unhindered, they always produce a unified, harmonious result. For their courses are not predetermined. The integration of the component parts in the resultant proceeds simply according to the law: different causes—a different effect. The group of causes may vary indefinitely. No limits are drawn to the form of their combination; ontologically there is no selection of the determining elements, each can combine with any other. And if certain elements, given at the same time, cancel one another, this only means a compensation for their working together, not their elimination or destruction, certainly not a disruption of the causal determination.

The finalistic trains are altogether different. Here the ultimate member of each one has been determined upon, and every displacement of the ultimate member is a cancellation of the train attached to it. Causes are indifferent as to the issue, means are not indifferent as regards their ends. If the end is frustrated, if it is made impossible by the crossing of another finalistic train in the same course of a complex event, the causes cease to be means to this end. In a process axiologically determined there is a selection of the integrating elements; they are selected by the end—by the value which has determined the end. Not all means can combine to an end. But this signifies that in the interlacing of a finalistic train not all trains are compatible with one another. Antagonistic ends exclude one another. They destroy not only themselves but also the entire trains reciprocally.

The co-existence of finalistic trains in one and the same limited event is only possible among similar or kindred ends which harmonize. The extent of ethical reality of course provides room for an unlimited variety of ends, but not in one and the same limited process, and not in one and the same volition. In the communal life of active persons this variety is always a limited one. It can exist only in so far as it is joined into a system, into a harmony of ends. Certain very general matters must be common ends for all. A community which is organized on this principle consists of a community of ends and interests. And the interlacing of finalistic trends in it is an interlacing of identical interests. But along with such there is, within certain limits, an interlacing of divergent interests. This consists of a community of means to different ends—of course only in so far as these ends do not directly contradict one another. The same elements can also be reciprocally means and ends for different finalistic trends and therefore for different persons. Every narrower community rests upon this kind of interweaving, although generally the whole is bound together by identical interests.

Here a wide field opens for possible adaptations and combinations which outwardly appear as compromises but, viewed metaphysically as a whole, are the only possible direct paths of the finalistic nexus and the true forms of a teleological individual in a community of such individuals.

(c) Purposive Contradictions and Valuational Conflicts

The question, however, concerns the interlacing of finalistic trends within an individual person, as well as among different persons within a community.

A man may find himself confronted with different tasks which his own valuational consciousness imposes upon him. And these may conflict with one another. Then behind the plurality of conflicting trends there exists a plurality of directions in the Ought-to-Be and ultimately a plurality in the values themselves. If there were a single concrete supreme value, from which all others could be derived, such a conflict could not properly arise—or at least only through some defect of the valuational consciousness. The unity of value would give a synthesis of values. But the realm of values is not thus constituted—at least so far as we know. There is no use in affirming and postulating a unity of the moral "good" above the valuational diversities; for its content is never present, only a variety of specific contents is ever given. In this fact are rooted the many cleavages in the purposes and strivings of men. They are due to the presence of valuational conflicts in the pure and ideally self-existent manifoldness itself.

According to ancient ethics, moral conflict was nothing but the antagonism between moral and immoral (or even only non-moral) impulses in man, or, as it were, between "duty and inclination." The "natural man," or an inborn tendency to evil in him, was made responsible for the immoral impulses. Antiquity saw their origin in the desires; Christian ethics in a kind of passive resistance, the "weakness of the flesh." In all these views there is something that is right. There is a conflict between natural instinct and the consciousness of values. And this conflict is a part of the concrete moral problem. But it is not the whole.

Along with it—or beyond it—there exists a conflict of another kind, the conflict of values themselves with one another. Certainly in the variety of values all do not stand in isolation from one another; the majority combine in a certain harmony—even if not in one value. But among them there are some which contradict one another, which in concrete cases by their contents exclude one another and which nevertheless can all, in one and the same situation, be things that ought positively to be done. Here arises a conflict of another, evidently of a higher, kind, not between moral and immoral, but between moral and moral. The alternative is here not that between wrong and right, but between wrong and wrong. Either way a value is violated and, again, either way a value is fulfilled. Whoever stands in such a predicament—and life continually places men in such—cannot escape without offence.

Only acquaintance with the general scale of values can throw light upon this extremely peculiar problem. But for the problem of teleology it means a new limitation. Human teleology—the only kind which we know with certainty—is limited not only by the bounds of prevision and predetermination, not only by the fact that they are embedded in the great causal stream of cosmic events, also not only by the antagonism among the finalistic trends in communal life; it is limited as well by the clash among the chief aspects themselves of the values —the aspects which alone can determine ends.

All other limitations are external and can, at least as a rule, be overcome. For they are relative to an external situation, of which the details are continually changing. But here arises an inner, essential limit to purposive activity, which is inherent in the realm of the possible objects of purpose. No teleology— that of man or any other, in case there be any other—can transcend this boundary; it exists not alone for purposive activity, as a real trend, but even for the setting up of ends.

Indeed, for all valuational consciousness, for the sensing of values and for their moral contents, this boundary encircles the whole realm of ends. It constitutes a metaphysical problem concerning the realm of values. Responsibility and accountability, conscience and the sense of guilt, approval and disapproval, find in it a barb which entangles and complicates immeasurably their problem, the root-problem of morality. Here a limit is set also to the most daring metaphysical concept of freedom. For these conflicts are not caused by man and he cannot put an end to them; his power, his freedom, react only to the real world. But the relations between values have their root not in the actual world, but in that of ideal self-existence.

They are of an axiological, not an ontological nature. All conflicts among values are clashes of axiological determinations as such. They would set a limit to the harmony even of a divinely perfect, of a world-ruling, providence and foreordination.

CHAPTER XXIII

THE MODAL STRUCTURE OF THE OUGHT

(a) THE PROBLEM OF MODALITY IN THE NATURE OF VALUE AND THE OUGHT

JUST how the mode of Being peculiar to values is constituted, is a question to which an answer cannot be given. The concept of ideal self-existence is one which is rather rigidly outlined. But it can conclusively be seen only by aid of the laws of knowledge. A firmer grasp of it is to be gained not by any definitions but only by a survey of the domain of idealistic knowledge.

As regards the mode of Being peculiar to values, nothing is so instructive as its close analogy to the theoretical essences, especially to the mathematical and logical structures. Thereby the unity of the ideal sphere for all departments is made incontrovertibly clear, however different in each the relation of the ideal to the actual may be.

But this analogy does not give a definition of the essence of ideal Being as such. Rather is it already presupposed. But what is presupposed is not structurally analysable; it is impenetrable to thought. Ideality in itself is as irrational as reality. The spheres of self-existence are indefinable. They can be approximately described, they can be definitely pointed to, they can be brought fully before us; but what is described or presented is always only the specific content, or the relation of the spheres. What is substantial or relational can be easily grasped, but not what is modal in them. Yet the point at issue is the modality.

No theory can make rational what is not so. But there is a reverse side to the Being of values, the modality of which is more accessible to thought: the ideal Ought-to-Be. From it we may approach the problem of the mode of Being. Three things of course must not be forgotten. In the first place, the Ought-to-Be does not exhaust the essence of values; it is a modality therein; but whether it is the standard modality for the self-existence of values is a question. Secondly, the Ought-to-Be is not characteristic for the ideal sphere as such, but only for a narrower section of it, the valuational sphere. From it, therefore, one cannot acquire a definition of the ideal as such, but only of the ethical ideal in distinction from the theoretical, where again the ideality itself as an indefinable mode is presupposed. But, thirdly, in this way one approaches the ideal forms only from the side of their connection with the real. For the Ought-to-Be of values, even the ideal Ought-to-Be, does not exist for the ideal sphere itself—in which values are not something that "ought-to-be" but something that "is"—but exclusively for the sphere of actuality (including the real actional sphere of the subject). The Ought-to-Be is through and through an Ought-to-be-Real. Possibly this circumstance is the metaphysical reason why the modal structure of the Ought is capable of being understood. For the pure modalities of the spheres do not allow of being understood.

However much or little may be attainable along this circuitous route, one must follow it, because it leads indirectly also to the ideal essences, to which the Ought-to-Be adheres. The connection of value with the Ought is by no means an external one. Ever since Kant, the ethical problem of principles has taken the path of the Ought and on many a question this has proved to be helpful. Only a proper modal analysis of the Ought has been lacking. That is due to the general neglect of the problem of modality in the philosophy of the nineteenth century. A thorough and new orientation of the theory of modality would be the concern of the doctrine of the categories, or of ontology. Here only the most essential points can be indicated.[1]

[1] Cf. Kantstudien, Volume XX (1915), p. 1–28, *Logische und Ontologische Wirklichkeit.*

(b) Ontological Necessity and Actuality

If one stands fast by the traditional series of modalities—possibility, actuality, necessity—a modal definition of the Ought is impossible. Precisely the tendency to pass over into the actual, which is the dynamic of the Ought, becomes incomprehensible. Necessity, as the only mode which can carry such a dynamic, lies already beyond the actual. In the Ought, however, we have a necessity on this side of the real and the unreal. The traditional series is aware of only a single positive mode below actuality—possibility. And this is absolutely undynamic.

If now this series should prove itself adequate in the domain of theory, one would have every reason for holding to it also in the domain of practice. But it has shown itself to be inadequate in more than one respect. It is not at all an ontological, but only a gnoseological series—that is, it points out not all the stages of Being, neither the ideal not the real, but only the stages of the knowledge of Being. And this knowledge is different from Being, and could have been anticipated a priori, previously to a proper investigation of the matter. In the nineteenth century, the problem of Being almost vanished behind the problem of knowledge. All question concerning objects had the (avowed or concealed) form of a question concerning the knowledge of objects. For no other department was this so fatal as for that of modality, and indeed, not only in regard to theoretical, but especially in regard to ethical questions.

The chief difference between ontological and gnoseological modality inheres in the relation of necessity to actuality. What I see to be actual, I do not on that account need to recognize as necessary. But, nevertheless, it can very well be necessary. And in so far as it is actual, it must also be necessary. Otherwise it would not have become actual. In the real world that only becomes actual for which the total series of conditions is complete. If only one condition be lacking, the whole cannot become real; but if all the conditions are given, its actualization is inevitable.

A knowledge of actuality therefore does not presuppose a knowledge of necessity; this can follow it or not, but in every case it constitutes a higher stage of knowledge. The ontological actuality of the object, however, presupposes (regardless of its being known) its necessity as much as its possibility. An object therefore can be real only if (1) it is possible—that is, if all the conditions for it are really at hand—and if (2) it is necessary—that is, if this chain of conditions involves it.

Ontologically, therefore, necessity is the presupposition of actuality. The latter is the higher, more conditioned, more complex mode, which contains possibility and necessity in itself as conditions; it rests on them and to a certain degree is their equilibrium, their breastwork. On account of this equipoise one can define ontological actuality point-blank thus: In it nothing is necessary which was not possible and nothing possible which was not necessary. Ontological possibility is indeed not mere self-consistency (as is the case with logical possibility): it consists of a series of conditions. So long as one is lacking, the object is impossible; but as soon as the object is possible— that is, as soon as the condition which was lacking is present —the object is also necessary (it can no longer fail to appear). And precisely this being at the same time possible and necessary is its actuality. Gnoseologically, on the other hand, necessity is evidently not a presupposition of actuality. To understand why a thing must be just as it is, is a different act from perceiving that it is as it is; and it is a higher and far more complex act.

We can give the argument the following more rigid form: If A actually is, possibility is clearly not adequate for its mode of Being; otherwise it could also be at the same time non-A —that is, A need not be actual. What, then, is added to possibility in the case of actuality? Is it perhaps contingency? If it be granted that in this sense contingency exists ontologically, it would disintegrate the world of the actual and destroy the great coherences, and would, therefore, be at variance with the phenomenon of actuality. Besides, a guarantee for the actual could never be found in it. Contingency is precisely the uncertain, which could also have been different and which allows cases to be indeterminate, to be not other than a possibility. What must be added to the possibility of A, in order to make it actual, is a mode which excludes the unreality of A, and at the same time fixes it in existence. But this inability to be non-A, the impossibility of non-existence, is nothing other than positive necessity, the must-be-actual. Necessity, therefore, belongs to the essence of actuality.

Thus actuality is to be graded ontologically as the higher mode. It is a synthesis of possibility and necessity, it is their equipoise, a blending of them in one and the same existent.

(c) The Abrogation of the Equipoise of Possibility and Necessity in the Positive Ought-to-Be

This ontological—not the gnoseological—series of modes must be made the foundation, if we would analyse the modal structure of the Ought. This goes without saying; the matter under consideration is not an Ought-to-Know, but the Ought-to-Be.

In the positive Ought-to-Be there is a tendency towards something, something which lies beyond the current actuality and is not actual. Therefore the modal structure of the actual must be annulled in the mode of Being peculiar to the tendency. The equipoise of possibility and necessity must be annulled, for in it subsists the modal structure of the actual. The Ought, therefore, as regards its mode of Being, is below actuality— and precisely for the reason that its content (that which is in itself of value) lies beyond the actual.

The annulment of the equilibrium means that possibility and necessity, in their contents, do not here coincide. One of them shoots beyond the other, the other remains behind. The question arises: Which of the two is in preponderance? It cannot be possibility; that would not involve a tendency.

Much rather is it evident, that what ought to be subsists independently of ontological possibility or impossibility. It directs its claim, without distinction, towards that, the conditions of which are not present in current reality, or are not wholly present, towards that, therefore, which is not really possible. It can, accordingly, be only an excess of necessity over possibility which constitutes the instability of the modes in the positive Ought-to-Be. Necessity is the only dynamic mode, it is that which includes a tendential element, or which can manifest such an element. Necessity can also indicate a claim which inheres in the Ought-to-Be. The positive Ought-to-Be, that which the given actuality does not satisfy, makes the demand that its content shall be actualized, and it thereby implies in the subject who is sensitive to its demands a tendency to actualize them. But in the actualization we have the subsequent provision of the conditions that were lacking —that is, a restoration of possibility, the possibility of what before existed only as a demand, that is, as a necessity detached from possibility.

In the modality of the positive Ought-to-Be the two fundamental factors can be clearly distinguished: a deficiency of possibility and an excess of necessity. The former is seen in the unreality of its content, in the fact that it cannot yet be; the latter in the no less existing categorial demand for the content, in the distinctive Ought-to-Be of what is not and therefore, ontologically, is also not yet possible.

The Ought-to-Be is the annulment of the equilibrium of the relational modes in favour of necessity. Herein consists the conceptual definition of its mode.

(d) THE MODALITY OF THE IDEAL OUGHT-TO-BE AND OF THE SELF-EXISTENCE OF VALUES

What holds good of the positive Ought-to-Be must also hold good, *mutatis mutandis*, of the ideal Ought-to-Be. The latter does not necessarily refer to the unactualized, it also does not unconditionally imply a demand. As regards the actuality or unactuality of its content, it is neutral. But this neutrality does not imply indifference, but only independence. If its content is unreal, it is immediately transformed into a positive Ought-to-Be.

Hence in another sense than the positive, the ideal Ought-to-Be stands on this side of actuality—that is, wholly on this side of both actuality and unactuality. And in this sense the characteristics of the positive modality of the Ought are transferred to its mode of Being.

The necessity of its content accordingly exists here quite independently of its ontological possibility. Even absolute impossibility, impossibility under any circumstances, would not annul it. On the other hand, one must not speak here of an actual thrusting of necessity beyond possibility; for in so far as the latter keeps pace with it and allows the actual to correspond to it, it does not annul the ideal Ought-to-Be. The Ought-to-Be then simply indicates the valuational emphasis upon the Actual; it means that this Actual ought to be just as it is (or that it is as it ought to be). But only the more ought one here to speak of a preponderance of necessity; for the valuational emphasis depends upon it alone. In the ideal Ought-to-Be exists the necessity of the content, although at the same time fully detached from possibility and thereby from actuality. For the valuational emphasis does not change according to whether it meets an actuality or not. Speaking modally, the ideal Ought-to-Be is necessity existing for itself on this side of possibility and impossibility.

This is the point at which there indirectly follows from the modal analysis something concerning the mode of existence peculiar to values. Value is inseparably joined to the ideal Ought-to-Be. The latter, of course, by no means exhausts the meaning of the former, but it always and directly adheres to it. The modality of the ideal Ought-to-Be must, therefore, be contained in that of the essence of value. That is, the valuableness of a content must indicate its necessity detached from any reference to real possibility or impossibility, at the same time floating free. Only then is it to be understood that an Ought-to-Be attaches universally to what is of value, issues from it and in direction and content is determined by the value—a determination which in the positive Ought-to-Be and in the Ought-to-Do that is directed to the subject, extends into ethical reality and there can become a real determinant. Precisely that free-floating of necessity must correspond to the ideality of the value. The hovering position above the actual sphere is indeed universally a characteristic of the forms of the ideal sphere. Only, in the domain of the theoretical ideal forms, it is not merely the hovering of naked necessity, but equally a hovering of pure possibility—not indeed of ontological possibility, which consists of the complete series of conditions, but of the logical, which as such does not involve real possibility, but, looked at from this point of view, is merely incomplete.

In the ideal ethical sphere, however, the limitation due to ideal possibility does not prevail in characteristic fashion, or at least not throughout. In the realm of values contradiction exists as an ideal fact, a conflict among values. Every value here has a certain existence for itself, a superiority over the relativeness of the whole sphere. The self-existence of value is not simply ideal Being in general, but is something specific. Ideality as such is withdrawn from modal determination here, as in the theoretical domain. But, in the structure of the Ought-to-Be, the specific quality of ethical ideality is accessible to thought. And this depends upon the specific unstable equilibrium of the relational modes, the domination of necessity.

But, once more, the fact that this domination is not confined to the ideal sphere but very emphatically reaches into the actual sphere—at least in the case of certain groups of values— does not in any way violate the modal characteristic of values. On the contrary, it is a clear sign of that positive relatedness of the spheres which constitutes the fundamental metaphysical bond in the ethical phenomenon. It is the inner condition of possibility for the axiological determination of the real, for the positive Ought-to-Be, for the living tendency in ethical actuality, for the teleology and personality of man as the bearer of ethical qualities.

Without doing violence to the phenomena, one could develop the whole ethical problem from the side of the question of modality—just as it is developed here from the side of the question of values and the Ought-to-Be, and as it has been developed in other interpretations from the point of view of acts. Thereby one would be brought to exactly the same fundamental questions. The group of ethical problems, fixed by the phenomena, is always the same, from whatever side one proceeds. Only the starting-point must not be converted into the point of view from which to survey the whole ground. As the matter is neutral in regard to the starting-point, so the investigation must also be kept neutral in regard to it.

(e) THE DIFFICULTIES OF FREE NECESSITY

Concerning the points just touched upon, two reflections arise. First, it seems to be a misconception, if one sees necessity in the Ought-to-Be. If that which ought to be is in fact necessary, then it must already "be." But what ought to be stands on this side of existence—at least on this side of the real. And it is fully positive only in so far as it is not real. But ontologically the necessary is *eo ipso* actual.

And, secondly: Is a necessity detached from possibility at all thinkable? Does not the ontological sense of necessity consist in the presence of all the conditions? But, then, it must, in contents, coincide with possibility, must be in equipoise with it and must involve actuality. This is indeed the proper sense of ontological necessity—in distinction from gnoseological necessity which here does not come into consideration. How, then, could a detached, free-floating, ontological necessity be possible?

The answer to the second of these questions is this: Such a

necessity is in fact not possible ontologically. It is never met with in the realm of the real—at least not in so far as it exists purely for itself without an axiological strain in it. In the proper sense the ontological excludes it; only ethical reality can contain it. In the wider sense the ethically real is also ontological, but it is not purely so. In the domain of nature only that is necessary which is also possible; and this is actuality. The ontologically real is modally defined by this safeguarding relation. But what ought to be, as such, is not at all an ontological actuality. In ontological actuality we meet only with necessity coupled with possibility; but here the relation is different. For the Ought-to-Be is by no means an ontological phenomenon.

It is therefore a blunder to seek for the ontologically modal relation in the Ought-to-Be. In it this has been annulled. Necessity is here detached, freed from possibility. It does not consist, like ontological necessity, of the series of conditions and is not implicated in them. There exists an involution from another side, in this case from that of ideal Being; that it does not directly penetrate into the real, that it is not immediately a real involution, agrees exactly with the broken form (previously analysed) of axiological determination.

This constitutes the changed character of necessity. Here it is not a Must-Be; for that, an Able-to-Be would be required. Fundamentally, it is, of course, the same necessity. It only presents another aspect—so changed that one does not recognize it as coming from the ontological and naturalistic group. And yet the transformation is only due to escape from the union with possibility, a union to which, as to an inviolable regularity, the untrained eye, bent alone on reality, is accustomed. This regularity is inviolable, but only for the actual; not for that which exists this side of actuality and unactuality. But here what-ought-to-be exists.

In ontological language: possibility and necessity are bound indissolubly together within the actual; but in themselves they are not inseparable. At the boundaries of the actual they fall apart. But in the positive Ought-to-Be the boundary of the actual is transcended.

In passing beyond the narrowly ontological problem, one strikes upon a new, a more fundamental meaning of necessity. Not the Must-Be, not the Unable-to-be-escaped-from, not the Being-involved through the totality of conditions (the *ratio sufficiens*) is its primary meaning, but the tendency towards something. If this tendency is unresisted, it implicates, involves, and stringently draws after itself. This is the case where the series of conditions is completely at hand—that is, where the ontological possibility also exists. Here, then, necessity is a Must-Be, a real Not-to-be-escaped-from, a Cannot-be-other-wise. We commonly name this implication "necessity"—as though there were no other. But it is only a special case, the necessity of that which is at the same time possible and, on that account, actual.

If any of the conditions is lacking, if the ontological possibility is not at hand, and if nevertheless there exists a tendency towards this thing which is not ontologically possible, we have tendency in the proper sense, the detached, free necessity, in which the character of a trend towards something becomes manifest. In nature this case does not exist; it exists only in axiological determination, in the Ought-to-Be, as also in its manifestation in ethical reality, in the teleology of man. If all reality were determined axiologically, teleologically, if the whole of ontology were based on a doctrine of duty, there would need to be everywhere the same free necessity of the non-possible in existence, in the realm of things and of natural processes.

That we do not meet with it there, that, even when we come upon it in the Ought-to-Be, it shows so strange an aspect and moves us like something unbelievable, is a further clear proof of the absolutely non-axiological structure of existent reality. That there is a necessity of the ontologically impossible (naturally not of the logically impossible) is and remains onto-logically a paradox. But the paradox is just the element of novelty, of the non-ontological in axiological determination.

This is the solution of the first difficulty. There was a displacement in the concept of the necessary. In the modal analysis of the Ought, necessity is restored to its original meaning, to its more general essence, which is found on this side of the ontological union with the possible. It is fundamentally an equivocation to describe by the same term the free and the ontologically bound necessity. Ontologically the necessary is actual *eo ipso*—that is, through its coupling with the possible. Axiologically, on the other hand, and on that account deontologically and teleologically, the necessary is *eo ipso* not actual.

(f) FREEDOM, ACTUALIZATION AND POSSIBILITY

The concept of freedom which comes to the fore in this modal structure of the Ought-to-Be is especially significant. It does not coincide with the much-disputed freedom of the will. This latter is the freedom of a personal subject in face of the Ought. But here the question refers to a freedom inhering in the Ought itself, as compared with existence and its determinations. It is the autonomy of the ethical principle. For from the principle, from the pure essence of value, proceeds the Ought-to-Be. The tendency which inheres in the Ought is free as against the actual; and this freedom is shared by every real tendency of the subject, by every striving act, which is determined by the Ought-to-Be. In this sense the freedom of necessity from union with ontological possibility is in fact an essential pre-condition even for the freedom of the will.

Characteristic of all tendency and striving, therefore of all genuine teleology, is self-dependence in face of present actuality —and consequently in face also of ontological possibility— the independence with which a goal, an end, an object that ought to be, something that transcends reality, is set up before one. Here is a self-determining factor which passes beyond the given. In the ancient theories it was an error to identify this freedom with volitional freedom of choice. Here is no question of a minimum of determination, but of a maximum, no question of an indeterminateness or an open possibility, but of a determination *sui generis*, which is added to the ontological determinations. But this means: It is not a freedom of possibility, but of necessity. On this ground, Kant (however differently he expressed it) rightly set aside freedom in the negative sense, as regards the autonomy of the principle, and allowed validity only to freedom in the positive sense, "freedom under the law." Indeterminism, even partial indeterminism, is a false theory; there is no actuality free from determinism.

But the proof of free necessity is the point of the problem which touches the real interpenetration of ontological and axiological determination in the one existent world, the efficacious activity of the positive Ought-to-Be in ethical actuality. This efficacious activity is the actualization of the unactual which has been set up, the realization of the ideal. That it takes place in the third stage of the teleological nexus, that it has causal structure like all real processes, and that it attaches itself to the latter without resistance, despite its reversed determination, has been shown in the analysis of the finalistic nexus. But now it is seen that in this process even free axiological necessity is added to ontologically bound necessity— and this by the very fact that it subsequently restores the missing ontological possibility, and produces the conditions of actuality which were lacking. In this restoration of possibility, in the making possible of what ought to be in the actual, it is indeed no longer free, or is only free to a limited degree— namely, free only within the limits of current reality in general; for instance, within the given actual situation, which comes in question as the point of impact with reality. The actualization of what ought to be is nothing else than its rendering of itself ontologically possible.

In the actualization begins again the balancing of necessity and possibility. The equipoise of both, which in the Ought-to-Be was disturbed, the stable level of the actual, is reinstated. But it is no longer entirely the same actual which is restored, but one which is changed in content; the Ought-to-Be and the disturbance of the balance have left traces of themselves. The projected necessity, behind which possibility lagged, does not flow back, but in the actualization it draws the halting possibility after it. Thus it actually subsists in making possible what ought to be. In the teleological nexus of reversed determination (that is, in its second stage) it discovers the means, which in their totality constitute the ontological possibility. By producing the possibility, by bringing about conditions, it actualizes, therefore, that which was set before it. And as the ontological necessity first sets in with the totality of the conditions, one may with equal right say: From the merely ethical, the free-floating and at the same time naked, necessity it leads over the real possibility to the ontologically bound necessity, which follows the possibility.

The third stage of the finalistic nexus is this real after-flooding of possibility. Here the conditions that were lacking are step by step "produced"—for this process is causal. Here a living energy is efficaciously active, a real work is accomplished. For the real, in the plane of which the process flows, has previously its ontological determinations. It offers resistance—indeed only a passive resistance—for it has no "tendencies" of its own, but even this passive resistance works as an inert substance, upon which the tendency of the process is forced. The actualization achieves this work, it draws the inert mass forward behind what-ought-to-be, sets it in motion and allows it again to come to rest only when it has reached, in content, the position of what ought to be. It is the mode of Being of an ideal energy in the sphere of reality. In the strict sense of the word, it makes possible the ontologically impossible.

CHAPTER XXIV

THE METAPHYSICS OF PERSONALITY

(a) PERSONALISTIC METAPHYSICS

TOGETHER with the concept of value and the Ought, that of personal being is the central concept of ethics. It became prominent in the problem of the positive Ought-to-Be, as every reaching forth of values out of the ideal realm into the actual depends upon the part played by the subject. Among all real entities only the subject has the power of mediation. Consciousness, knowledge—of the world as well as of values ("reason")—activity, Will, self-determination, purposive activity, and prevision and predestination, which are involved in such activity, all these are elements of this power of the subject.

But it was further shown that the subject in this sense is something more than a subject; he is a person. He is characterized not only by the existence of such acts, but also by a specific quality of value and disvalue, which adheres to them and only to them. He is no longer a mere ontological entity, he is also an axiological entity. The subject is a person in so far as he is, in his transcendent acts—that is, in his conduct—a carrier of moral values and disvalues.

To this extent a personal entity may be distinguished purely by the ethical phenomenon. However metaphysical this delineation in itself may be, however little the essence of personality— and its peculiar mediation between values and actuality—may be discerned from it, the boundary of facts given in the ethical phenomenon has not been overstepped. To this extent the metaphysic of personality lies still within the nature of what is demonstrable and nothing in any way speculative has been added to it. It contains a critical minimum of metaphysics.

Such unavoidably metaphysical factors, however, have in

them something seductive for philosophical thought. They easily rob it of critical moderation; they exercise a kind of impulsion towards the removal of limits even in the case of quite modest interpretations. The inducement to explain the world in terms of personality, to personalize the world, has its root in the problem of the personal entity.

Since ancient times, this view of the world has been widely held. The Stoic doctrine of the Logos, although itself not yet properly personalistic, prepared the way for it and created its categories. Here the concept of a world-spirit had its immediate predecessor—in Neo-Platonism it was identified with the νοῦς of Aristotle; here arose the concept of that συμπάθεια, which, as the common feeling of finite beings for one another, permeates the cosmic whole and binds it into the unity of a collective spiritual entity. And here also was developed the view that the finite spirit (man) is embedded in a universal infinite spirit, the divinity—a thought which already contains in a nutshell the ordered gradation of spiritual units from man upwards to Godhead.

Personalistic metaphysics may be of different origins. Something of it lurks in every theistic view of the world. But in theism its basis is not ethical but religious. Ethics cannot involve itself in any speculative philosophy of religion, so long as the latter does not set up tenets contrary to ethics. But the case is different when such speculation thinks it can base itself on the ethical nature of personality, and when a universal cosmic personalism is derived from the unavoidable metaphysic of the person as a moral being. Then ethics must take sides. For in the tenability of such a derivation its own foundations are at stake.

Among contemporary theories, the chief example of such a personalism based on ethics is furnished by the very theory to which the investigation of values owes its greatest advancement —the ethics of Scheler. With his view we must necessarily come to grips just at the very point where, in fundamental matters, we are at one with him.

(b) Scheler's Doctrine of Person and Act

His theory starts from the position that person and act belong indissolubly together, that the two are not in consciousness, not in the "ego," that neither is an object of psychological reflection and that neither appears in "experience." "A person is not an empty starting-point of acts, but is a concrete being, without which any talk about acts never touches the full and adequate essence of any act." The person is not something behind or above the acts, but is already contained in them; he is their real unity, inseparable from their essence. And this unity is concrete, it subsists "for acts of every possible variety." It is presupposed as the consummating essence of every single act. In the unity of this consummation the acts are fundamentally joined. An isolated act is a psychological abstraction. In actuality—and the consummation of an act is its actuality —there is no isolation.

Phenomenologically, these propositions embrace the essence of a person—in distinction, on the one side, from a thing, and, on the other, from a subject. But they do not, of course, touch the positive essence of personality. All appearances, contents, functions of consciousness, so far as they can be psychologically conceived, do not coincide with acts and certainly not with their concrete unity in execution. As the genuine act is only in its fulfilment, so the person is only in the unity of the fulfilment and therefore not in any, even an inner, manifestation, nor in any experience.

Here an absolute limit is set to psychological understanding. There is no proper psychology of the person. Indeed, there is not even a psychology of acts. The essence of remembering, expecting, hoping, loving, eludes reflection directed upon the facts of consciousness. If consciousness is the field of psychological objectivity, the proposition must hold good that acts have a superconscious existence. And if in regard to them there is no question as to any other than this psychological objectivity, the further proposition must also hold good, that, in general, acts are not objects and cannot be given in any objective presentation. The same then holds naturally in a higher degree of their consummating unit—the person.

Scheler draws this latter inference. According to him, the person, because he "exists and lives only in the fulfilment of intentional acts," is, in his essence, not an object. We may very well have an inner experience of the ego and its functions, but not of the person and his acts. In this the presupposition always is that inner experience in the psychological sense is the only kind of knowledge about anything that is here under question.

But precisely this presupposition may be disputed. If there were no possibility of a presentation of acts and persons as objects, ethics would itself be an impossibility. For man as a person is the object of ethics. And his actively transcendent acts (disposition, will, conduct) are just what is subjected to valuational judgments, they are what constitute the object of the judgment of value. Ethics takes as its object what Scheler says is incapable of becoming an object. The attitude of ethics is in this not a fictitious one, not, as it were, one which is first set up by philosophical theory; rather does ethics take over this attitude from concrete moral life itself. The evaluating attitude towards actions and acting persons is a thoroughly solid one, characteristic of man in general. Indeed, one might say it is the primal attitude, infinitely more natural and general than psychological reflection and certainly at least just as natively original as the attitude towards things. For the unsophisticated man, the latter is always conditioned by his attitude towards persons; for in life persons are always the more actual.

But such a primitive attitude towards persons is thoroughly objective. However essentially different it may be from the attitude towards things and the relations of things, it is in its objectivity in no respect different. The difference between ontological and axiological, between theoretical and practical reference, stands on this side of all conceivable limits of objectivity in general. All reference is to a something referred to;

and all intuition or immediacy is an intuition or an immediacy of objects. That those acts which here constitute the object are themselves in turn acts referring to something and therefore on their side have objects to which they are directed, does not in the least prevent them from being themselves objects. There are acts *sui generis*, which are referentially directed to acts. And the phenomenon of moral consciousness consists precisely in this, that there are such acts.

(c) Acts and Persons as Objects

This phenomenon, as was said, is an elemental one, not to be traced back to other phenomena. Whether one can explain it by the help of any theory may be regarded as questionable. But its existence and its phenomenological describability are indisputable. The description of it would alone fill a whole chapter. Here it is cited only as evidence for the following facts of the moral life.

Man, understood in the sense of a natural presentation of him, discovers himself as a person among persons. He belongs to a world of persons. Anyone who enters into the domain of his personal life is primarily, as such, presented intuitively to him. Not by reflection does he first come upon the fact that there is another person, but from the outset he sees himself placed in a living actional relation with the person, which is at the same time a relation of disposition, conduct and evaluation. Thus for him every "other man" is an immediate object of conduct, inward and outward; and he sees that every other man in the same way makes him himself an object of conduct, irrespective of whether this conduct be merely inward or of a kind that shows itself in actions.

For one another, persons are from beginning to end embedded in a communal world of real objects. They share the same mode of reality with things and the relations of things. That they do not exist except in the fulfilment of acts makes no difference. For the acts themselves share the same reality with events of every kind. But it inheres in the essence of the real in general, to be a possible object of knowledge. Whether in fact there is a knowledge which grasps a specific reality depends upon other conditions. In itself it might be that there were no knowledge of persons because no real knower was adjusted towards persons as objects. But such a personalistic agnosticism does not tally with the facts. We have a consciousness of persons, and indeed one as elemental as of things—an immediate knowledge that these beings surrounding us do not stand there, as things do, indifferent to us, but in every situation of life take up an attitude towards us, turn away from us or recognize us, bear us ill-will or love us. Precisely in the fulfilment of such acts consists the personal element in them, and it is exactly these acts of taking sides for or against, of which we have an immediate consciousness—a consciousness which may be deceived like any other consciousness of an object, but which exists in even the most simple-minded.

We have a primary perception of other persons, it is of the most vivid, concrete and individualized kind, a knowledge of the acts of inner preference on the part of other persons; chiefly of acts which are directed towards ourselves, but also of acts which are directed towards others than ourselves. This knowledge has nothing to do with psychological reflection, nor is it essentially furthered by psychological knowledge when such is added to it. It is something immediate and in its immediacy supremely puzzling. For, however much it may be conditioned by external experience and thoughtful reflection, it can never be resolved into these as its elements. Besides this, there is contained in it a direct attitude of feeling for the actional consummation of another person—that is, for the peculiarly personal element in him.

In this sense persons and genuine personal acts are in fact objects. Persons, as well as things, are objects. The difference between person and thing has no bearing on the matter. Persons are no more transcendent than things. Whatever is real equally transcends the subject who knows it, is equally independent of him, equally self-existent. Persons may be knowable in a more limited sense than things; but, like things, they are objects of possible knowledge.

Nor has this gradation anything to do with the opposition of the outer and inner worlds. For every person, every other person belongs to the outer world; and, once more, every person is in himself an inner world, he is the subject for which other persons are objects. The whole ontological interpenetration of inner and outer worlds is already presupposed here. It is a condition of the mode of existence for personal beings.

(d) PERSONALITY AND SUBJECTIVITY, "I" AND "THOU"

But persons are, of course, objects of a different kind. This difference does not affect their modality and proper objectivity; but it does, of course, affect their structures and their metaphysical essence. Persons are not chiefly objects of knowledge, but of interest, of disposition and action. And they are so for this reason, that they themselves are, likewise, beings who are interested in others. They are interwoven into another texture than that of cognitive relationship. The correlation of subject and object does not exhaust their concrete connection with life. To be sure, things also are woven into the many-sided context, but always in one aspect only. An attitude can be taken towards them, but they themselves take no attitude. For this reason the attitude towards them is different. They are not objects of disposition and action, they are only means in the connection of possible actions. Actional intentions pass beyond them to persons. Ethical or axiological consideration applies only indirectly to them. But to persons and acts it applies directly.

The two correlations "person and thing" and "subject and object" do not coincide, but are not indifferent to each other; they do not simply overlap each other, like spatial dimensions. For things are never subjects, but objects may very well be persons. Things are not necessarily on this account objects (to a subject), they can—just like persons—be trans-objective, indeed trans-intelligible. Everything real is fundamentally neutral concerning the limits of its objectification or capability of being objectified. But persons are necessarily subjects of possible objectification. For acts, in the unitary achievement of which personality consists, are nothing but transcendent acts; they are directed to objects, and herein they carry in themselves the centrality of the subject. None the less subjectivity and personality are fundamentally different. One and the same entity, in which subject and person coalesce, is one thing as subject and another as person. As subject he is a purely ontological entity and stands over against the real external world which is in part objectified. But, as a person, he is at the same time an axiological being; in his transcendent acts he is at the same time the carrier of specific values and disvalues which are peculiar only to him. But this distinguishes him from the thing with which, ontologically, he shares reality, and, gnoseologically, shares the peculiarity of being an object of knowledge.

A person stands in a twofold relationship—to the world of things on the one side, and the world of persons on the other. In the former, as a "self," he stands over against the "not-self," in the latter as "I" over against "Thou."

It is a widespread psychological error to refer the correlation of I and Thou to the subject. Rather is it the peculiar relationship existing only among persons, which above all other relations everyday speech indicates by the personal pronouns. I and Not-I constitute a gnoseological, and indirectly also a psychological, contrast: I and Thou a purely ethical contrast. This subsists only among act-fulfilling, personal beings, and is really present only in the execution of transcendent acts directed by a person to a person. It is a distortion of this relation, in itself so simple, when Scheler affirms that an "I" can neither act nor take a walk. Only an "I" can do either. Naturally not as a subject—a subject never acts nor takes a walk—but surely as a person. The terminology which applies the word "I" to the subject is linguistically forced and entirely arbitrary. Language says "I act," and "I take a walk." Here the personal sense of the "I " is clear. And in so far as the speech, disposition and conduct of an "I" are necessarily directed to a "Thou," so the same thing which holds good of the "first person" necessarily holds good of the "second person."

The error becomes still more serious if with Scheler one separates the essence of the person from that of the subject and makes it independent. The failure to appreciate the personal significance of the concept "I" intensifies the evil. The person, if taken out of the correlation of I and Thou—in which alone we know him—becomes transformed into something absolute which is no longer referred back, is no longer relative to anything at all. "God, for instance, can be a person but not an I, since for him there is neither a Thou nor an external world." Such an argument betrays its untenability in this, that it finds itself at home in what is most unknown and most impenetrable (in what is never an object of definite thought) and carries over to what is known and alone is given that which it assumes to behold in the most unknown. We do not know whether such a personal Being exists or even can exist—a person not in the presence of a second and similar person and not confronted by an actual world. Just as little as we may on this account deny his possibility, so little may we assume it. And even if there be such a Being, nothing follows as to the essence of personality as such. For even this may have been utterly transformed in him.

If God be a person—in the only meaning of the word accessible to us and given in the phenomenon—he must also be a subject. For a person is a fulfiller of acts; and the existence of acts consists in their execution. But the acts, which alone are under consideration, are transcendent acts; they are directed towards persons as objects and thereby they mark their fulfiller as a subject. As a categorial form, a subject is a presupposition of a person. Personality is the higher and therefore the more fully conditioned; but the subject is the lower, and therefore the conditioning, form. In the subject the ethical carriership of values is lacking; the subject, as such, is not a fulfiller of acts ethically relevant.

In itself a subject might exist even without personality: a purely mirroring, representing entity, without any sensing of values, any disposition, any preferences. We do not know of such a being, and have no right to assume its existence; but it is conceivable without inner contradiction; philosophically it has often been constructed from the point of view of epistemology, in order, then, to lead in theory a shadow-like existence incapable equally of being confirmed or denied. But the converse, a personal being without subjectivity, is in any case not possible. It is conceivable only by stripping both concepts of their fulness of content and by detaching them outwardly and abstracting them from each other. But if one means the personal being in its concreteness, as a unity and as a fulfiller of transcendent acts directed towards persons, one immediately sees that one has presupposed in it the transcendent relation "subject-object." A person who is not a subject is an empty abstraction.

Personality exists only on a basis of subjectivity, just as subjectivity exists only on a basis of organic life, and life only on a basis of the whole subordinate uniformity of nature. This categorial gradation is not reversible. Nor does it mean a bringing-forth of the higher out of the lower, but only that the higher is conditioned by the lower. The novelty of the higher form is autonomous as compared with the lower, it introduces new uniformities and formations which are not in any way contained in the lower. But it cannot exist without them. It has free play only "upon them," it cannot displace or nullify its own basis. The higher category is always the weaker, the more dependent—in spite of its autonomy; the lower is the stronger, it cannot be ever again destroyed by any power—in spite of its paucity of content and indefiniteness of outline. For the higher form it is only material, but it is necessary material. Without it the higher remains an abstraction. Every inversion of this categorial law—however plausibly it can be done by abstraction from the specific content of the forms—is a fundamental misunderstanding of the metaphysical facts, a distortion of the problem, a falsification of the given coherence of phenomena, an empty play with thoughts. And even if one should by such sport arrive at desired results, the thing desired would not on that account have been demonstrated to be true. The result would have crept in surreptitiously.

(e) PERSON AND WORLD

Scheler's further thesis concerns the correlation of person and world. According to him a world is always relative to a person whose world it is; it is "only a concrete world and only as the world of a Person." Consequently, an individual world corresponds to an individual person. And, again, in such a world only individual truth is valid; for instance, metaphysical truth itself must have for every person a different content, "since the content of cosmic existence itself is for every person a different one." Therefore absolute truth also can be only "personal"; and the fact that it is so is grounded not in the nature of truth but in the nature of existence. As for the person, he does not belong to the world, he is not part of it, he for ever remains over against it.

If one takes this proposition exactly in the connection in which it stands, it has a distinctive merit. For it is directed against the assumption of a "transcendental reason," a "consciousness in general", a "universal" to which the world is said to be relative. Such an assumption is, of course, unfounded, particularly if one means to base the super-personal unity of the world upon it. But the mistake lies not in the impersonality of the world-correlate, but in its subjectivity; and ultimately in the presupposition that in general the world is relative to a correlate. For such a relativity permits in no way of being demonstrated ontologically. There exists no phenomenon which corresponds to it.

But this latter consideration turns against Scheler's proposition itself. In its polemical meaning this is far from being exhausted. It is throughout a positive, highly metaphysical proposition. Remarkably enough there is at work here a motive inspired by that very idealism which Scheler is attacking. It is only transformed from the transcendental-subjectivistic scheme to one which is equally a transcendental-personalistic scheme; a shifting which is very slight, since personality presupposes subjectivity. Nor is the inference lacking which directly follows from it—namely, that there is a transcendental person, the inference that there is an "infinite and perfect spiritual person" to which alone the proposition was directed.

Above all: A world, concrete, intuited, given, can of course only be the world of a person, must be "relative" to that person, and all truth valid in regard to it must necessarily be a "personal truth." But it does not inhere in the nature of the world simply as existent, to be either concrete and intuited or to be given. Its existence and that of all things in it has its mark in this, that it subsists independently of any discernment of it or any presentation of it; indeed, there is no single phenomenon of discernment and objectiveness, in which the self-existence of the thing discerned and given is not involved. Every kind of insight—be it experience or aprioristic discernment, emotional certainty (as in the sensing of value) or inference according to the understanding—carries in it this index of the self-existence of its object as an essential factor; and only so far as it bears this index in itself does it at all manifest the specific character of an insight. It regards its object as something self-existent. That a real self-existence corresponds to the self-existence which is implied may of course be questioned, but only in the sense of universal scepticism, or of a universal subjectivism. But neither of these corresponds in any way to Scheler's "relativity to a person."

Each is besides a mere assertion in contradiction to fact, an assertion the tenability of which is still to be proved.

The real world exists, even when it is not beheld, even when it is present to no one. Subjects, to which alone it, or rather a part of it, can be presented, themselves emerge only in it, they are entirely embedded in it, they are carried by it. But it itself, as also those parts of it which are observed, exists quite apart from the emergence of a subject. The world and its parts do not stand or fall with their being discerned, with their being objects, but they arise and vanish according to quite differently constructed laws of universal existence—not otherwise than do the subjects who also are embedded in their environment. But this self-existent world is likewise in itself "concrete," as is every member of it; it is ontologically concreted, independently of any concreteness of a possible intuition or presentation. Concreteness is just as little relative to an experiencing subject, or to a person, as is the texture of life itself, which has incorporated the person into the whole of the cosmic texture. Concreteness is not at all an affair of experience, like beholding and presentation, but is a peculiarity of all ontological reality as such.

If we wish to draw the "world" at all into the realm of ethical investigation, we must accept as true what is true of it ontologically: that it is in no wise a correlate of anything. What is meant by the world is precisely the whole, which plainly embraces all correlations. If we do not wish to describe this whole as the world, we must call it something else; but that would not remove the problem of the cosmos. "The world," this eternal singular one, is far from being merely the world of things—not to mention the world merely of objects, for even things in their self-existence are indifferent as to whether they be objects for anyone or not—this same world is just as primarily a world of persons; it embraces the real living texture of persons, including their specifically ethical relations; these are just as originally in it as is the universal context of reality in general. If we wanted to banish personal entities from this cosmic context, we should thereby rob them not only of their concrete environment, but even of their reality. For the cosmic context is the context of all reality.

"Person and thing" constitute a relation of opposites within the real world. But the contrast is by no means concerned with existentiality, it is exclusively constitutive, structural, and, besides that, axiological; it is a contrast as regards the carriership of values. It cannot therefore be so extended as to apply to "person and world." For the "world" is as much a world of persons as of things. Accordingly, it is erroneous not to wish to acknowledge persons to be on a level with things as parts of the world. And whether there also exists a person outside of the world to whom "the world" as a whole could be a correlated thing is beyond human judgment. We know only the phenomenon of persons existing in the world, living in it, entities which will and act, and it is a fundamental phenomenon of such a personal entity—since it exists in the unifying fulfilment of its acts; but its acts, again, presuppose a living context of persons—it can only exist in a world of persons (and things), but can never stand wholly over against the world as a correlate.

And, finally, as for the concept of "personal truth," it is in a certain sense, of course, correct: namely, as an expression of the scope of transcendent acts on the part of a single person —a realm that is actually most specifically conditioned. What we may rightly call the "personal world" of the individual is always a segment of the self-existent world, and is therefore conditioned by its larger connections, as well as by the special position which the individual person holds towards persons and things.

The segment as such, as well as the special perspectives and objectifications of which it consists for the individual, are of course relative to the person. But the mode of existence of the persons and things themselves, which lie within the segment, is by no means relative to the individual, but is wholly independent, like everything real. For the "personal world," for the segment as such and for its mode of objectivity, "personal truth," which exists only for the person, must hold good. But even this sort of validity is not that which pertains to truth as such. Only in an inexact sense is there such a thing as "personal truth"; rightly speaking, it is not truth at all. It is of the essence of the existent, as something determined for all time in itself and unequivocal, that there can be only one, and indeed only an absolute, truth in regard to it. Every other concept of truth is a substitute which does not deserve the name.

Were the fulness of content of the "personal world" a fulness existing only for one person, there would not be, above the relative and personal, an absolute truth; and the orientation of man in the world would sink in a shoreless relativism. But if all forms which are drawn into the orientation are ontologically rooted in the common self-existent world, every personal enclosure of sections and, with it, all discernment, all experience, are something secondary. Above the questionable "personal truth" rises an absolute truth, which for the individual person remains, of course, an Idea, but nevertheless gives the foundation to his insight and his orientation in the world.

CHAPTER XXV

METAPHYSICAL PERSONALISM

(a) THE IDEA OF THE WORLD AND THE IDEA OF GOD

IF one starts from Scheler's correlation between "person and world," the "world" lacks the all-embracingness and absoluteness which everybody involuntarily understands in the concept of it. The limited personality therefore is confronted with the idea of the "macrocosm," to which it is related as the part to the whole. But if correlativity continues in force as a law, there must be a corresponding personal counterpart for the macrocosm. The idea of God formulates such a correlate, the idea of "an infinite and perfect spiritual person." The existence of such a person indeed does not follow from the idea; but his acts, in their essential outlines, are for us conceivable from actional phenomenology, in so far as this considers acts not of specific, empirical persons, but of all "possible" persons. "Thus with the unity and identity and individuality of the world the idea of God is given on the ground of an essential coherence." These words give expression to metaphysical personalism.

Scheler regards it as irrational to posit a single concrete world as actual, without positing at the same time the idea of a concrete spirit; one could not believe in the former without at the same time believing in God.

What justifies such a statement? In the first place, there are found here once more the disguised metaphysical outgrowths of idealism which occasion the statement—such assumptions as "universal reason," the "moral governor of the world," the "logical subject." These are indeed only surrogates for a macrocosmic correlate of the world; and in the polemic against them Scheler's proposition has a certain justification. But the fundamental presupposition is still that "the" universe as such requires a correlate, that to be a world for someone inheres in the very mode of the world's existence. The statement shares this presupposition with the idealistic theses.

But this presupposition has been shown to be erroneous. There is no such essential law. It contradicts the plain and evident meaning of all objectivity, theoretical as well as practical. Just as little does the concreteness of the world depend upon the concreteness of a personal counterpart. Conversely, a personal being which was not a member of a concrete, real world would itself be an abstraction. For in the fulfilment of its act —transcendent throughout and directed upon self-existent objects—it is necessarily set in the real cosmic context as a real part of it; but it is never "over against" the world as a whole.

The basic error here has nevertheless a deeper root. It lies in the universalization of personality beyond its natural sphere of validity and objectivity, in the detaching of it from its presupposition, from subjectivity, and from its whole ontological sphere, the real world itself.

The phenomenology of the person intensifies this universalization. It gives only the essential features of personality, considered in themselves and at the same time isolated. However objectively these may be regarded, they are only half discerned so long as they are not viewed in the context of persons and, ultimately, of reality. The entire ineptness of the extension given to their range of validity has its ground here. This kind of transcendence of boundaries takes place wherever essential features, correctly seen in a particular phenomenon, are carried over, without noticing it, to the totality of all phenomena, even of those which are fundamentally different. Materialism, logicism, psychologism, are such one-sided views of the world, justified in the narrow limits of their native problem, totally wrong as interpretations of the whole. Personalism belongs to this series. What holds good for an aspect of the world, which exists only relatively to a real individual person, for instance, its relativity to a person, is evidently not transferable to the world itself, of which it is a section and a partial aspect. Aspects of the world are relative to persons, and even this is true only in so far as the persons are members of a real world; but the one real world itself is not on that account related to any person. But, conversely, all persons are onto-logically relative to the world. If out of this relation of depen-dence one makes a correlation by a forced passage beyond bounds, one stands immediately in the conceptual construction of metaphysical personalism.

(b) The Individual Person and the Communal Person

Metaphysical personalism has a deeper ethical root in the thought of a "collective person." That the individual, isolated and for himself, is an abstraction, that he does not emerge except in larger contexts of persons and is conditioned not only in his existence but also in his ethos by his context, is an ancient view. But Scheler conceives of these contexts—in so far as they are not merely biological communities, not mere societies of individuals but spiritual unities of a peculiar kind —as persons of a higher order, as "collective persons." They also are fulfillers of action and carriers of actional values, and indeed in such a way that the acts of individual persons are always conditioned by those of the collective person. This relationship finds expression in the solidarity of individual persons and of their joint responsibility for one another as well as for the collective person. What binds man and man, whether it be reciprocal understanding, striving or love, communal knowledge, work or the aim of life, is not a derived organiza-tion of individuals originally independent, but the fact that they are rooted in a personal unit of a higher order. If to this we add that such higher orders always take on further potentialities —up to an absolute and all-embracing corporate person—the personalistic picture of the world culminates in the idea of God.

The magnificence of this metaphysical perspective must be

fully acknowledged. But it is precisely such views that, on account of their vastness, are more likely to mislead than to convince.

It is true that the acts of individual persons, and the persons themselves, are always variously conditioned by the greater collective structure in which they are rooted; it is also true that understanding and love have a transcendent character which, from the point of view of the individual, is irrational. Ever since the profound thought of the Stoic συμπάθεια there have been many worthy metaphysical attempts to explain spiritual co-operation. Equally indisputable is it that the phenomena of joint responsibility and solidarity are something which transcends the limits of the individual. It would be a blunder to decide authoritatively how these eternal riddles of the human ethos are to be solved. In the metaphysic of morality there are more problems than these that are not solved. At the present-day stage of investigation we have still a long way to go. If all previous solutions were premature, we have a double reason for leaving them on one side for a time and attending to more immediate questions. The personalistic solution, despite its peculiar charm, is no better than the older errors of speculation. For the ascription of personality to the higher social units—to nation, State, cultural circle, humanity —is a theory which but feebly withstands criticism.

The conditioning of the individual person and his acts by a narrower or wider community does not by any means imply the personal character of the latter—just as little as the conditioning of individual knowledge by the prevalent level of public opinion implies that the latter is a conscious communal subject. It is true that those social units in a certain sense are also fulfillers of acts, and that to a certain extent the carriership of ethical fulfilment inheres in them. But the very question is whether this fact alone is sufficient ground for attributing to them personality in the full and intensified sense.

It would be much more conceivable that they possessed only a borrowed, pale and lowered degree of personality. There is no doubt, for example, that a nation as such can act, execute tasks, quarrel and have debts; but it remains questionable whether all this holds good of it in the same sense as of a single individual, whether with the community the real initiative does not always issue from single persons, whether communal ends are not seen by individuals and whether wrongdoing and guilt do not fall conspicuously upon them. So long as the question is considered only in general outlines, it can of course only be said that it may be so. But all this is changed as soon as one enters into a consideration of the principles, the categories, involved in the problem. Here we find that very definite limits are set to the possible extension of personality.

(c) "Persons of a Higher Order" and the Consciousness of such an Order

For Scheler the question was simpler than it is in itself, because he removed the essential condition of the relation which subsists between person and subject. If one takes free-floating personality, without any categorial basis, there is nothing to prevent one from allowing gradations of personality to mount as high as one pleases. But if we see that personality is based upon a subject which carries it and cannot exist without such a basis—for since acts achieved by persons are directed to objects, they must proceed from subjects—if we see this, then with one stroke such a gradation finds its limits. Personality can only inhere in such structures as already have the categorial form of subjects. The reversal or dissolution of this connection means an inversion of the fundamental law of categories.

This law declares that a higher form always has the lower as its presupposition, rests upon it, is therefore dependent upon it as upon a *conditio sine quâ non*. Now, as a person, in comparison with a subject, is indisputably the higher form— by virtue of his axiological nature he belongs to a sphere of existence in which a subject as such cannot participate—it follows that personality cannot exist without subjectivity, therefore that it can never exist as a detached personality. A person can be only a subject, an "I," a consciousness, an entity which has its inner world in contrast to the outer world, and to which the former is presented in an inward aspect— an entity which can know, feel, love, hate, tend towards a goal, will and do. One may say in the words of Leibniz: apperception is the condition of personality.

There is no use in citing the nature of God as an argument against this position. Categorical laws, in so far as they are discerned at all, are evident. But we know nothing about the nature of God. Only in accordance with the categorial relations, which rule our thought and intuition, can we hold anything before our minds, but never without them or in opposition to them. Categorial elements, torn from their context, may indeed be easily built up without this basis into something logically harmonious with itself—but in the way in which a fabulous world may be self-consistent. For such a construction no ontologically real mode of possibility exists.

Now if personality is bound to a consciousness, "persons of a higher order" can evidently be attached only to a consciousness of a higher order. But it is very questionable whether and in how far there exists a consciousness of a higher order above the individual consciousness. In this direction the fantasy of idealism has been inexhaustible; the "transcendental subject," the "consciousness in general," the *intellectus infinitus* are apparently brought against personalism. But they are little suited as characterizations of such corporate entities as nation, cultural group, humanity. Scheler expressly sets them aside. Taken literally, such assumptions stand on a very insecure footing; they are free forms without categorial support, quite incapable of supporting themselves, still less of sustaining the far heavier burden of collective persons.

But if one starts rather from the given phenomenon, if one finds one's bearings where solidarity and joint responsibility are found, it becomes clear that these do not at all establish a consciousness of a higher order. Rather are they functions which can evidently exist without a binding collective consciousness. Both lie in an internal and unique connection which subsists between acts and actional values of individual persons. How such a connection is metaphysically possible is indeed very puzzling. But an over-arching consciousness is in any case not the binding force; therefore, also, a collective person is not. For actional consciousness, valuational consciousness, and the sense of responsibility are always features of an individual person only, whether they exist in oneself or another or in a community of persons. In any case we know every consciousness of that kind only as the consciousness of an individual, however much it may reappear in other individuals in the same form or variously modified. But that it is a shared consciousness of the acts and actional values of others, that acts of many directed to the same end coalesce and work like a collective act of a communal person and can possess value or disvalue, all this signifies anything but their centralization in a corporate personality; it indicates only common participation in the ethos and the ontological and axiological connection among the individual personal subjects. A consciousness of common possession, on the other hand, subsists exclusively in the individuals, and not in the community.

There are, of course, collective spiritual structures; there is an "objective mind"—even if not in the Hegelian sense—which never is absorbed in the individual consciousness, but in which all participate. Art, science, the morality of an age, the national, political or religious life, is a collective spirit in this sense. The mode of existence of such structures is a thoroughly real one, as they have their beginning and end, their history and their laws of development. They are a macrocosmic spiritual power, which stands in closest reciprocity with the individual mind. They subsist above the individuals, but they rest entirely upon them, and every development in them is the work of individuals; the individual, on his side, is again determined by their structure, and indeed so much so that he finds scope for his individuality only in it, or, at least, very little beyond it. But the real structures of the group-mind possess the character neither of a subject nor of a person. Just as little as they amount to a collective consciousness or can be represented as a mere sum, so little may we describe them as a consciousness, in the proper sense of the word, superimposed upon the individual consciousness. Only the individual has a consciousness of them—and that only an imperfect consciousness. Complete consciousness is absent.

The unity of this really super-individual structure has its root not at all in a subjective unity, but in a unity of content, a unity of object. It is therefore in any case not a personal unity.

(d) Ascending Orders of Corporate Bodies and Descending Orders of Personality

Above the individual person there are corporate bodies which in fact show a certain analogy to personality proper: family, race, nation, State. Such corporations can collectively entertain convictions, can strive, act, be disposed, like persons; and the objects of their behaviour are, as a rule, corporations of the same order, just as the objects of the acts of individual persons are always in turn persons.

These structures, however, are not persons of a higher order, but only analogues of a person. Individuals are bound together in them and carry in common a responsibility for the communal behaviour. But as for personality proper, they lack a fundamentally essential element—not all the categorial factors of a person reappear in them. They lack the binding consciousness of the whole—the subject of a higher order. The real carriers of communal responsibility are ultimately the single persons, however widely the entire burden may be shared among them.

But that these communities show at least an analogy to a person, that they conduct themselves "as if" they were in fact persons of a higher order, this rests upon the fact that their members are personal beings. The real persons, the individuals, must lend their personality to the higher structures in order to make personal conduct possible for them. For in such quasi-personal forms there are always representative persons who act in the name of the whole: leaders and thinkers, who foresee and determine the goals. That their representative Will is not unconditionally "the will of all," that the community can set itself in opposition to it, can deny it, and can find a substitute in the will of another individual person, this simply proves how entirely there is here not a person but a surrogate. Only a person can represent the whole, but the whole is never itself a person. The principle of representation and delegation —even when the representative is legitimately elected—is not a complete substitute for personality.

Still a representative lends to the community at least a certain mediate personality. But the higher the grade of collectivity, so much the more does the principle of representation and delegation miss fire and so much the more impersonal becomes the communal form. We might therefore with some justification make the statement: the higher orders of communal life are not higher orders of personality, but lower.

It is here as it is in mathematics with infinity and rationality. Rationalism is always prone to believe that the higher orders of the infinite and therefore of the "irrational" may at the same time be higher orders of the rational. In this it is presupposed that the *ratio* itself is capable of rising with the orders. This is an assumption entirely without foundation. We know only the human ratio; and this does not mount beyond itself. It remains fixed within its own boundaries and what transcends these is hopelessly irrational. It is just so with personality. We know only the personality of man and can speak intelligently only of it. It also does not advance beyond itself, however far the ethical problems may grow into the macrocosmic with the expanding orders of corporate life. Just as the mounting orders of the infinite are necessarily at the same time descending orders of the rational—for even accessibility to knowledge diminishes progressively—so the rising orders of collective life are always and necessarily descending orders of personality —for exactly the specific unity of the fulfiller of acts, as it can inhere only in a subject, diminishes progressively with every upward step.[1]

It is an almost ineradicable heritage of rationalism that we are disposed, wherever there is a gradation of advancement of form towards cosmic extent, not only to transfer subconsciously the attributes of the lower of the only given grades to the higher and more comprehensive, but also to magnify them to a proportionately higher degree. Metaphysical personalism is entirely built upon this bias. It finds repeated in the ascending orders of collectivity certain fundamental features which it knows in man's personality, the only one presented to us; and this analogy is enough for it to hazard the assertion that those higher collective units must also be persons of a higher potency.

Personalism takes no account of the quite evident fact that here the categorial foundation of personality, the subject, the unit of knowing, willing and doing—in short of the act-fulfilling entity—is lacking or reappears only in a few of the next higher grades and only vicariously and devitalized. The ethical problem is hereby wrongly wrenched from its ontological basis. If we draw this into the network of problems, and if in reflection we go back to the whole series of categorial presuppositions without which the ethical problems do not at all exist, the more general categorial laws of gradation and dependence are seen in their power, and we become aware that the increments of the power in the collective unit are at the same time diminutions in the power of personality.

(e) ETHICS AND THEOLOGY

In the total perspective which is hereby disclosed, it becomes immediately clear that the two extremes are the limits of

---

[1] Cf. *Metaphysik der Erkenntnis*, Chapter V (b).

personality. In the full, primary sense of the word, a person is and remains only the lower extreme, the individual subject, the man. The opposite extreme, the universal, absolute and all-embracing entity, if such exist, is so far removed from being the highest order or person that it must be much rather the lowest order of person, the absolute minimum as regards personality, at the same time the *status evanescens* (= o) of personality in general. But this means that the well-understood categorial coherence of this whole perspective proves exactly the opposite of that which personalism tries to prove by it: God—if one succeeds in drawing Him into this perspective —is not the highest and absolute person, but the absolutely impersonal being. The concept of Him, seen from this point of view, would be the negative limiting concept of personality in general.

Whether one should presume to draw God into this relation appears more than doubtful. One has also no ground for expecting from ethical problems that they should produce any theological corollaries. Even Kant's procedure, in basing theological concepts upon morality, has brought upon itself the disapproval of thoroughgoing theological thought. Scheler's personalism, although it sets aside Kant in general and especially the doctrine of postulates, perpetrates a quite analogous leap beyond limits. But the concept of a person does not tolerate such action, at least not in so far as it is an ethical concept. Whether it has some other meaning, and whether this applies to a divinity, does not admit of being either affirmed or denied by ethics. By a metaphysical intensification of the ethically personal, one only renders its possibility ambiguous.

The whole doctrine of personalism, together with its theologically questionable consequence, would be ultimately a matter of indifference to ethics if it did not indirectly foster an axiological prejudice. If there be persons of a higher order, it is a temptation to assume—since persons are carriers of moral values—that the higher values attach to the persons of the higher order; the highest value therefore attaches only to an infinite person, but to man only the lowest moral values are attached. Scheler actually sees in the "saint" such a highest value, the superiority of which over all other values—and not only over those that are ethical—is said to be rooted in an objective dependence. Here, behind the moral theology, peeps forth theological morality, a tendency which leads straight to the abrogation of all independence on the part of the ethical in general, because it touches the autonomy of moral values.

But irrespective of the personalistic idea of God and its all-depressing preponderance, the higher classes of value are thus so distributed among the average grades that collective persons must necessarily be the carriers of higher values than individual persons. This is a point of view which degrades man in comparison with the collective entities that are built upon him, and which elevates them at his expense. Nation, State, humanity thus appear as valuational carriers in a higher sense than man himself, whose personality they in truth reflect but feebly. Thus a distorted picture is given. Nation and State, it goes without saying, are not good or bad, not honourable or mean, not lovable or hateful, in the same primal sense as is the individual man. Always and everywhere they are so only in a secondary sense. And indeed only through the individual man, of whom they are a function.

The moral being is not the Absolute nor the State nor anything else in the world but, singly and alone, man, the primal carrier of moral values and disvalues.

INDEX FOR VOLUMES I-III